Beginning NFC
Near Field Communication with Arduino, Android, and PhoneGap

Tom Igoe, Don Coleman, and Brian Jepson

Beijing · Cambridge · Farnham · Köln · Sebastopol · Tokyo

Beginning NFC

by Tom Igoe, Don Coleman, and Brian Jepson

Printed in the United States of America.

Published by O'Reilly Media, Inc., 1005 Gravenstein Highway North, Sebastopol, CA 95472.

O'Reilly books may be purchased for educational, business, or sales promotional use. Online editions are also available for most titles (*http://my.safaribooksonline.com*). For more information, contact our corporate/institutional sales department: 800-998-9938 or *corporate@oreilly.com*.

Editors: Rachel Roumeliotis and Allyson MacDonald	**Indexer:** WordCo Indexing Services
Production Editor: Nicole Shelby	**Cover Designer:** Randy Comer
Copyeditor: Jasmine Kwityn	**Interior Designer:** David Futato
Proofreader: Kiel Van Horn	**Illustrator:** Rebecca Demarest

January 2014:   First Edition

Revision History for the First Edition:

2013-01-13:   First release

See *http://oreilly.com/catalog/errata.csp?isbn=9781449372064* for release details.

ISBN: 978-1-449-37206-4

[LSI]

This book is dedicated to Red Burns.

Table of Contents

CHAPTER 1

Introduction

This book started life innocently enough in an email from Brian to Tom in March 2011. Brian thought it would be a good idea to add a couple of lines to the second edition of another book about near field communication, *Making Things Talk*, which we were working on at the time. There was already a chapter on radio frequency identification (RFID) in the book, so how hard could it be? Two and a half years later, we've learned a lot about NFC along the way and picked up an excellent and knowledgeable collaborator, Don Coleman, author of the NFC plug-in for PhoneGap.

Even though NFC has a lot of potential, most of the material written about it so far hasn't been written for the casual programmer. Everything out there assumed that if you wanted to know about NFC, you were prepared to do it from the silicon up. You had to understand the details of the various RFID specs involved, and you had to be prepared to write code that interpreted the byte stream from an NFC reader one byte at a time. While it's useful to understand that, we figured NFC would see wider use if programmers could concentrate on what they were using it for, rather than the low-level details. Don's PhoneGap library was the best tool we found to do just that. It lets you design NFC exchanges in the way we imagine the NFC forum designers intended: you think about the messages being exchanged and don't worry about the rest.

Most of this book is written in that spirit. You'll learn about the basics of the NFC Data Exchange Format (NDEF) by reading and writing messages from device to tag and from device to device. You'll see a few sample applications—some written for PhoneGap, some for Arduino, and some for Node.js—running on embedded devices like the Raspberry Pi and the BeagleBone Black. You'll learn some of the use patterns of NDEF, and you'll get a taste of how you might think about the physical interaction of NFC-driven applications.

The state of the art varies from platform to platform, however. Not everything that the NFC Forum specifications describe is accessible to the casual programmer on every platform yet. We've attempted to give you a roadmap in this book, particularly in the

1

later chapters, as to what the current state of development is, and where there is still room for usability improvement.

We hope that this book will help the casual programmer get a sense of what can be done using NFC, and that it will inspire more professional developers to create simple-to-use tools to help spread its use.

Who This Book Is For

You don't have to be a trained professional programmer to read this book. We tried to write it for programming enthusiasts—people who've picked up some knowledge along the way, but maybe not in a formal learning setting. You won't learn to write enterprise-level code here, but you will get a practical introduction to what near field communication is and how to program applications using it on Android, Arduino, and embedded Linux.

We assume you have some familiarity with programming, however. You will want to be familiar with JavaScript and HTML for most of the examples in the book. You'll get introduced to a little C in the Arduino projects, but if you're familiar with JavaScript or Java, it will look familiar enough. For those latter projects, you should be a little familiar with electronics, but you don't have to be.

Recommended Reading

"What? I have to read other books in order to read this book?" No, but there are a few books that we found helpful in writing this one. We thought you might find them useful as well.

If you're new to JavaScript, read Douglas Crockford's *JavaScript: The Good Parts*. Come to think of it, read it if you're an old hand at JavaScript. It'll make you a better programmer. He explains the theoretical underpinnings of the language and the best use patterns clearly and definitively.

For PhoneGap and Android, the online Getting Started Guides are the most up-to-date references; see the PhoneGap developer portal (*http://phonegap.com/developer/*) and the Android developer site (*http://developer.android.com/*). For more in-depth introductions to Android, see *Professional Android 4 Application Development* or *Android Programming: The Big Nerd Ranch Guide*.

For an in-depth introduction to NFC from an engineering perspective, the NFC Forum Specifications (*http://bit.ly/nfc-tech-specs*) are the original source material (we have reproduced some of them in Appendix A for handy reference). We also found *Professional NFC Application Development* by Vedat Coskun, Kerem Ok, and Busra Ozdenizci to be a good reference, particularly for experienced Java programmers. We have deliberately taken a more populist approach than that book, since many of our readers are hobbyists, hackers, and other self-identified dilettante programmers.

If you're new to Arduino, Massimo Banzi's *Getting Started with Arduino* is an excellent starting place. Tom Igoe's *Making Things Talk, 2nd Edition* is a good book for experienced programmers to learn about connecting Arduino projects to networks. Michael Margolis' *Arduino Cookbook* has some handy recipes for Arduino programs as well.

For an introduction to Node.js, which pops up later in this book, Brett McLaughlin's *What is Node?* is a nice essay-length introduction with no code. Manuel Kiessling's *The Node Beginner Book* and Pedro Teixeira's *Hands-On Node.js* are helpful and short guides to getting started with the actual code.

For a good introduction to the Raspberry Pi or the BeagleBone Black, which you'll encounter in Chapter 9, you can find material for getting started on Adafruit's tutorials (*http://learn.adafruit.com*). The books *Getting Started with Raspberry Pi* by Matt Richardson and Shawn Wallace and *Getting Started with BeagleBone* by Matt Richardson are also good introductions.

What's Covered in This Book

Chapter 2 gives you an introduction to near field communication (NFC) by comparing it to radio frequency identification (RFID). Simply put, NFC is a superset of RFID. It can do most things short-range RFID can do, and more. You'll get a preview of the most important terms, a look at the architecture of an NFC system, and learn what tools you need and where to get them.

Chapter 3 introduces you to PhoneGap and the NFC plug-in for PhoneGap. You'll install the tools necessary to develop PhoneGap applications for Android and build and run your first couple of applications. By the end of this chapter, you'll have read your first NFC tag using an Android device.

Chapter 4 is an in-depth overview of the NFC Data Exchange Format (NDEF). You'll learn how it's structured and see it in practice by writing an application that performs the same basic task using different types of NDEF records, to see how each record type affects user interaction on Android.

Chapter 5 covers how to listen for NDEF messages on Android. You'll learn how to filter for different types of tags and messages, and how the Android Tag Dispatch system can be used to your advantage when developing NFC apps.

In Chapter 6, you'll build a full NFC application on Android that features a full user interface, audio playback, and control of web-connected lighting, all mediated by NFC tags. The goal of this chapter is to show you how to plan the interaction design and data formatting of an application to best take advantage of NFC.

Chapter 7 brings another platform into play: the Arduino microcontroller development platform. You'll learn how to read and write NDEF messages using the Arduino NDEF library. You'll also develop another full application using Arduino and Node.js.

Chapter 8 introduces you to peer-to-peer exchanges using NFC on Android. You'll learn how the record types you're exchanging through peer-to-peer affect the receiving device, and you'll learn about how NFC can negotiate the handoff of larger exchanges to alternate carriers like Bluetooth and WiFi.

Chapter 9 gives you the state of the art on NFC development on embedded Linux platforms using the Raspberry Pi and BeagleBone as examples. You'll get an understanding of what's possible on embedded Linux, and see a few sample applications in Node.js. There's still a lot of room for usability improvements in this context, so be warned that this chapter is not for the technically timid. You'll want some familiarity with the Linux command-line interface to get the most out of this chapter. This is where some of the most exciting possibilities for NFC use lie, though, so it's good territory to know.

What You'll Need

To do the exercises in this book, you'll need some hardware and software. All of the software is free, fortunately. The most expensive piece of hardware used here is an NFC-enabled Android device. The following sections list what you'll be using.

Hardware

To follow along with the book overall, you'll need the following hardware:

- An Android NFC-enabled device
- Several NFC-compatible tags (check compatibility with your devices; "Device-to-Tag Type Matching" on page 19 includes a chart showing which devices work with which tag types)

For Chapter 6, you'll need:

- A Philips Hue lighting system (*https://www.meethue.com*)
- A Bluetooth Music Receiver (e.g., Belkin Bluetooth Music Receiver (*http://bit.ly/belkin-bmr*) or HomeSpot's NFC-enabled Bluetooth Audio Receiver (*http://amzn.to/homespot-receiver*))

For Chapter 7, you'll need:

- An Arduino Uno microcontroller, available from many outlets, including Arduino (*http://store.arduino.cc*), Adafruit (*http://www.adafruit.com*), Seeed Studio (*http://www.seeedstudio.com*), RadioShack and others

- An NFC Shield (you can use Adafruit's PN532 NFC/RFID Controller Shield for Arduino (*http://www.adafruit.com/products/789*) or Seeed Studio's NFC Shield (*http://bit.ly/seeed-shield*) or NFC Shield v2.0 (*http://bit.ly/seeed-nfc-shield*))

- If you're using the Adafruit shield, you may want to get some shield stacking headers (*https://www.adafruit.com/products/85*) from Adafruit as well.

- A solenoid-driven door lock, 12V or less. We used an Amico 0837L DC 12V 8W open frame type solenoid for electric door lock (*http://amzn.to/amico-lock*) bought on Amazon, but you can also get solenoids from other retailers. Adafruit sells a similar lock-style solenoid (*http://www.adafruit.com/products/1512*) and Seeed Studio sells several models, so if you're ordering a shield from them, you can get a solenoid from them as well.

- A TIP120 Darlington transistor (*http://www.adafruit.com/products/976*)

- A 12V, 1000mA power supply (*http://www.adafruit.com/products/798*), with 2.1mm ID, 5.5mm OD, center-positive connector to power the solenoid circuit

- Jumper wires (*http://www.adafruit.com/products/759*) or 22AWG solid-core wire

- Two LEDs (one red, one green). These are available from any electronics retailer, but for reference, check out Adafruit's red LED pack (*http://www.adafruit.com/products/299*) or green LED pack (*http://www.adafruit.com/products/298*).

- Two 220Ω resistors for the LEDs

For Chapter 9, you'll need:

- A BeagleBone Black or Raspberry Pi embedded Linux microcontroller

- 1 amp or greater power supply for your board

- An SLC3711 Contactless USB Smart Card Reader (*http://bit.ly/usb-reader*)

- Optional but useful:
  - A USB WiFi adapter for your board (Adafruit's Miniature WiFi (802.11b/g/n) Module (*http://www.adafruit.com/products/814*) works well)
  - A USB A-to-A extender for your NFC adapter
  - A USB to TTL serial cable—debug/console cable (*http://www.adafruit.com/products/954*)

Table 1-1 lists the electronics components for this book with part numbers from some of the electronics distributors we use regularly, in case you want alternatives to those listed previously.

Table 1-1. Electronic components used in this book

Part	MakerShed	Jameco	Digikey	SparkFun	Adafruit	Farnell	Arduino	Seeed
220Ω resistor		690700	220QBK-ND			9337792		

Part	MakerShed	Jameco	Digikey	SparkFun	Adafruit	Farnell	Arduino	Seeed
Solderless breadboard	MKEL3	20723	438-1045-ND	PRT-00137	64	4692810		STR101C2M or STR102C2M
Red hookup wire	MKSEEED3	36856	C2117R-100-ND	PRT-08023		1662031		
Black hookup wire	MKSEEED3	36792	C2117B-100-ND	PRT-08022		1662027		
Blue hookup wire	MKSEEED3	36767				1662034		
12V 1000mA DC power supply (or equivalent)		170245		TOL-00298	798	636363		
Arduino Uno rev3 Microcontroller Module	MKSP11	2121105	1050-1017-ND	DEV-09950	50	1848687	A000046	ARD132D2P
Green LED	MKEE7	333227		COM-09592		1334976		
Red LED	MKEE7	333973		COM-09590		2062463		
Blue LED		2006764		COM-00529		1020554		
Yellow LED	MKEE7	34825		COM-09594		1939531		
MIFARE RFID tag	MKPX4			SEN-10128				
NFC shield	MKAD45				789			SLD01097P
TIP120 Darlington transistor		10001_ 10001_ 32993_-1	TIP120-ND		976	9294210		
3.3V USB/TTL serial debug cable				DEV-09717	954			
BeagleBone Black	MKCCE3	2176149	BB-BBLK-000-ND		1278	2291620		ARM00100P
Raspberry Pi Model B	MKRPI2			DEV-11546	998	43W5302		

Software

To follow along with the book overall, you'll need the following software:

- The Android software development kit (see "Setting Up the Development Environment" on page 24)
- The Cordova CLI, your toolbox for PhoneGap (see "Install Cordova CLI for PhoneGap" on page 28)
- Node.js and the Node Package Manager (npm)

- A text editor (we like Sublime Text 2 (*http://www.sublimetext.com/2*) as a cross-platform GUI editor, but you can use anything that can generate a plain-text file)

For Chapter 6, you'll need:

- The Zepto jQuery library, available from Zepto.js (*http://zeptojs.com*)

For Chapter 7, you'll need:

- The Arduino IDE (*http://bit.ly/arduino-software*)
- The Seeed-Studio PN532 library (*https://github.com/Seeed-Studio/PN532*)
- The Arduino NDEF library, available from Don Coleman's GitHub repository (*https://github.com/don/NDEF*)
- The Time library (*http://bit.ly/time-library*) for Arduino by Michael Margolis

Don't worry about setting all this up right now; we'll let you know when you need to install a piece of software.

Other Useful NFC Apps

The following will be useful throughout the course of the book:

- NFC TagInfo by NXP (*http://bit.ly/nfc-taginfo*) allows you to read any NFC or Mifare tag and examine the NDEF record on it.
- NFC TagWriter by NXP (*http://bit.ly/nfc-tagwriter*) allows you to do many of the same things as TagInfo. It can also write tags, and unformat tags, which is really handy.
- NFC Research Lab's NFC TagInfo (*http://bit.ly/nfc-taginfo-nfcrl*) will show you all the info about a given tag. It's more advanced than NXP's TagInfo, in that it will also allow you to see a memory dump from the tag. It's invaluable for troubleshooting your applications.

For Chapter 4, you'll need:

- Trigger (*http://bit.ly/trigger-app*) by TagStand
- NFC Writer (*http://bit.ly/nfc-tagstand*), also by TagStand
- TecTiles (*http://bit.ly/samsung-techtiles*) by Samsung (functional in the United States and Canada only)
- App Lancher NFC Tag Writer (*http://bit.ly/app-lancher*) [sic] by vvakame
- A Foursquare (*http://www.foursquare.com*) account if you don't have one already, and Foursquare for Android (*http://bit.ly/foursq-android*)

Conventions Used in This Book

The following typographical conventions are used in this book:

Italic

Indicates new terms, URLs, email addresses, filenames, and file extensions.

`Constant width`

Used for program listings, as well as within paragraphs to refer to program elements such as variable or function names, databases, data types, environment variables, statements, and keywords.

This icon signifies a tip, suggestion, or general note.

This icon indicates a warning or caution.

Using Code Examples

Supplemental material (code examples, exercises, etc.) is available for download at *https://github.com/tigoe/beginningnfc*.

This book is here to help you get your job done. In general, if example code is offered with this book, you may use it in your programs and documentation. You do not need to contact us for permission unless you're reproducing a significant portion of the code. For example, writing a program that uses several chunks of code from this book does not require permission. Selling or distributing a CD-ROM of examples from O'Reilly books does require permission. Answering a question by citing this book and quoting example code does not require permission. Incorporating a significant amount of example code from this book into your product's documentation does require permission.

We appreciate, but do not require, attribution. An attribution usually includes the title, author, publisher, and ISBN. For example: "*Beginning NFC: Near Field Communication with Arduino, Android, and PhoneGap,* by Tom Igoe, Don Coleman, and Brian Jepson. Copyright Tom Igoe, Don Coleman, and Brian Jepson 2014 978-1-4493-6307-9."

If you feel your use of code examples falls outside fair use or the permission given above, feel free to contact us at *permissions@oreilly.com*.

Safari® Books Online

 *Safari Books Online* is an on-demand digital library that delivers expert content in both book and video form from the world's leading authors in technology and business.

Technology professionals, software developers, web designers, and business and creative professionals use Safari Books Online as their primary resource for research, problem solving, learning, and certification training.

Safari Books Online offers a range of product mixes and pricing programs for organizations, government agencies, and individuals. Subscribers have access to thousands of books, training videos, and prepublication manuscripts in one fully searchable database from publishers like O'Reilly Media, Prentice Hall Professional, Addison-Wesley Professional, Microsoft Press, Sams, Que, Peachpit Press, Focal Press, Cisco Press, John Wiley & Sons, Syngress, Morgan Kaufmann, IBM Redbooks, Packt, Adobe Press, FT Press, Apress, Manning, New Riders, McGraw-Hill, Jones & Bartlett, Course Technology, and dozens more. For more information about Safari Books Online, please visit us online.

How to Contact Us

Please address comments and questions concerning this book to the publisher:

O'Reilly Media, Inc.
1005 Gravenstein Highway North
Sebastopol, CA 95472
800-998-9938 (in the United States or Canada)
707-829-0515 (international or local)
707-829-0104 (fax)

We have a web page for this book, where we list errata, examples, and any additional information. You can access this page at *http://oreil.ly/beginning-nfc*.

To comment or ask technical questions about this book, send email to *bookquestions@oreilly.com*.

For more information about our books, courses, conferences, and news, see our website at *http://www.oreilly.com*.

Find us on Facebook: *http://facebook.com/oreilly*

Follow us on Twitter: *http://twitter.com/oreillymedia*

Watch us on YouTube: *http://www.youtube.com/oreillymedia*

Acknowledgments

We've received generous assistance from many people and organizations during the writing of this book. The PhoneGap-NFC plug-in was Kevin Griffin's brainchild; he and Don wrote the first version of it and presented it at PhoneGap Day 2011. Kevin Townsend of Adafruit has been an invaluable resource for his in-depth knowledge of NXP's software and hardware. Yihui Xiong of Seeed Studio and author of the Seeed Arduino NDEF library, was crucial to the success of Chapter 7. Philippe Teuwen made fast patches to libfreefare, clearing roadblocks in Chapter 9. Derek Molloy's pages on the BeagleBone Black (*http://derekmolloy.ie/beaglebone/*) were a handy resource. The images in this book are better thanks to Jody Culkin and Fritzing.org. Early readers Ben Light, Sae Huh, Gabrielle Levine, Alex Kauffmann, Fil Maj, and Dominick Gruntz offered valuable feedback.

This book was made possible by the patient support of our employers and colleagues at NYU's Interactive Telecommunications Program (ITP), Chariot Solutions LLC, Maker Media, and Arduino. We would also like to acknowledge the even more patient support of our families and partners.

CHAPTER 2

NFC and RFID

Radio frequency identification (RFID) is becoming commonplace in everyday life these days. From tap-and-go payment cards and transit passes to E-ZPass devices used on toll roads to the tags stuck on and sewn into consumer goods to manage inventory and deter theft, most of us encounter RFID tags at least a few times a week and never think about what can be done with this technology.

In the past few years, a new term has started to bubble up in connection with RFID: *near field communication* (NFC). Ask your average techie what it is and you'll probably hear "Oh, it's like RFID, only different." Great, but how is it different? RFID and NFC are often conflated, but they're not the same thing. Though NFC readers can read from and write to some RFID tags, NFC has more capabilities than RFID, and enables a greater range of uses. You can think of NFC as an extension of RFID, building on a few of the many RFID standards to create a wider data exchange platform.

This book aims to introduce you to NFC and its capabilities in a hands-on way. Following the exercises in these chapters, you'll build a few NFC applications for an NFC-enabled Android device and for an Arduino microcontroller. You'll learn where RFID and NFC overlap, and what you can do with NFC.

What's RFID?

Imagine you're sitting on your porch at night. You turn on the porch light, and you can see your neighbor as he passes close to your house because the light reflects off him back to your eyes. That's passive RFID. The radio signal from a passive RFID reader reaches a tag, the tag absorbs the energy and "reflects" back its identity.

Now imagine you turn on your porch light, and your neighbor in his home sees it and flicks on his porch light so that you can see him waving hello from his porch. That's active RFID. It can carry a longer range, because the receiver has its own power source, and can therefore generate its own radio signal rather than relying on the energy it absorbs from the sender.

RFID is a lot like those two porches. You and your neighbor know each other's faces, but you don't really learn a lot about each other that way. You don't exchange any meaningful messages. RFID is not a communications technology; rather, it's designed for identification. RFID tags can hold a small amount of data, and you can read and write to them from RFID readers, but the amount of data we're talking about is trivial, a thousand bytes or less.

What's NFC?

Now imagine another neighbor passes close, and when you see her, you invite her on to the porch for a chat. She accepts your invitation, and you sit together, exchange pleasantries about your lives, and develop more of a relationship. You talk with each other and you listen to each other for a few minutes. That's NFC.

NFC is designed to build on RFID by enabling more complex exchanges between participants. You can still read passive RFID tags with an NFC reader, and you can write to their limited amount of memory. NFC also allows you to write data to certain types of RFID tags using a standard format, independent of tag type. You can also communicate with other NFC devices in a two-way, or duplex, exchange. NFC devices can exchange information about each other's capabilities, swap records, and initiate longer term communications through other means.

For example, you might tap your NFC-enabled phone to an NFC-enabled stereo so that they can identify each other, learn that they both have WiFi capability, and exchange credentials for communication over WiFi. After that, the phone will start to stream audio over WiFi to the stereo. Why doesn't the phone stream its audio over the NFC connection? Two reasons: first, the NFC connection is intentionally short range, generally 10cm or less. That allows it to be low-power, and to avoid interference with other radios built into devices using it. Second, it's relatively low-speed compared to WiFi, Bluetooth, and other communications protocols. NFC is not designed to manage extended high-speed communications. It's for short messages, exchanging credentials, and initiating relationships. Think back to the front porch for a moment. NFC is the exchange you have to open the conversation. If you want to talk at length, you invite your neighbor inside for tea. That's WiFi, Bluetooth, and other extended communications protocols.

What's exciting about NFC is that it allows for some sophisticated introductions and short instructions without the hassle of exchanging passwords, pairing, and all the other more complicated steps that come with those other protocols. That means that when you and your friend want to exchange address information from your phone to his, you can just tap your phones together. When you want to pay with your Google Wallet, you can just tap as you would an RFID-enabled credit card.

When you're using NFC, your device doesn't give the other device to which it's speaking access to its whole memory—it just gives it the basics needed for exchange. You control what it can send and what it can't, and to whom.

How RFID Operates

An RFID exchange involves two actors: a *target* and an *initiator*. The initiator, a tag reader or reader/writer device, starts the exchange by generating a radio field and listening for responses from any target in the field. The target, a tag, responds when it picks up a transmission from an initiator. It will respond with a *unique identifier number* (UID). RFID has two *communication modes*: active and passive. *Passive RFID* exchanges involve a reader/writer and a tag that has no power source on board. The tags get their power from the energy of the radio field itself. It's generally a very small amount, just enough to send a signal back to the reader. *Active RFID* exchanges involve a target that's an independently powered device. Because the target is powered, its reply to the reader can travel a much greater distance. E-ZPass and other traffic ID systems use active RFID.

RFID tags have a small amount of memory on board, usually less than 1 kilobyte. An initiator device can read this data, and if it's a reader/writer device, it can write to the tag as well. This allows you to store small amounts of information associated with the card. For example, it's sometimes used in transit systems that use RFID, to keep track of how much value is left on the card. However, since RFID systems generally are networked to a database, it's more common to store a data record indexed by the tag's UID in a remote database, and store all information about the tag in that remote database.

RFID Standards

Contrary to popular belief, there is no single universally interoperable RFID protocol or technology. There are dozens. RFID standards are developed by the International Standards Organization (ISO), in conjunction with major participants in the RFID market. ISO works as a mediating body to help competitors in many different industries develop interoperable standards so that even when they compete, their technologies can sometimes work together. The various RFID standards define the radio frequencies used, the data transfer rates, the data formats, and more. Some of these standards define layers of a single interoperable stack, as you'll see with NFC. Other standards define a whole different class of applications. For example, the ISO-11784 standard was originally developed for animal tracking. It operates in frequencies between 129 and 139.4kHz, and its data format features fields suited to describing the animals to be tracked. You can also find EM4100 procotol readers and tags that operate in the 125kHz range. These are often used as proximity cards, and feature very limited information in their data protocol, usually just a UID. The ISO-14443 standards were developed for use with payment systems and smart cards. They operate at 13.56MHz. They include features in their data format for incrementing and decrementing values and for encrypting data, for example. Within the 14443 family, there are several different formats including Philips and NXP Mifare tags, Sony FeliCa tags, and NXP DESFire. ISO-14443A tags are compatible with NFC, so you'll see a lot of them in the pages that follow.

How NFC Operates

NFC can be thought of as an extension of RFID. NFC exchanges also involve an initiator and a target like RFID. However, it can do more than just exchange UIDs and read or write data to the target. The most interesting difference between RFID and NFC is that NFC targets are often programmable devices, like mobile phones. This means that rather than just delivering static data from memory, an NFC target could actually generate unique content for each exchange and deliver it back to the initiator. For example, if you're using NFC to exchange address data between two phones, the NFC target device could be programmed to only provide limited information if it's never seen this particular initiator before.

NFC devices have two *communications modes*. If the initiator always supplies the RF energy and the target gets powered by the initiator's field, they're said to be engaging in *passive* communication mode. If both target and initiator have their own energy sources, they're in *active* communication mode. These modes are the same as regular RFID communication modes.

NFC devices have three *operating modes*. They can be *reader/writers* that read data from a target and write to it. They can be *card emulators*, acting like RFID tags when they're in the field of another NFC or RFID device. Or they can operate in *peer-to-peer mode*, in which they exchange data in both directions.

NFC Data Exchange Format (NDEF)

Data exchanged between NFC devices and tags is formatted using the *NFC Data Exchange Format* (NDEF). This is a term you'll hear a lot; NDEF is one of the key advancements that NFC adds to RFID. It's a common data format that operates across all NFC devices, regardless of the underlying tag or device technology. Every NDEF message contains one or more NDEF records. Each record has a particular record type, a unique ID, a length, and a payload of data. There are a few well-known types of NDEF records. NFC-enabled devices are expected to know what to do with each of these types:

Simple text records

These contain whatever text string you want to send. Text messages generally don't contain instructions for the target device. They also include metadata indicating the language and encoding scheme (e.g., UTF-8).

URIs

These contain network addresses. An NDEF target device that receives a URI record is expected to pass that record to an application that can display it, such as a web browser.

Smart Posters

These contain data you might attach to a poster to give it more information. This can include URIs, but might also contain other data, like a text message to be sent about the poster, telling your friends about it. A target device that receives a Smart Poster record might open a browser, SMS, or email application, depending on the message's content.

Signatures

These provide a way to give trustworthy information about the origins of data contained in an NDEF record.

You can mix and match records in an NDEF message, or you can send only one record per message, as you choose.

NDEF is one of the important technical differences between RFID and NFC. Both NFC and many of the RFID protocols operate on 13.56MHz, but RFID tags do not have to format their data in NDEF format. The various RFID protocols do not share a common data format.

Think of NDEF messages like paragraphs and records like sentences: a paragraph is a discrete chunk of information that contains one or more sentences. A sentence is a smaller chunk of information that contains just one idea. For example, you might write a paragraph that indicates that you're having a birthday party, and gives the address. The NDEF message equivalent might contain a simple text record to describe the event, a Smart Poster record containing the physical address, and a URI for more information on the Web.

The Architecture of NFC

In order to understand NFC in depth, it helps to have a mental model of the architecture. There are several layers to consider. The lowest layer is the physical, namely your CPU and the radios that are doing the communication. In the middle, there are data packetization and transport layers, then data format layers, and finally, your application code. Figure 2-1 shows the various layers of the NFC stack.

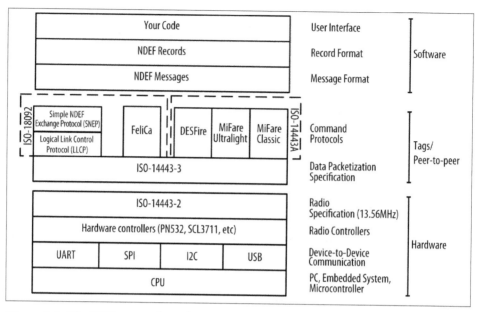

Figure 2-1. The NFC protocol stack

At the physical layer, NFC works on an RFID radio specification, ISO-14443-2, that describes low-power radios operating at 13.56MHz. Next comes a layer that describes the framing of data bytes sent over the radio, ISO-14443-3. Any of the radios you might use are separate hardware components, either inside your phone or tablet, or attachments to your microcontroller or personal computer. They communicate with the main processor of your device using one or more standard inter-device serial protocols: *universal asynchronous receive-transmit* (UART), *serial peripheral interface* (SPI), *inter-integrated circuit communication* (I2C), or *universal serial bus* (USB). If you're a hardware enthusiast, you probably know the first three, but if your focus is software, you may only know USB.

Above that are several RFID command protocols, based on two specifications. The original RFID control specification that NFC tag reading and writing is built on is ISO-14443A. The Philips/NXP Semiconductors Mifare Classic and Mifare Ultralight and NXP DESFire protocols are compatible with ISO-14443A. The NFC peer-to-peer exchange is built on the ISO-18092 control protocol. Sony FeliCa RFID cards and tags, mostly available in Japan, are based on this standard as well. You can read from and write to tags using these standards and still not be using NFC, however.

The first major difference between NFC and RFID is the peer-to-peer communications mode, which is implemented using the ISO-18092 standard. There are two protocols, a *logical link control protocol* (LLCP) and a *simple NDEF exchange protocol* (SNEP) that manage peer-to-peer exchanges. These are shown in the stack alongside the control protocols, since they operate on the same standard as one of them.

The second major difference between RFID and NFC, the NFC Data Exchange Format (NDEF), sits atop these control protocols. NDEF defines a data exchange in messages, which are composed of NDEF records. There are several different record types, which you'll learn more about in Chapter 4. NDEF makes it possible for your application code to deal with data from NFC tag reading and writing, peer-to-peer exchanges, and card emulation all the same way.

Most of this book focuses on the use of NDEF messaging. Although we'll discuss the lower layers so that you understand them, we think that the advantage to NDEF is that it frees you from thinking about them.

NFC Tag Types

There are four types of tags defined by the NFC forum, all based on the RFID control protocols described previously. There's a fifth that's compatible, but not strictly part of the NFC specification. Types 1, 2, and 4 are all based on ISO-14443A, and type 3 is based on ISO-18092. You can get tags from many vendors, and you've probably run across them in everyday life without knowing it. Their details are as follows:

Type 1

- Based on ISO-14443A specification.
- Can be read-only, or read/write capable.
- 96 bytes to 2 kilobytes of memory.
- Communication speed 106Kb.
- No data collision protection.
- Examples: Innovision Topaz, Broadcom BCM20203.

Type 2

- Similar to type 1 tags, type 2 tags are based on NXP/Philips Mifare Ultralight tag (ISO-14443A) specification.
- Can be read-only, or read/write capable.
- 96 bytes to 2 kilobytes of memory.
- Communication speed 106Kb.
- Anti-collision support.
- Example: NXP Mifare Ultralight.

Type 3

- These are based on the Sony FeliCa tags (ISO-18092 and JIS-X-6319-4), without the encryption and authentication support that FeliCa affords.

- Configured by factory to be read-only, or read/write capable.
- Variable memory, up to 1MB per exchange.
- Two communication speeds, 212 or 424Kbps.
- Anti-collision support.
- Example: Sony FeliCa.

Type 4
- Similar to type 1 tags, type 4 tags are based on NXP DESFire tag (ISO-14443A) specification.
- Configured by factory to be read-only, or read/write capable.
- 2, 4, or 8KB of memory.
- Variable memory, up to 32KB per exchange.
- Three communication speeds: 106, 212, or 424Kbps.
- Anti-collision support.
- Example: NXP DESFire, SmartMX-JCOP.

A fifth type, proprietary to NXP Semiconductors, is probably the most common in NFC use today:

Mifare Classic tag (ISO–14443A)
- Memory options: 192, 768, or 3,584 bytes.
- Communication speed 106Kbps
- Anti-collision support.
- Examples: NXP Mifare Classic 1K, Mifare Classic 4K, Mifare Classic Mini.

Where to Get Tags

Mifare and NFC tags are increasingly easy to get. To make the most of this book, you should have some NFC Forum tags and some Mifare Classic tags as well.

Many mobile phone stores now carry Samsung's TecTiles, which work well for many of the applications in this book. They're expensive, but convenient. The original TecTile tags are Mifare Classic, which work well on Arduino in Chapter 7 and the USB NFC reader on the BeagleBone Black and Raspberry Pi in Chapter 9. It's not clear, but it would appear that Samsung is abandoning TecTile in favor of TecTile 2. There is a general shift among hardware vendors away from Mifare Classic and toward the official NFC Forum tag types.

If you want tags in different form factors, Adafruit has a wide variety in their NFC category (*http://adafruit.com/category/55*). SparkFun (*http://www.sparkfun.com*) and

Seed Studio (*http://www.seeedstudio.com*) also have plenty of Mifare tags; search for "NFC" or "Mifare" and you'll find plenty.

You can also get tags from TagAge (*http://www.tagage.net*), but shipping can be slow from Finland, depending on your location. Customer service has been excellent for us, however.

Identive NFC (*http://bit.ly/identivenfc*) can deliver tags overnight. They are a bit more expensive, but they arrive quickly and they have a cool android on them.

Device-to-Tag Type Matching

Not all NFC-compatible tags work with all NFC devices. In the course of working on this book, we've tested many different devices and tags, and have found some combinations work, and some don't. Though Table 2-1 isn't an exhaustive table, it's intended to give you enough information to choose your devices and tags appropriately.

The most common issue you'll run into is that some devices will read Mifare Classic tags, while others won't. Mifare Classic is not actually an NFC Forum standard tag type, and recently, major hardware vendors like Broadcom and Samsung have started to drop support for it on their devices. You're likely to get unpredictable results when you try to read Mifare Classic tags with some of these newer tags. For example, the Nexus 4 will read Mifare Classic as a generic tag, but the Samsung S4 (Google Edition) displays an error saying it can't handle the tag. When possible, we recommend going with one of the official NFC Forum tag types. In the chapters ahead, we'll make more specific recommendations where appropriate.

If you're coming to NFC because you're interested in using it for embedded hardware projects on the Arduino, Raspberry Pi, or BeagleBone Black (which you'll learn more about in Chapter 7 and Chapter 9), you should make sure you have both NFC tags and Mifare Classic tags. The libraries for those platforms were developed starting with Mifare Classic support, and as of this writing, they don't handle all the NFC Forum types. We've added Mifare Ultralight (NFC type 2) read support for the Arduino NDEF library (which Don wrote), and there is partial Ultralight and DESFire support (NFC types 2 and 4) in libfreefare, one of the libraries we'll show you in Chapter 9.

While we hope to see additions to those libraries to support all of the NFC Forum tag types, it's not there yet. Growing pains like these are common with emerging technologies, but so far, signs point to the industry moving toward a standardized set of tag types.

Table 2-1. Device-to-tag compatibility

Device	Type 1	Type 2 (Mifare Ultralight)	Type 3 (Sony FeliCa)	Type 4 (Mifare DESFire)	Mifare Classic
Samsung Galaxy S	Yes	Yes	Yes	Yes	Yes
Google Nexus S	Yes	Yes	Yes	Yes	Yes
Google Galaxy Nexus	Yes	Yes	Yes	Yes	Yes
Google Nexus 7 version 1	Yes	Yes	Yes	Yes	Yes
Google Nexus 7 version 2	Yes	Yes	Yes	Yes	No
Google Nexus 4 (phone)	Yes	Yes	Yes	Yes	No
Google Nexus 10 (tablet)	Yes	Yes	Yes	Yes	No
Samsung Galaxy S4 (tablet)	Yes	Yes	Yes	Yes	No
Samsung Galaxy SIII	Yes	Yes	Yes	Yes	Yes
Adafruit NFC Shield	No	Partial	No	No	Yes
Seeed Studio NFC Shield for Arduino	No	Partial	No	No	Yes
NFC USB Dongle (libnfc)	No	Partial	No	Partial	Yes

What You Can Do with NFC

There are many possible applications for NFC. Its tag emulation functionality is showing up in monetary transactions like Google Wallet, and in payment and ticketing systems for public transport. There are several mobile phone apps that allow you to save configuration data for your phone to a tag, and use the tag to automatically change the context of your phone (e.g., set the quiet settings for meetings, turn on WiFi and configure for a given network by tapping a tag). Home audio equipment is coming on the market that allows you to automatically pair your phone or tablet with your audio player or TV, to use the former as a remote control for the latter. Healthcare systems have implemented patient ID and record linking using NFC, and the NFC Forum recently released a Personal Health Device Communication (PHDC) technical specification to aid in that development. Inventory management can be improved by using NDEF records written to the goods being shipped, about their journey, shipping times, and so forth. Fleet tracking can also be enhanced using NFC tags and readers by storing route information, travel times, mileage, maintenance, and fuel information on tags, or transferring it from vehicle to mobile device through peer-to-peer.

In the course of working on this book, we've seen NFC-compatible tags in many locations, from New York City's Citi Bike key fobs to metro passes in China and Norway to hotel room keys, and more. Although not all of these applications are using the tags to the full potential NFC affords, they all could be enhanced or simplified through some of its features.

The combination of peer-to-peer messaging between devices with minimal negotiation, and a common data format between device and tag messages makes NFC a potentially powerful tool for data-intensive applications in the physical world.

Conclusion

Near field communication adds some promising new functionality to RFID technologies. Most notable of these is the NFC Data Exchange Format, NDEF, which provides a common data format across the four different NFC tag technologies. NDEF can be used for both tag-to-device data exchange and for device-to-device data exchange. This distinguishes NFC as more than just an identification technology; it is also a useful technology for short data exchanges. The method by which NFC devices and tags interact—by means of a single tap—affords a spontaneity of interaction between users.

There are four physical NFC tag types. These are based on existing RFID standards; three of the tag types are based on the ISO-14443A standard, and the fourth is based on the ISO-18092 standard. This makes NFC tags at least partially compatible with many existing Mifare and FeliCa RFID systems. Although these older systems do not support NDEF, they can still identify those NFC Tags that are compatible with them. An RFID reader that can read Mifare Ultralight tags, for example, would still be able to read the UID of an NFC type 2 tag, even though it couldn't read any NDEF data encoded on the tag.

In its current state, there are some incompatibilities between some NFC devices and older Mifare Classic tags. Some NFC radios support Mifare Classic as an unofficial fifth tag type, while others don't. As NFC matures and more devices come on the market, these incompatibilities will hopefully come to affect users less. For now, however, it's best to check the compatibility between the readers and tags you plan to use in a given application.

CHAPTER 3

Getting Started with PhoneGap and the PhoneGap-NFC Library

PhoneGap is a development framework that allows you to build apps for iOS, Android, BlackBerry, Windows Phone 7 and 8, Symbian, and Bada all using (mostly) HTML5 and JavaScript. The folks at PhoneGap have created what is essentially a basic browser application, but with no interface. You implement the interface in HTML5 and Java-Script, then compile the app for your given platform. They've also developed a system for plug-ins so that developers can extend the basic browser application using native features of the various platforms. It's handy because it means you don't have to know the native application frameworks for the various mobile platforms in order to write applications that can run on them all.

For this book, you'll be using PhoneGap to write apps for Android and a plug-in that allows you to access the NFC hardware that's built into many Android phones. The code you write to listen for tags and to interact with the user will be written in JavaScript and the interface will be laid out in HTML5. The application shell is written in Java, as is the NFC plug-in, but you won't have to change any of the shell code for the projects in this book.

Why Android?

PhoneGap-NFC also supports Windows Phone 8, BlackBerry 7, and BlackBerry 10. We chose Android for this book because it has the largest market share and the most NFC phones, and most users of the PhoneGap-NFC plug-in have been Android users. If you have a Windows Phone or BlackBerry, you should be able to modify some of the examples to follow along. However, there are some limitations. Windows Phone 8 can read, write, and share NFC tags, but only has access to the NDEF data. It can't see tag type, tag UIDs, or any other tag metadata. BlackBerry 10 has similar restrictions: it can read and share NFC tags, but currently cannot write them.

PhoneGap-NFC for BlackBerry 7 supports more NFC features than BlackBerry 10, but you'll need to use older releases to make it work since PhoneGap 3.0 dropped support for BlackBerry 7.

You can use any text editor you want to write your code, but you'll use the Android software development kit (SDK) and its associated tools to compile your code and deploy it to your device. You'll also get to know the Cordova command-line interface (CLI), which is a set of tools for compiling PhoneGap applications using the Android SDK. You'll need a little familiarity with the command-line interface of your computer as well.

The instructions assume you're working in a command-line interface, such as the Terminal on any Linux machine or OS X. For Windows users at the Command Prompt, there are some slight differences that we'll call out.

Hello, World! Your First PhoneGap App

For the projects in this chapter, you need:

- A text editor (if you don't have a favorite text editor, we recommend Sublime Text 2 (*http://www.sublimetext.com/2*), as it's a good cross-platform code editor)
- An NFC-enabled Android phone (see Table 2-1 for a list of usable phones)
- A few NFC tags (for best results across multiple devices, stick with the NFC Forum types; see "Device-to-Tag Type Matching" on page 19 for more on which tags work with which devices)
- The Android software development kit
- The Cordova CLI, your toolbox for PhoneGap ("Install Cordova CLI for PhoneGap" on page 28)
- Node.js and the Node Package Manager (npm); you'll use this to download the Cordova CLI (see "Install Node.js and npm" on page 27)

Setting Up the Development Environment

First you need to download the Android SDK from the Android Developer site (*http://bit.ly/sdkandroid*). Android recommends that you download the Android Developers Toolkit (ADT) bundle, which includes a bundled version of the Eclipse development environment. We're not using Eclipse for this book, however, so you can just download the SDK tools for your platform, which should take less time to download. To do that, click "Use an Existing IDE" at the bottom of the "Download" page and you'll get a link to download just the SDK tools without Eclipse.

On OS X or Linux

Extract the Android SDK and put it somewhere on your computer where you know you can find it again. For example, if you put it in your Applications folder on OS X, the path to it would be */Applications/android-sdk-macosx*.

On Windows

You'll need to install a Java Development Kit (JDK) first by downloading it from the "Java SE" link on the Oracle website (*http://java.oracle.com*). After you install Java, you can run the Android SDK installer.

You'll need one more thing on Windows: Apache Ant, which manages the build process for Android programs. Download the Ant ZIP file from the Apache Ant website (*http://bit.ly/apacheant*), extract the file to the *C:* drive, and rename the top-level folder (such as *apache-ant-1.9.1-bin*) to *Ant*. If you did this correctly, you should find subdirectories such as *C:\Ant\bin* and *C:\Ant\lib*.

On Windows, the Android SDK installer will default to a hidden directory in your home directory: *C:\Users\Username\AppData\Local\Android\android-sdk*, which will make it hard to find later. We suggest you change this to *C:\Users\Username\Android\android-sdk*.

Install the Android Platform Tools

On OS X or Linux

Open up a Terminal window and change directories to the SDK directory (i.e., use `cd /Applications/android-sdk-macosx`). The SDK doesn't come with a version of the Android platform tools, so you need to install them by typing the following:

```
$ tools/android update sdk --no-ui
```

On Windows

If the Android SDK installer can't find your Java installation (a common problem on 64-bit Windows), quit the installer, and set your JAVA_HOME environment variable as directed later in this section. Try the installer again and it should find your Java installation.

You'll be given the opportunity to install the tools when the installer is finished. Leave the checkbox labeled "Start SDK Manager" checked and click "Finish." When the SDK manager appears, click "Install *n* Packages" (where *n* is whatever number of packages happen to be offered by default). If you accidentally unchecked the checkbox before clicking "Finish," open a Command Prompt, change directory to the SDK location (i.e., `cd Android\android-sdk`) and run the following command:

```
C:\Users\Username\Android\android-sdk>tools\android update sdk --no-ui
```

This will update the Android SDK and install the latest versions of the platform tools. You may be asked to accept some software licenses before you proceed. This will take a while, so you may want to take a minute to stretch and get some refreshment while it's installing.

Next you need to change the PATH variable for your environment to include the Android SDK tools. The tools directory covers most of the tools for compiling, uploading, and running your app on your device, and in platform tools, you'll find an important tool called adb that you'll use for debugging purposes later.

 In the examples that follow, if you put the tools in a location other than the one shown, change the paths as needed. Also note that you are creating two paths: one for the *tools* subdirectory and one for *platform tools*.

On OS X or Linux

Change directories to your home directory and edit the *.bash_profile* or *.profile*. If the file doesn't exist, you can just create it. Add the following lines to that file:

```
export ANDROID_HOME=/Applications/android-sdk-macosx
export PATH=$PATH:$ANDROID_HOME/tools:$ANDROID_HOME/platform-tools
```

Change the *ANDROID_HOME* path if you stored the SDK somewhere other than the Applications directory, of course. Then save your profile file, and log out of the Terminal and log back in to reset the PATH variable.

On Windows

You have to find your way to the "System Properties Advanced" dialog box:

Windows XP

Open the Start Menu, then right-click on "My Computer" and choose "Properties," then go to the "Advanced" tab.

Windows 7 or Vista

Open the Start Menu and right-click on "Computer." Choose "Properties," then choose "Advanced System Settings" from the list on the left.

Windows 8.1

From the desktop, right-click or tap and hold on the Start Menu, then choose "System." Select "Advanced System Settings" from the list on the left.

Click the button at the bottom labeled "Environment Variables." Find the PATH entry under "User Variables" (*not* "System Variables") and click "Edit." If there is no PATH entry, click "New" and name the new variable PATH.

Append all three of the following to the end of the path with *no space* between them (the last two entries let you run Java and Ant from the command line):

```
;%ANDROID_HOME%\tools
;%ANDROID_HOME%\platform-tools
;%JAVA_HOME%\bin
;C:\Ant\bin
```

Be sure to include the ; separator as shown (if you had to create a new PATH variable, you can skip the leading ;). Don't change anything that's already there: you must add this to the end. If you make a mistake, click "Cancel" and try again. Stay out of the "System Variables." If you make a mistake in the system PATH setting, you can cause serious problems for Windows.

While you're on this screen, you must also set your ANDROID_HOME and JAVA_HOME environment variables:

1. Click "OK" to dismiss the PATH dialog, then click "New" under "User Variables."

2. Set the name to JAVA_HOME and the value to C:\Program Files\Java \jdk1.7.0_25 (or whatever the installation directory of your JDK is).

3. Click "OK" to dismiss the PATH dialog, then click "New" again.

4. Set the name to ANDROID_HOME and the value to C:\Users\%USERNAME%\Android \android-sdk.

If you installed Java or the Android SDK in a different location, change the variables as necessary.

Finally, click "OK" until all the dialogs are gone.

Install Node.js and npm

Node.js is a platform for developing network applications in JavaScript. It also has a great system for installing packages (such as PhoneGap). Node's package manager (npm) is the fastest way to install the Cordova CLI for PhoneGap. You'll also see Node used in projects in Chapters 7 and 9.

To install Node.js:

Windows
    Download and install Node.js (*http://nodejs.org*).

If you have any trouble running Node from the command line in Windows after you install it, you may need to log out and log in again for its PATH changes to take effect.

Linux

Install Node.js using your package manager. If npm is in a separate package from Node.js, install it as well. For example, on Ubuntu, you'd run the command `sudo apt-get install nodejs npm`.

Mac OS X

You can either use the Node.js installer on the website, or install it with a package manager such as Homebrew (*http://brew.sh*). If the installer doesn't add the npm module binary directory to your PATH, you may need to add it to your PATH by putting something like this in your *.bash_profile* or *.profile* and then open a new Terminal window:

```
export PATH=/usr/local/share/npm/bin:$PATH
```

You'll also need Git installed. It's installed by default on OS X and most Linux distributions. If not, install it with your package manager. You can get command-line Git for Windows (*http://git-scm.com/downloads*), and the Git installer will ask if you want to install Git into the system PATH environment variable. We suggest that you do so, because this will let you run Git from the Command Prompt.

Install Cordova CLI for PhoneGap

Open a Terminal or Command Prompt and install the Cordova package (this gives you the PhoneGap framework).

On OS X or Linux

Run the following command at a Terminal prompt:

```
$ npm install -g cordova
```

On Windows

Run the following command in a Command Prompt window:

```
> npm install -g cordova
```

The `-g` option installs the Cordova command-line utility to a location in your PATH.

You can now create a PhoneGap project just by typing the following:

```
cordova create project-location package-name app-name
```

In the command, `project-location` is the path to your new Cordova Android project, `package-name` is the package name for the app you'll create, using reverse domain-style notation (e.g., com.example.myapp), and `app-name` is the name of your application.

You'll then need to `cd` into the project directory and add the Android platform:

```
cd /path/to/project-location
cordova platform add android
```

You'll see these steps frequently in the chapters that follow. For most of this book, we'll refer to the preceding steps simply by saying "use the `cordova create` command to create a project."

Now you're all ready to make your first PhoneGap project!

PhoneGap or Cordova?

What's the difference between PhoneGap and Cordova? PhoneGap was originally developed by Nitobi, which was later bought by Adobe. Before Nitobi was purchased, they donated the PhoneGap codebase to the Apache Software Foundation to ensure good open source stewardship of the code. As part of the transition from Nitobi to Apache, the project name was changed from PhoneGap to Cordova. PhoneGap is now Adobe's distribution of Cordova.

Historically, PhoneGap and Cordova, the open source project behind PhoneGap, were almost identical. This has changed with the release of 3.0. Now, the Cordova distribution provides the core functionality to embed a webview (browser) into a native application. Cordova is distributed without any of the plug-ins installed. This allows you to only install the functionality you need, simplifies your code base, and reduces the amount of code in your app.

PhoneGap is a distribution of Cordova, similar to how Safari and Chrome are based on WebKit. The PhoneGap distribution of Cordova comes with all of the core plug-ins installed. Additionally, the PhoneGap command line adds features like PhoneGap Build support. If you don't have a native SDK installed, the compiling of the project can be delegated to PhoneGap Build.

In this book, we use the terms PhoneGap and Cordova interchangeably. For code samples, we use the open source Cordova version.

Creating a PhoneGap Project

Change directories to whatever directory you like to keep projects in (perhaps your Documents directory) and use the `cordova create` command to create a project:

```
$ cordova create ~/Hello com.example.hello Hello
```

There is no output from `create` if it succeeds, but it will create a new directory. This command will create a directory in your working directory called *Hello*. Change directories to it and list the files:

```
$ cd ~/Hello
$ cordova platform add android
$ ls
```

 If Cordova requests that you install a specific Android target (other than the ones that were installed by default), type `android` to start the SDK manager, then install the SDK that Cordova requested. The version numbers of the SDK may not always match up (e.g., Cordova may ask for the Android 4.2 SDK, but the SDK manager only offers you 4.2.2), but the Android target that Cordova asks for (e.g., target 17) will match the API number listed in the SDK manager, as in Android 4.2.2 (API 17). After you install the Android target, try running the `cordova create` command again.

On Windows, the commands will be a little different. Open a Command Prompt (by default, it will place you in your home directory, usually *C:\Users\username*), but to be sure, you might want to change directory to it first with `cd /D %userprofile%` (in most configurations, the `%USERPROFILE%` environment variable contains your home directory). You can, of course, run these commands in another working directory:

```
> cd /D %userprofile%
> cordova create Hello com.example.hello Hello
> cd Hello
> cordova platform add android
> dir
```

On all three platforms, the directory will contain the following structure:

www
> The content files for the project: images, HTML, and so on. This is what you'll work with most.

platforms
> Support files for various platforms, such as Android.

plug-ins
> Any plug-ins you've installed.

merges
> Platform-specific web assets merged during the prepare phase.

The *platforms/android* directory contains the following:

AndroidManifest.xml
> The manifest file describing the app's structure, permissions, and so on.

ant.properties
> The compiler properties file.

assets
>A copy of the main *www* directory for the project.

bin
>Any binary files that are built in the compiling process.

build.xml
>The details needed by the compiler to build the project.

cordova
>A directory containing the various scripts that Cordova uses to automate the build process.

gen
>Files generated during the compile.

libs
>Any additional PhoneGap libraries needed, such as the PhoneGap-NFC library.

local.properties
>Properties of your development environment on your computer.

proguard-project.txt
>Properties for a tool for shrinking and obfuscating your code.

project.properties
>The project properties file.

res
>Resources used to build the project. You'll modify some files in this directory later.

src
>The Java source files for the app. You won't bother with these.

On Windows, you may need to install a USB driver for your device. When you updated the SDK earlier, you got USB drivers for many devices. However, even flagship devices like the Nexus 7 may require a separate driver installation. For example, you can download the Nexus 7 driver from ASUS (*http://bit.ly/1eMJkp0*). See Android's USB Drivers page (*http://bit.ly/usb-drivers*) for instructions on installing drivers that are included with the Android SDK.

You've got everything you need here to run a very basic app that does nothing but display a splash screen. To compile and install it on your device, connect the device over USB and run the following command if you are on OS X or Linux:

```
$ cordova run
```

If you're on Windows, run this command:

```
> cordova run
```

When everything's ready, you'll be running your app directly on your Android phone or tablet.

 Can't find developer options on Android version 4.2 or later? Open "Settings" and scroll down to "About Device" (it's "About Tablet" on the Nexus 7). Tap the "Build" number seven times. This will enable developer options. Then return to the previous screen to find "Developer Options" and turn it on. In particular, you want to enable "Stay Awake" while charging and "USB Debugging." If you have a password set for your device, you may want to disable it while you're coding, as it removes the need to unlock your device every time you upload a new version of your app.

Finally, open the phone and launch the Hello Application. You should see a screen like that in Figure 3-1. Once you've got the basic "Hello, World!" application running, try modifying the *index.html* to make it more fancy. It lives in the *www* directory. Add buttons, images, and all the other things you'd add to an HTML page. Then save your files, run it again, and see how it changes on your phone.

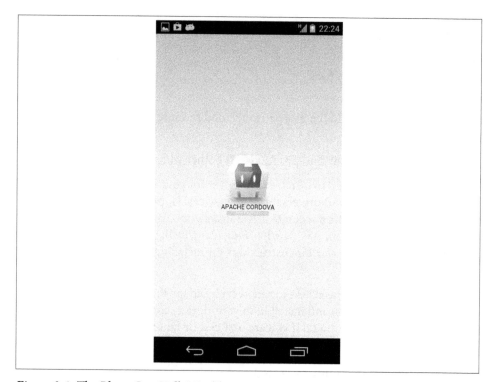

Figure 3-1. The PhoneGap HelloWorld app

The Important Files

There are two files you'll work with frequently in your PhoneGap projects: the *index.html* in the *www* directory, and the *index.js* file in the *www/js* directory. You can add other HTML and JavaScript files, but by convention, these will be the root of your application. These are the files you'll modify to make your app do what you want.

The *index.html* page will include the graphic layout of your application, just as it would for any website. The *index.js* contains event handlers, like `onDeviceReady()`, `initialize()`, and so forth. Later on you'll add some functions to it, like `onNfc()` for when a tag is read.

You can always get an unmodified version of the default file structure by creating a new project.

There are a few other JavaScript files that affect your application that you'll likely never see: the *cordova.js* file, the *cordova_plugins.js* file, and its companion, the *cordova_plugins.json* file. The *cordova.js* file is the main PhoneGap library. The *cordova_plugins.js* and *cordova_plugins.json* files initialize the plug-ins you install, giving you access to the PhoneGap-NFC library and the NFC hardware. These show up in *platforms/android/assets/www* when you install plug-ins and run your app.

A Word on JavaScript Idioms

The default coding idiom, or pattern of programming, for PhoneGap may look strange to you if you're still new to JavaScript. In many JavaScript programs, you'll see functions initialized like this:

```
function toggleCompass() {

}
function init() {

}
```

If you've programmed in C or Java, this pattern probably looks familiar to you. These functions are global to your application, and can be called from anywhere like this:

```
toggleCompass()
```

In the default Cordova *index.js* file, on the other hand, you'll see that all functions are created inside one giant variable called `app`. In JavaScript, variables can contain functions, and you can pass functions as parameters of functions. Since they're elements of the `app` object, they're written as an *object literal*, like so:

```
var app = {
    initialize: function() {

    },
```

```
    bindEvents: function() {

    },

    onDeviceReady: function() {

    }
}
```

An object literal is a pair of curly braces surrounding name/value pairs, which are separated by commas inside the braces. If you've seen *JavaScript Object Notation* (JSON), you've seen this before. JSON is the syntax for writing object literals. These are still functions, just in a different notation. To call these functions, which are local to the app object, you do it like so:

```
app.initialize();
app.bindEvents();
app.onDeviceReady();
```

Writing all your functions inside the app object means that you know they're all local and you won't accidentally overwrite functions from other JavaScript libraries with the same names you may choose to use in more complex apps.

For more on JavaScript, check out Douglas Crockford's *JavaScript: The Good Parts*. It does a nice job of describing how JavaScript is structured and how it works.

A Simple Locator App

Since the "Hello, World" template is such a handy reference, keep it intact and make a new project for your first custom app. This project will contain the bare minimum you need in your HTML and JavaScript files to get things running. To make it interesting, you'll make an app that starts and stops tracking your latitude and longitude on a click.

 In the following examples, OS X and Linux (indicated by a leading $) and Windows (indicated by a leading >) variants of the commands are shown one after another. On Windows, we're using %userprofile %, which points to your home directory in most Windows installations, but you can use another location if you wish.

In future chapters, unless the commands are radically different, we'll only show the OS X and Linux version, and Windows users should assume the commands are differentiated as shown here.

Make a new project called Locator just as you did before. Use `cordova create` again:

```
$ cordova create ~/Locator com.example.locator Locator ❶
```

❶   Windows users should type `%userprofile%\Locator` instead of `~/Locator`.

Then add the Android platform and the geolocation plug-in to the project. Plug-ins for PhoneGap/Cordova extend the framework's functionality. Plug-in authors register their plug-ins' URLs with the Cordova project so they can be added to the plug-in database. Many plug-ins add access to a device's hardware, like this one, which gives you access to a device's geolocation system. The NFC plug-in, which you'll see shortly, gives you access to the NFC radio. You'll see how plug-ins fit into the file structure a bit later, but for now, here's how to install the geolocation plug-in:

```
$ cd ~/Locator ❶
$ cordova platform add android
$ cordova plugin add \  ❷
    https://git-wip-us.apache.org/repos/asf/cordova-plugin-geolocation.git
```

❶   Windows users should type `/d %userprofile%\Locator` instead of `~/Nfc ReaderLocator`.

❷   `\` is the line continuation character in Linux, OS X, and other POSIX systems.

Now change directories to the project's *www* directory. Edit the *index.html* file and delete everything. The following is a minimal HTML file that includes only the basics you'll use for most apps. There's a main div element called `app` where all the action will take place. You'll see it and its subelements modified quite a bit in the *index.js* file. At the end of the file, include the *cordova.js* script and your application's *index.js* script. Finally, call the `initialize()` function from *index.js* to run the app:

```
<!DOCTYPE html>

<html>
   <head>
      <title>Locator</title>
   </head>
   <body style="font-size: 1.4em;">
      <div class="app">
         <div id="messageDiv"></div>
      </div>
      <script type="text/javascript" src="cordova.js"></script>
      <script type="text/javascript" src="js/index.js"></script>
      <script type="text/javascript">
        app.initialize();
      </script>
   </body>
</html>
```

Edit the *index.js* file and delete everything. You'll replace it with the following script. All the functions and variables in this script are local to an object called `app`, by convention. Start out by initializing a variable called `app`:

```
var app = {

};
```

Next, add a few functions you need for initialization, to set up listeners for startup events, button touches, and the like. Replace the code you just added with this:

```
var app = {
/*
   Application constructor
*/
   initialize: function() {
      this.bindEvents();
      console.log("Starting Locator app"); ❶
   },
/*
   bind any events that are required on startup to listeners:
*/
   bindEvents: function() {
      document.addEventListener('deviceready', this.onDeviceReady, false); ❷
   },

/*
   this runs when the device is ready for user interaction:
*/
   onDeviceReady: function() {
      app.display("Locating...");
      app.watchLocation();
   },
```

❶ console is defined by your browser. Every modern browser features a JavaScript console viewer in its interface.

❷ document is defined by your browser and the HTML document that you're viewing.

Next, add a function to get the device's location. This function has two callbacks, one for success and one for failure. If it succeeds, it displays the device's coordinates using a function called display(). If it fails, it displays a failure message:

```
/*
   Displays the current position in the message div:
*/
   watchLocation: function() {
      // onSuccess Callback
      // This method accepts a `Position` object, which contains
      // the current GPS coordinates
      function onSuccess(position) {
         app.clear();
         app.display('Latitude: ' + position.coords.latitude);
         app.display('Longitude: ' + position.coords.longitude);
         app.display(new Date().toString());
```

```
        }

        // onError Callback receives a PositionError object:
        //
        function onError(error) {
            app.display(error.message);
        }

        // Options: throw an error if no update is received every 30 seconds.
        //
        var watchId = navigator.geolocation.watchPosition(onSuccess, onError, {
          timeout: 30000,
          enableHighAccuracy: true
          });
    },
```

Finally, you need to connect these functions to the user interface. The functions that follow, `display()` and `clear()`, write to an HTML `div` element in *index.html*. You'll see these same two functions in many apps in this book:

```
    /*
        appends @message to the message div:
    */
    display: function(message) {
        var label = document.createTextNode(message),
            lineBreak = document.createElement("br");
        messageDiv.appendChild(lineBreak);      // add a line break
        messageDiv.appendChild(label);          // add the text
    },
    /*
        clears the message div:
    */
    clear: function() {
        messageDiv.innerHTML = "";
    }
};      // end of app
```

The full source listing for this application can be found on GitHub (*http://bit.ly/master-locator*).

Save the files you edited, then `cd` to the project root, and run the app on your phone with the following commands:

```
$ cd Locator
$ cordova run

> cd /d %userprofile%\Locator
> cordova run
```

When you run the app on the phone, you'll get a screen as shown in Figure 3-2.

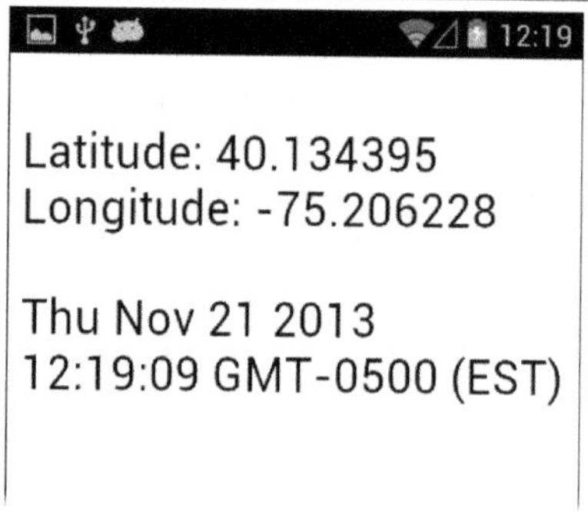

Latitude: 40.134395
Longitude: -75.206228

Thu Nov 21 2013
12:19:09 GMT-0500 (EST)

Figure 3-2. The Locator app showing location

You can modify the HTML and JavaScript just as you would for any other HTML-, JavaScript-, or CSS-based application on the Web. So feel free to experiment. Once you understand the basics of making a PhoneGap app, you're ready to move on.

Ways to Debug

There are a few useful tools for debugging while you're working on PhoneGap apps. Use whichever of these you find most helpful.

First, you might want to install jshint to check your code before running it. To install it, type:

```
$ npm install -g jshint
```

Then to run it, type:

```
$ jshint /path/to/js/file
```

When you run your code through jshint, it will pick up errors and formatting mistakes before you even run it.

When your device is still tethered to your computer, you can also get a log output when your app runs using adb logcat. After you run your app with cordova run, type:

```
$ adb logcat
```

This will give you the log of everything that happens on your Android phone. It's pretty detailed, and includes more than just your JavaScript *console.log* messages. It can be useful, but it can also be overwhelming. For example, here's the output from the launch of the previous app:

```
I/ActivityManager(  393): START u0 {act=android.intent.action.MAIN
        cat=[android.intent.category.LAUNCHER] flg=0x10200000
        cmp=com.example.locator/.Locator} from pid 590
D/dalvikvm( 2883): Late-enabling CheckJNI
I/ActivityManager(  393): Start proc com.example.locator for activity
```

```
com.example.locator/.Locator: pid=2883 uid=10080
gids={50080, 1006, 3003, 1015, 1028}

... twenty or so lines cut for brevity's sake ...

D/SoftKeyboardDetect( 2883): Ignore this event
I/ActivityManager( 393): Displayed com.example.locator/.Locator: +475ms
D/CordovaLog( 2883): file:///android_asset/www/js/index.js: Line 7 :
        Starting Locator app
I/Web Console( 2883): Starting Locator app at file:///android_asset/
        www/js/index.js:7
```

If you want to filter out all but the web console messages, run it through grep (OS X or Linux) or findstr (Windows) like so:

```
$ adb logcat | grep "Web Console"
```

```
> adb logcat | findstr /C:"Web Console"
```

When you do this, any of the console.log() statements in your JavaScript will show up in the console. It'll focus on things that you need to know most of the time. The output is stripped down to:

```
I/Web Console( 2335): Starting Locator app
        at file:///android_asset/www/js/index.js:7
```

You can also filter by any of the other message types this way. To quit it, press ctrl+C. When you disconnect your device from your computer, it will stop automatically.

Some programmers prefer to keep it running in a separate Terminal or Command Prompt window so they can compile and run without having to start and stop it. You can differentiate between runs of your app by hitting Enter several times in that window to create a break. Others prefer the stop/start method because it gives you a clearer record for each time you test your app.

You can also use the Android Debug Monitor to watch everything going on. This is a graphic user interface that lives in the *tools* subdirectory of your Android SDK. Because you added that to your path earlier on, you can simply type the following to launch it:

Linux or OS X:

```
$ monitor &
```

Windows:

```
> start monitor
```

The ampersand will cause monitor to run in the background and return you to the Command Prompt after launching. If you are using Windows, the batch file starts the monitor in the background. You can filter the logcat messages using the "Web Console" tag, or any other log tag you want to look for. You can also see the status of the other logs as well. There's also a performance monitor, a file explorer, and more. Figure 3-3 shows the interface.

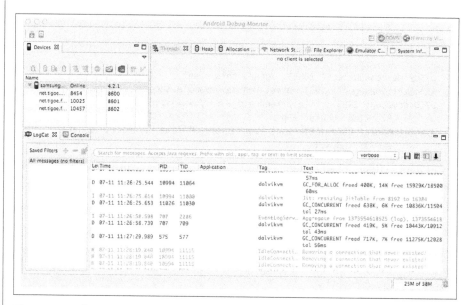

Figure 3-3. The Android Debug Monitor

If your device is connected to the Internet, you can also find a JavaScript console at *http://debug.phonegap.com*. Just put in a unique name like "kramnitz" in the field entry on that page, then include the script link in your *index.html* file. The next time you run your app, you'll see your JavaScript console at *http://debug.phonegap.com/client/#kramnitz*. It's handy and familiar, but it does require a network connection.

The advantage of *debug.phonegap.com* is also its disadvantage: you only see your JavaScript errors there. Sometimes you catch bugs from Android's messages using adb logcat that you'd otherwise miss if you were only looking for JavaScript errors. You may also find that *debug.phonegap.com* runs a bit slower when there's a heavy load of other programmers on it.

PhoneGap Meets NFC: NFC Reader

Now that you've got a handle on PhoneGap, it's time to extend it to include the NFC plug-in. For this you'll need the same software as the first app, the PhoneGap-NFC plug-in, and a few NFC tags as well. The first NFC app you create will read just the unique ID of any tag it sees.

The same structure will be used for all PhoneGap apps, so keep this app handy to use as a template. Create a new app called NfcReader:

```
$ cordova create ~/NfcReader com.example.nfcreader NfcReader ❶
$ cd ~/NfcReader ❷
$ cordova platform add android
```

❶   Windows users should type `%userprofile%\NfcReader` instead of `~/NfcReader`.

❷   Windows users should type `/d %userprofile%\NfcReader` instead of `~/NfcReader`.

Installing the NFC Plug-In

There are a number of changes needed to add NFC support to your project. These are all automated by the command:

```
$ cordova plugin add /path/to/plugin
```

The one you'll use commonly throughout the book is:

```
$ cordova plugin add https://github.com/chariotsolutions/phonegap-nfc.git
```

So you understand what's going on under the hood, here's what's installed:

- The plug-in's files live in your project's *plugins/* subdirectory (in this case, it's called *com.chariotsolutions.nfc.plugin*). It also gets installed in *platforms/android/assets/www/plugins/*.
- Your project's *AndroidManifest.xml* file and the resource config files also need modification so your app can use the NFC reader hardware on your device. This file lives in your project's *platforms/android/* directory.
- The file *platforms/android/res/xml/config.xml* gets modified as well. Here are the modifications to those two files:

```
<feature name="NfcPlugin">
    <param name="android-package"
      value="com.chariotsolutions.nfc.plugin.NfcPlugin" />
</feature>
```

- The *AndroidManifest.xml* file gets the NFC permission added at the end of the other permissions tags:

```
<uses-permission android:name="android.permission.NFC" />
<uses-feature android:name="android.hardware.nfc"
                 android:required="false" />
```

Since that's a lot to remember, it's nice that the one-line plug-in add command does it all for you.

You've already created your project using the create command, as directed earlier. Next, change directories to the root of your project and add the plug-in as described at the beginning of this section like so:

```
$ cd ~/NfcReader
$ cordova plugin add https://github.com/chariotsolutions/phonegap-nfc.git

> cd /d %userprofile%\NfcReader
> cordova plugin add https://github.com/chariotsolutions/phonegap-nfc.git
```

This installs the NFC plug-in from its online repository in the current working directory.

Writing the NFC Reader App

Now that you've got all the assets in place, it's time to make the application itself. You'll have two files you need to edit for this project:

- *index.html* in the *www* directory
- *index.js* in the *www/js* directory

This app will listen for NFC-compatible RFID tags and print their IDs on the screen.

Start with *index.html* as before. Here's a bare-bones page, much like the Locator app's index page. The changes are that you're adding a call to the Cordova script at the end of the body and you're changing the elements of the app div in the body. The latter is where tag IDs will be displayed.

Open *index.html* and replace it with the following code, then save the changes:

```html
<!DOCTYPE html>

<html>
    <head>
        <title>NFC tag ID reader</title>
    </head>
    <body style="font-size: 1.5em">
        <div class="app">
            <div id="messageDiv"></div>
        </div>
        <script type="text/javascript" src="cordova.js"></script>
        <script type="text/javascript" src="js/index.js"></script>
        <script type="text/javascript">
          app.initialize();
        </script>
    </body>
</html>
```

The *index.js* file will have an event handler to listen for NFC tags and rewrite the message div when it gets a tag. As before, start by initializing the app variable, and adding an `initialize()` function and a `bindEvents()` function:

```javascript
var app = {
/*
    Application constructor
*/
```

```
    initialize: function() {
        this.bindEvents();
        console.log("Starting NFC Reader app");
    },

/*
    bind any events that are required on startup to listeners:
*/
    bindEvents: function() {
        document.addEventListener('deviceready', this.onDeviceReady, false);
    },
```

The onDeviceReady() function is a bit more complex this time. You need to add a listener for when tags are discovered by the NFC reader. The nfc.addTagDiscovered Listener() function tells the NFC plug-in to notify your app when any NFC tag is read. The first argument is the event handler that is called when a tag is scanned. The second and third arguments are the success and failure callbacks for the plug-in initialization. When it succeeds, it will call the onNfc() function. When the listener is initialized, it'll let you know, and when it fails, it'll give you failure messages as well.

The addTagDiscoveredListener() handler is one of a few different listeners you can use from the NFC library. It's the most generic. It doesn't care what's on the tag, it just responds whenever it sees a compatible tag:

```
/*
    this runs when the device is ready for user interaction:
*/
    onDeviceReady: function() {

        nfc.addTagDiscoveredListener(
            app.onNfc,              // tag successfully scanned
            function (status) {     // listener successfully initialized
                app.display("Tap a tag to read its id number.");
            },
            function (error) {      // listener fails to initialize
                app.display("NFC reader failed to initialize " +
                    JSON.stringify(error));
            }
        );
    },
```

The onNfc() function takes the tag read in an NFC event and prints it to the screen using display(), just as you saw in the Locator app. These are the last functions in the app:

```
/*
    displays tag ID from @nfcEvent in message div:
*/
    onNfc: function(nfcEvent) {
        var tag = nfcEvent.tag;
        app.display("Read tag: " + nfc.bytesToHexString(tag.id));
```

```
        },
    /*
        appends @message to the message div:
    */
        display: function(message) {
            var label = document.createTextNode(message),
                lineBreak = document.createElement("br");
            messageDiv.appendChild(lineBreak);          // add a line break
            messageDiv.appendChild(label);              // add the text
        },
    /*
        clears the message div:
    */
        clear: function() {
            messageDiv.innerHTML = "";
        }
    };      // end of app
```

The full source listing for this application can be found on GitHub (*http://bit.ly/tigoe-nfcreader*).

That's all the changes. Save both files, then change directories to the root of the project if you're not already there, and compile and install the application:

```
$ cd NfcReader
$ cordova run

> cd /d %userprofile%\NfcReader
> cordova run
```

This launches the NFC Reader application. When it's up and running, bring a tag close to the phone, and you should get a message saying "Read tag" followed by the UID, in hexadecimal notation, as shown in Figure 3-4. Try with another tag and you'll see another UID.

Project Repository Housekeeping

Once you've got a project working, if you're going to save it in a Git repository or any other version control system, you may not want to store the build files, binaries, and so forth. It's a good idea to delete or `.gitignore` the file *platforms/android/local.properties* in your project directory so it's not uploaded to the repository. If you've got the PATH variables set in your login profile as shown in "Install Node.js and npm" on page 27, you'll never need the *local.properties* file. If you don't, then when you're updating the project from a remote repository, you'll need to:

```
$ cd projectDirectory
$ android update project -p platforms/android/
```

Here's a list of everything you can safely omit from your repository. If you're using Git, you can simply .gitignore these:

```
platforms/android/local.properties
platforms/android/bin
platforms/android/gen
platforms/android/assets/www
```

Figure 3-4. The NFC Reader app reading a tag

This will work with any RFID tag that's compatible with your NFC reader. That includes all tags compatible with the ISO-14443A format, including Philips and NXP Mifare tags, Sony FeliCa tags, NXP DESFire. You're not yet reading or writing data to the tag; you're just reading the tag's unique ID. For this application, compatible tags are not as much of an issue as when you start to write NDEF records to the tags. You'll find that this app can read Mifare Classic tag IDs even on those devices that are supposedly incompatible with Mifare Classic.

You've proven that your device's reader works, and can be programmed to read tags. In the next chapter, you'll learn how to read from and write to tags using the NFC Data Exchange Format, NDEF.

Troubleshooting

If your app doesn't read any of your tags, here are a few things to check:

Is your device NFC-enabled?
> To check, go to "Settings" on your device and tap "More…" If you don't see NFC there, you're out of luck. If you do see it, make sure it's enabled. When you scan a tag, you should get an acknowledgment melody. A successful read melody ends on a high note, and a failed read ends on a low note. The PhoneGap-NFC plug-in will report in the error if NFC is disabled or if NFC is not available. This app prints that info to the screen. Others may not.

Are you using compatible tags?
> If you get no acknowledgment melody when you scan a tag, make sure it's a compatible tag. If it's not, your reader won't read it.

Did you make good contact?
> The NFC reader on most devices is only part of the back of the device, usually near the upper part. If you don't get a read, try moving the tag around the back to find out where the reader's antenna is. It sometimes takes a second or so to get a good read.

Are your tags damaged?
> Ripped, wrinkled tags won't work, nor will tags placed perpendicular to the surface of the device. Make sure your tags are in good condition and are flat against the device.

Conclusion

The steps you followed in this chapter will be used in all of the PhoneGap-NFC projects that follow in this book, so here's a quick summary to use for future reference:

- Initialize a generic PhoneGap app with the `cordova create` command
- Add the platform using `cordova platform`
- Add the PhoneGap-NFC assets using `cordova plugin`

Your app needs, at minimum, the following files:

- *index.html*, in the *www* directory
- *index.js*, in the *www/js* directory

Your *index.html* file needs to include the following JavaScript scripts:

- *cordova.js*

- *index.js*

Your main JavaScript file should include the following elements from the PhoneGap-NFC library:

- An NFC listener handler
- A function to respond to NFC events

If you've got all of those elements, you're ready to go.

By now, you should be familiar with the structure of a PhoneGap app, and with the steps necessary to add the PhoneGap-NFC plug-in to an app. You'll see this same structure replicated in the rest of the projects in this book. What you've seen so far, though, is really just RFID—there's been no real NFC action yet. In the next chapter, you'll learn about the data exchange format that defines all NFC transactions.

CHAPTER 4

Introducing NDEF

In order to understand NFC, you need to know about the NFC Data Exchange Format (NDEF), which is the lingua franca for NFC devices and tags. In this chapter, you'll learn about the structure of NDEF and the records it carries. You'll also write a couple of apps that read and write NDEF-formatted messages.

NDEF Structure

NDEF is a binary format structured in *messages*, each of which can contain several *records*, as shown in Figure 4-1. Each record is made up of a *header*, which contains metadata about the record, such as the record type, length, and so forth, and the *payload*, which contains the content of the message. Think of an NDEF message like a paragraph, and records like the sentences within it. A well-formed paragraph is made up of sentences pertaining to one topic. Similarly, it's good practice to use one NDEF message made up of several records to describe one subject, say, an address book entry.

NFC transactions are generally short. Each exchange generally consists of only one message, and each tag carries just one message. Keep in mind the physical circumstances of an NFC exchange: you tap your device to another device or tag, and the whole exchange happens while you're in contact with the other device or tag. You don't want to send a whole novel in a single exchange, so think of your NDEF messages as paragraph-length, not book-length. You'll see a workaround to this for sending large files in one of the final chapters of this book, but for now, consider one NFC exchange as one NDEF message, and think of one NDEF message as one or more short records.

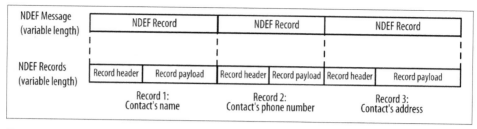

Figure 4-1. The structure of an NDEF message made up of several records; this is a typical example—an address book entry with three records (name, phone number, address)

An NDEF record contains a payload of data and metadata describing how to interpret the payload. Each record's payload can be one of several different *data types*. The header for each record contains metadata describing the record and its place in the message, followed by its type and ID. After the header comes the payload. Figure 4-2 gives you the full picture of the bits and bytes of an NDEF record.

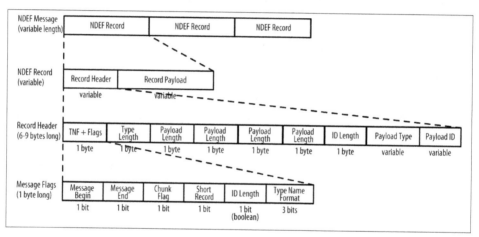

Figure 4-2. NDEF message structure, with details about the bytes of the header

As you can see from Figure 4-2, an NDEF record consists of a type name format (TNF), payload type, payload identifier, and the payload. The payload is the most important part of an NDEF record; it's the content that you're transmitting. The TNF tells you how to interpret the payload type. The payload type is an NFC-specific type, MIME media-type, or URI that tells you how to interpret the payload. Another way to think about this is that the TNF is the metadata about the payload type, and the payload type is the metadata about the payload. The payload identifier is optional and allows multiple payloads to be associated or cross referenced.

Type Name Format

NDEF records begin with a type name format. The TNF indicates the structure of the value of the type field. The TNF tells you how to interpret the type field. There are seven possible TNF values:

0 Empty
> Empty record that has no type or payload.

1 Well-Known
> One of several pre-defined types laid out in the NFC Forum RTD specification.

2 MIME media-type
> An Internet media type as defined in RFC 2046.

3 Absolute URI
> A URI as defined in RFC 3986.

4 External
> A user-defined value, based on rules in the NFC Forum Record Type Definition specification.

5 Unknown
> Type is unknown. Type length must be 0.

6 Unchanged
> Only for middle and terminating records of chunked payloads. Type length must be 0.

7 Reserved
> Reserved by the NFC Forum for future use.

For many applications, you'll probably use TNF 01 (Well-Known) or TNF 02 (MIME media-type) for various Internet media. You'll see the TNF 04 (External) frequently as well, since Android uses an External type called an Android Application Record to trigger apps to open.

Payload Type

The Payload type, also known as the Record type, describes the content of the payload more specifically. The TNF defines the format of the payload type. The type can be an NDEF-specified type, MIME type, URI, or External type. The NDEF Record Type Definition (RTD) specification describes Well-Known Record types and sets the rules for creating External types. The MIME RFC and the URI RFC set the rules for the other types.

For example, a record of TNF 01 (Well-Known) could have a Record type of "T" for a text message, "U" for a URI message, or "Sp" if the payload is a Smart Poster. A record of TNF 02 (MIME media-type) might be one of several different Record types, among them "text/html," "text/json," and "image/gif." A record of TNF 03 (Absolute URI) would have a literal URI, *http://schemas.xmlsoap.org/soap/envelope/*, as the type. A record of TNF 04 (External) might also have one of several different Record types, the most common of which you'll see in this book is "android.com:pkg."

For more detail, consult the NDEF Specification document on formats for NFC Forum Record Type Definitions (*http://bit.ly/specs-rtd*). You can find a list of common NFC RTD specifications in Appendix A as well.

NDEF messages can contain multiple Payload types, but by convention, the type of the first record determines how the whole message is processed. For example, Android's intent filtering for NDEF messages only looks at the first record.

URIs in NDEF Messaging

You'll hear the terms URI, URL, and URN frequently in this book. A URI, or uniform resource identifier, is a string of characters that identifies a web resource. A URN, or uniform resource name, names the URI. A URL, or uniform resource locator, also tells you the type of transport protocol needed to get the resource. If the URN is your name, then the URI is your address, and a URL is telling someone to take the bus to get to your address. Or in web terms:

URN

   mySpecialApp

URI

   net.tigoe.mySpecialApp (in reverse domain format)

URL

   http://tigoe.net/mySpecialApp

The type name format "Absolute URI" is a bit misleading. The Absolute URI TNF means that the *Record type*, not the *payload*, is a URI. The URI in the type field describes the payload, similar to the way a MIME type describes the payload for TNF 02. For example: Windows and Windows Phone use TNF 03 (Absolute URI) for LaunchApp records using the URI "windows.com/LaunchApp." LaunchApp records prompt the user to launch an app, much like Android uses Android Application Records to launch apps. If the app is not installed, the user is prompted to download it from the store.

Android breaks the NDEF specification a bit with Absolute URI records. Although the NDEF specification says the type describes the payload, Android devices handle TNF 03 (Absolute URI) records by opening the browser with the URI in the type field; basically, Android treats the URI in the type field as if it were the payload. BlackBerry and Windows Phone do not open the browser when an Absolute URI tag is scanned.

If you want to send a URI or URL as a *payload*, then you shouldn't use TNF 03 (Absolute URI). You should encode them as TNF 01 (Well-Known) with NFC RTD "U" (URI). The NDEF specification provides a URI Record Type Definition specification with URI Identifier Codes for encoding URIs more efficiently. For example, 0x01 is the code for *http://www*. 0x02 is the code for *https://www*. In "Writing Different Record Types" on page 66 you'll see an example in which you add a URL to a payload, then add a single byte with the value 0x01 to add the *http://www*. You'll see these in more detail in the application that follows, and you can see them all in Appendix A.

You can also encode URIs onto a TNF 01 (Well-Known) with NFC RTD "Sp" (Smart Poster). Using Smart Poster records allows additional information to accompany the URI, such as text descriptions in multiple languages, icons, and optional processing instructions.

Payload Identifier

The payload identifier, which is an optional field, should be a valid URI. It can be a relative URI, so even "foo" would work. It's used to let your applications identify the payload within the record by ID or to allow other payloads to reference other payloads. It's up to you to decide on the payload ID, but you also don't have to include it.

Payload

The payload is your content. It can be anything you want that fits in a stream of bytes. A properly constructed NDEF library doesn't care what's in the payload, it just passes it on. You can encrypt your payload, you can send plain text, you can send a binary blob, or anything else you can think of. It's up to the sending application and the receiving application to agree on what the payload means and how it's formatted.

Figure 4-2 provides some more details about the binary format of the record header's first byte. You will hopefully never need to use this information, since any well-written NDEF library should handle all of this for you. If you're using the software libraries in this book, this is true. The finer details of the binary formatting will be taken care of for you, and can safely skip ahead to "NDEF in Practice" on page 56. If you want to understand more of the structure of messages and records, read on.

Record Layout

The first five bits of the NDEF record are flags that tell how to process the record and information about the record's location in the message.

The bit flags in the first byte of the record header are as follows:

MB (Message Begin)
    True when this is the first record in a message.

ME (Message End)
True when this is the last record in a message.

CF (Chunk Flag)
True when this record is chunked.

SR (Short Record)
True if the short record format is used for payload length.

IL (ID Length is present)
True if the ID Length field is present.

Note that the IL bit is not the length of the ID field, it just indicates the presence of the length field. If the IL bit is 0, there is no ID length field or ID field.

The Message Begin and Message End bit flags are used for processing the records within a message. Since an NDEF message is just a collection of one or more NDEF records, there is no binary format for an NDEF message. The MB and ME flags let you determine when the message begins and ends. The first record in a message will have its MB flag set to true. The middle records will have both flags set to false. The end record in a message will have the ME set to true. A message with one record will have both the Message Begin and Message End bits set true.

Since there are only eight possible type name formats, you only need 3 bits to store it. The TNF is stored in the last three bits of the Message Flags byte.

Record Header

NDEF records are variable length data structures. The record header contains the information required to read the data.

An NDEF record begins with the TNF byte, which includes the bit flags. After the TNF, the NDEF record header includes the type length. The type length is a one byte field that specifies the length of the payload type in bytes. The type length is required, but may be zero.

The payload length comes next. The Short Record (SR) bit flag in the first byte of the record header determines the length of the payload record. If SR is true, the payload length is one byte, otherwise it's four bytes. Payload length is required, but may be zero.

If the ID length field is present and the (IL) flag is true, the next byte in the header is the ID length.

The record type field is a variable length field after ID length field (or after the payload length field if the IL flag is false). The type length field determines how many bytes should be read.

If there is a record ID, it comes after the type. This variable length field is determined by the ID length byte.

This is the end of the header. The payload comes next.

How Big Can an NDEF Message Be?

NDEF record payloads are limited in size to $2^{32}-1$ bytes long, which is why the payload length field of the header is four bytes (or 2^{32} bits). However, records can be chained together in a message to form longer payloads. In theory, there is no limit to the length of an NDEF message. In practice, the capabilities of your devices and tags define your limits. If you're exchanging peer-to-peer messages between devices and no tags are involved, your NDEF messages are limited only by the computational capacity of your devices, and the patience of the person holding the two devices together. If you're communicating between a device and a tag, however, your messages are limited by the tag's memory capacity.

When you're using NFC tags, the size limits of your records are well below the $2^{32}-1$ byte limit. NFC tag types are based on a few different RFID tag standards. Most NFC tag types are based on ISO-14443A standard. These vary from 96 bytes of memory, expandable to 4K depending on the tag type. The Philips/NXP Mifare family of tags are compatible with NFC, including the Mifare Ultralights, Mifare Classic 1K and 4K tags, and the Classic Mini. There is one type of NFC tag based on the Japanese Industrial Standard (JIS) X 6319-4. These have up to 1MB of memory. Sony FeliCa tags are typical of this type. For more details on the tag type specifications, see the specifications section of the NFC Forum website.

Generally, NFC exchanges are short. A person holds her device to a tag or another device, a brief exchange happens, and she moves on. It's not a protocol designed for long exchanges, because the devices need to be held literally in contact with each other. When you send large messages, the user has to hold the device in place for as long as the message takes to transfer. This can get tedious, so people generally prefer to use NFC to exchange capabilities between devices, then switch, or handover, to WiFi or Bluetooth to exchange data or media files.

Here's a typical example of where NFC and WiFi might work in tandem: imagine you've got an NFC-enabled home music player that can sync tracks with your smartphone or tablet via WiFi from a central home media server. You're listening to an album on the home stereo, but you have to leave for work. You tap your phone to the stereo, and the stereo tells the phone via NFC what track is playing and what time it's up to in the song. Your phone then checks to see if it's got the song in its playlist, and if not, downloads the song via cellular or WiFi. You go out the door, and when you've got your headphones on, you pick up the album where you left off.

Record Chunking

If you need to send content that's larger than the $2^{32}-1$ byte limit, you can break a payload into chunks and send it in several records. When you do so, you set the Chunk Flag (one of the TNF flag bits) to 1 for the first chunked record and all following records that are chunked, except the last chunk. You can't chunk content across multiple NDEF messages.

The TNF is set in the first chunked record. Subsequent chunks must use TNF 06 (Unchanged). Middle and terminating chunks must have a *type length* of 0.

The payload length of each record indicates the payload *for that chunk*.

Having a message that exceeds 500MB (that's 2^{32} bits) seems unlikely, so you may not use chunking for that too often. However, chunking can also be used for dynamically generated content, especially where the payload length is not known in advance.

Chunking is used relatively rarely. The libraries used in this book don't implement chunking. Android's parser will read chunked messages and combine them into logical NDEF records.

Additional Info

For more on the structure of NDEF, including a handy set of tests for writing your own NDEF parsing engines, visit the NFC Forum specifications page (*http://bit.ly/nfc-tech-specs*).

NDEF in Practice

In order to see NDEF in practice, it's useful to look at how existing applications do it. For this section, you'll need to download a few existing apps to your device so you can write some tags with them and compare their work.

One of the most common tasks in many popular tag writer apps is the Foursquare check-in. When you tap a tag formatted with this task, your device will automatically connect to the social media app Foursquare and check you in at a venue. However, each app manages this task slightly differently, and the differences show up in their results.

For this project, you need the following:

- An NFC-enabled Android phone
- Five NFC tags
- The apps that are listed next (you can install these to your device directly from Google Play on your computer or other device)

We also expect that you've gone through Chapter 3 and installed all the software needed to complete the examples in that chapter.

 For best results across multiple devices, stick with the NFC Forum tag types; Mifare Classic tags won't work with many newer devices. See "Device-to-Tag Type Matching" on page 19 for more on which tags work with which devices. Avoid Type 2 (Mifare Ultralight) tags as they don't have enough memory for this project.

For this comparison, the following apps were used:

- Trigger (*http://bit.ly/trigger-app*) by TagStand
- NFC TagWriter (*http://bit.ly/nfc-tagwriter*) by NXP
- NFC Writer (*http://bit.ly/nfc-tagstand*), also by TagStand
- TecTiles (*http://bit.ly/samsung-techtiles*) by Samsung (functional in the US and Canada only)
- App Lancher NFC Tag Writer (*http://bit.ly/app-lancher*) [sic] by vvakame

You'll also need NXP TagInfo (*http://bit.ly/nfc-taginfo*) to read the tags back, Foursquare for Android (*http://bit.ly/foursq-android*), and a Foursquare (*http://www.four square.com*) account.

Be sure to log in to the Foursquare app before you test any of these. If you run into any problems (such as the Foursquare app flashing on the screen and disappearing), go back to the app and log in again. This is a good example of the sort of problems that can occur entirely outside of your control. After the payload is handed off to Android, an app (such as Foursquare) is responsible for what happens next. If that app doesn't deal with it gracefully, you might be scratching your head.

Don't worry if you're not really in the location you're checking into. For one, each app will have to request permission to use Foursquare before actually performing the check-in, and you can always go and delete the check-in on the Foursquare website afterward. There's nothing worse than confusing your friends as to your whereabouts while you're testing NFC!

The process of writing the tags for each of these apps is fairly straightforward, with the exception of TagWriter. Here are the basic steps:

NFC Task Launcher
Open the app and click the + at the top to make a new task. Choose "NFC" from the task category list. Name your task, then click the + button. From the list, choose "Social Media," then "Foursquare Check-in at a venue." Choose a venue by typing in a name, or click the magnifying glass and the app will look for nearby venues.

Click "OK," then click "Add to Task." Click the right arrow to write to tag. Place the phone over the tag, and the app will write to the tag.

TagStand Writer

Open the app, click "Foursquare Venue," and pick a venue. When the screen changes to the writing screen, click the venue name to see the tag content. Write down the URL as shown in Figure 4-3 because you'll need it for NXP TagWriter. Place the phone over the tag and the app will write to the tag.

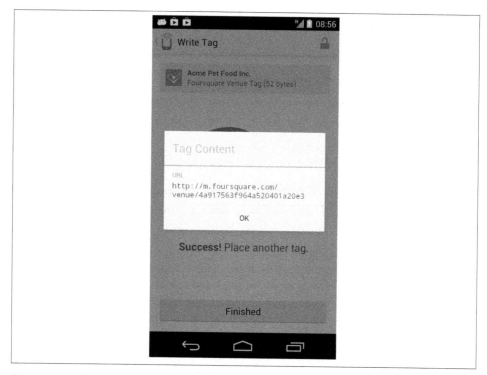

Figure 4-3. When you're on the tagwriting screen of TagStand Writer, you can click on the venue name to see the full URL of the venue

NFC TagWriter

Open the app and choose "Create, Write, and Store." Choose "New," and from the menu, choose "URI." Enter "Foursquare Check-in" in the description field. A description is required for this exercise so that a Smart Poster record is written to the tag. Enter the Foursquare venue as follows: *http://m.foursquare.com/venue/venueid* where *venueid* is a long hexadecimal string. Copy it from the one you wrote down from TagStand Writer previously. Don't forget the *http://*. Click "Next." Place the phone over the tag, and the app will write to the tag.

Samsung TecTiles

Make sure you already have Foursquare installed. Open the TecTiles app and click "New Task." Name it, then click "OK." Click "Add" to create a new task. Click "Application." Choose Foursquare from the list of apps. Click "Write to Tag." Place the phone over the tag, and the app will write to the tag.

AppLauncher NFC

Open the app, choose Foursquare. Place the phone over the tag, and the app will write to the tag.

Once you've written and labeled five tags, try them out. Close all apps and place the phone over the tag. They should respond as detailed in Table 4-1.

Next, open NXP TagInfo. Place the phone over the tag, and the app will read the tag. Choose NDEF and you can see the NDEF details of any tag (as illustrated in Table 4-1).

Table 4-1. The output of each app

App	Record	TNF	Record type	Payload	Action
NFC Task Launcher	1	MIME	x/nfctl	enZ:Foursquare;c: 4a917563f964a520401a20e3	Attempts to launch Task Launcher app; if successful, passes URL to Foursquare app
	2	External	android.com:pkg	com.jwsoft.nfcactionlauncher	
Tagstand Writer:	1	Well-Known	U	*http://m.foursquare.com/venue/ 4a917563f964a520401a20e3*	Launches Foursquare app, takes you to venue check-in screen
NXP TagWriter	1	Well-Known	Sp		Launches Foursquare app, takes you to venue check-in screen
	1.1		U	*http://m.foursquare.com/venue/ 4a917563f964a520401a20e3*	
	1.2		T	Foursquare check-in	
Samsung TecTiles	1	Well-Known	U	tectile://www/samsung.com/tectiles	Attempts to launch TecTiles app
	2	Well-Known	T	·enTask····Foursquare·com.joelapenna…[a]	

App	Record	TNF	Record type	Payload	Action
App Launcher NFC	1	External	android.com:pkg	com.joelapenna.foursquared	Launches Foursquare app only

[a] The Samsung TecTiles message contains unprintable characters. The actual characters are not important and have been replaced with a middle dot. The line was also truncated with an ellipsis. You can see the full byte stream for these tags by writing a tag from TecTiles and reading it with NXP TagInfo.

As you can see, each app does the job differently. There are four basic approaches represented here, however:

- Launch the Foursquare app and let the user do the rest (App Launcher NFC)
- Send a URI and let the operating system do the rest (Tagstand Writer)
- Launch the original app which in turn launches the Foursquare app (NFC Task Launcher, Samsung TecTiles)
- Send a Smart Poster (NXP TagWriter)

The first method just uses one NDEF record, with the TNF set to "External." The record type is then the Android Application Record for the application you want to launch, and the content is the actual name of the app, like so:

```
TNF: External
Record type: android.com:pkg
com.joelapenna.foursquared
```

Using the first method, you're telling Android what application to launch only.

The second method also uses just one NDEF record, with the TNF set to "Well-Known" and the record type set to "U" for URI. Again, the content is the actual address, like so:

```
TNF: Well-Known
Record Type: U
http://m.foursquare.com/venue/4a917563f964a520401a20e3
```

Using the second method, you're telling Android the URI of the thing you want to open and letting the operating system decide what application is best to open it. It's a bit like letting Windows decide what application opens a file with a particular extension. If Foursquare weren't on your device, Google Play would open to handle these URLs.

The third method uses an NDEF message composed of two NDEF records. For both NFC Task Launcher and Samsung TecTiles, the original application handles the tag read and then launches Foursquare. NFC Task Launcher uses a MIME-type record that includes the Foursquare venue information and an External AAR record that ensures that the application is installed. TecTiles takes a similar approach with a different implementation. TecTiles uses a URI record with a custom *tectile://* URL to launch the application. It encodes the Foursquare information into a second text record. Unfortunately, TecTiles only launches the application; it does not store the venue information. Both applications use intent filters to launch when their tag is scanned. NFC Task Launcher registers for MIME-type x/nfctl. TecTiles registers for their custom *tectile://* URI. You'll learn more about intent filters in "Android's Tag Dispatch System" on page 89.

The fourth method uses a Smart Poster record. Smart Posters are a more complex type of NDEF record, where the payload is actually another NDEF message. The message embedded in the Smart Poster payload contains two NDEF records of its own, a URI and a text record. Since Smart Poster records have multiple records, they can deliver additional information about the URI, such as a title, icon, or suggested processing actions.

You can see that some of the applications, like TecTiles and NFC Task Launcher, write Android Application Records to launch their own app, not Foursquare. They then have their app launch Foursquare. This presumably allows them to track when their app is used, even if the end result is to open a different app. It's more complicated, but it arguably allows for gathering metrics about your app's use.

A Tag Writer Application: Foursquare Check-In

In this section, you'll write your own tag writer app in order to get a better understanding of how this works in practice. This app is very simple; it looks for a tag that can be formatted as an NDEF tag, and if it finds one, it writes an NDEF message to the tag.

For this project, you need the following:

- An NFC-enabled Android phone
- Five RFID tags
- Foursquare for Android (*http://bit.ly/foursq-android*) and a Foursquare (*http://www.foursquare.com*) account

Start by making a new project as you did in Chapter 3. Use Cordova to create a project, add the Android platform, and install the plug-in:

```
$ cordova create ~/FoursquareCheckin com.example.checkin FoursquareCheckin ❶
$ cd ~/FoursquareCheckin ❷
$ cordova platform add android
$ cordova plugin add https://github.com/chariotsolutions/phonegap-nfc
```

❶ Windows users should type %userprofile%\FoursquareCheckin instead of ~/FoursquareCheckin.

❷ Windows users should type /d %userprofile%\FoursquareCheckin instead of ~/FoursquareCheckin.

Now you're ready to write your app by editing the HTML and JavaScript files. The *index.html* file is in the *www* directory of the app directory you just created and the *index.js* is in *www/js*. Open them both and delete everything to start your own app from scratch. Start with an *index.html* file like so:

```html
<!DOCTYPE html>

<html>
  <head>
    <title>Foursquare Check-In Tag Writer</title>
    <style>body { margin: 20px }</style>
  </head>
  <body>
    <p>Foursquare Check-In Tag Writer</p>

    <div class="app">
      <div id="messageDiv">No tag found</div>
    </div>

    <script type="text/javascript" src="cordova.js"></script>
    <script type="text/javascript" src="js/index.js"></script>
    <script type="text/javascript">
          app.initialize();
      </script>
  </body>
</html>
```

Writing an NDEF Record to a Tag

Next, you're going to write the *index.js* file to format an NDEF record and write an NDEF message to any tag it encounters. For now, you'll keep it simple and hardcode most of the parameters. You've seen many methods for triggering a Foursquare check-in; to start with, just do the simplest thing: launch the Foursquare app using an Android Application Record.

Start with a variable to write when a tag shows up:

```javascript
var app = {
    messageToWrite: [],     // message to write on next NFC event
```

Next comes an `initialize()` function to start things off and a `bindEvents()` function to set up an event listener to detect when the device is ready:

```javascript
// Application constructor
initialize: function() {
   this.bindEvents();
   console.log("Starting Foursquare Checkin app");
},
/*
   bind any events that are required on startup to listeners:
*/
```

```
bindEvents: function() {
    document.addEventListener('deviceready', this.onDeviceReady, false);
},
```

After that comes a handler to clear the screen and add an event listener to listen for discovered tags:

```
/*
    this runs when the device is ready for user interaction:
*/
onDeviceReady: function() {
    app.clear();

    nfc.addTagDiscoveredListener(
        app.onNfc,              // tag successfully scanned
        function (status) {     // listener successfully initialized
            app.makeMessage();
            app.display("Tap an NFC tag to write data");
        },
        function (error) {      // listener fails to initialize
            app.display("NFC reader failed to initialize "
                + JSON.stringify(error));
        }
    )
},
```

The NFC event handler, onNfc(), will write to the tag, like so:

```
/*
    called when a NFC tag is read:
*/
onNfc: function(nfcEvent) {
    app.writeTag(app.messageToWrite);
},
```

Next come the display() and clear() functions, just as you wrote them in "PhoneGap Meets NFC: NFC Reader" on page 40:

```
/*
    appends @message to the message div:
*/
display: function(message) {
    var label = document.createTextNode(message),
        lineBreak = document.createElement("br");
    messageDiv.appendChild(lineBreak);      // add a line break
    messageDiv.appendChild(label);          // add the text
},
/*
    clears the message div:
*/
clear: function() {
    messageDiv.innerHTML = "";
},
```

The methods for the `makeMessage()` and `writeTag()` functions that follow make use of functions from two objects defined by the NFC plug-in. These are the NFC object, which gives you access to your device's NFC reader, and the NDEF object, which defines and formats NDEF records and messages.

```
makeMessage: function() {
    // Put together the pieces for the NDEF message:
    var tnf = ndef.TNF_EXTERNAL_TYPE,           // NDEF Type Name Format
        recordType = "android.com:pkg",          // NDEF Record Type
        payload = "com.joelapenna.foursquared",  // content of the record
        record,                                  // NDEF record object
        message = [];                            // NDEF Message to pass to writeTag()

    // create the actual NDEF record:
    record = ndef.record(tnf, recordType, [], payload);
    // put the record in the message array:
    message.push(record);
    app.messageToWrite = message;
},

writeTag: function(message) {
    // write the record to the tag:
    nfc.write(
        message,              // write the record itself to the tag
        function () {         // when complete, run this callback function:
            app.display("Wrote data to tag.");   // write to the message div
        },
        // this function runs if the write command fails:
        function (reason) {
            alert("There was a problem " + reason);
        }
    );
}
};     // end of app
```

You already know that an NDEF record consists of a TNF, a record type, and a payload. The NDEF object has functions for creating NDEF#Records. An NDEF#Message is simply an array of NDEF#Records. To create a new NDEF record, you need to pass in four parameters:

Type name format
    A 3-bit value. The TNF values are contained as constants in the NDEF object, so you can refer to them using those constants.

Record type
    A string or byte array containing zero to 255 bytes, representing the record type. The NDEF object has built-in constants for many of these as well, though not all, as you can see in this example.

Record ID

A string or byte array containing zero to 255 bytes. As you read earlier, record IDs are optional, so you can use an empty array, but this value must not be null.

Payload

A string or array containing zero to $(2^{32}-1)$ bytes. Again, you can use an empty array, but this must not be null.

In the makeMessage() function, the TNF is TNF_EXTERNAL_TYPE, using the constants defined in the NDEF object; the record type is android.com:pkg, meaning that your payload will be an Android Application Record; the record ID is not specified, so an empty array is sent; and the payload is the name of the application to launch, com.joe lapenna.foursquared.

Save both the *index.html* and *index.js* files, then change directories to the root of your new app, and run it:

```
cordova run
```

When you run the app and tap your device to a tag, you should get the tag ID as shown on the left side of Figure 4-4. Click the link and the app will write to the tag and give you the notification seen on the right side of Figure 4-4. Close the app, tap your device to the tag, and it should launch Foursquare.

The full source code can be found on GitHub (*http://bit.ly/4square-checkin*).

Figure 4-4. The Foursquare check-in app; waiting for a tag (left) and writing to a tag (right)

Writing Different Record Types

Your app can now write a tag to launch another app from that tag, but it doesn't do all the things you saw in the previous examples. It would be great if you could emulate all five of the other apps, for comparison. To do that, make a new project called "FoursquareAdvanced." Install the NFC plug-in, then copy the *index.html* and *index.js* from the previous Foursquare Check-In app example:

```
$ cordova create ~/FoursquareAdvanced com.example.advanced FoursquareAdvanced ❶
$ cd ~/FoursquareAdvanced ❷
$ cordova platform add android
$ cordova plugin add https://github.com/chariotsolutions/phonegap-nfc
$ cp ~/FoursquareCheckin/www/index.html ~/FoursquareAdvanced/www/.
$ cp ~/FoursquareCheckin/www/js/index.js ~/FoursquareAdvanced/www/js/.
```

❶ Windows users should type %userprofile%\FoursquareAdvanced instead of ~/FoursquareAdvanced.

❷ Windows users should type `/d %userprofile%\FoursquareAdvanced` instead of `~/FoursquareAdvanced`.

Start by modifying the *index.html* page by adding a form with an option menu that lets the user choose the app she wants to emulate. Here's the new *index.html* page:

```html
<!DOCTYPE html>

<html>
    <head>
      <title>Foursquare Check-In Tag Writer - Advanced</title>
      <style>
          body { margin: 20px }
      </style>
    </head>
    <body>
      <p>Foursquare Check-In Tag Writer - Advanced</p>
      <div class="app">
        <form>
          Write a tag like: <br />
          <select id="appPicker">
            <option value="1">NFC Task Launcher</option>
            <option value="2">TagStand Writer</option>
            <option value="3">NXP TagWriter</option>
            <option value="4">Samsung TecTiles</option>
            <option value="5">App Launcher NFC</option>
          </select>
        </form>
        <div id="messageDiv"></div>
      </div>
      <script type="text/javascript" src="cordova.js"></script>
      <script type="text/javascript" src="js/index.js"></script>
      <script type="text/javascript">
        app.initialize();
      </script>
    </body>
</html>
```

When the user picks one of the apps in the menu, you'll now have a convenient form element that you can read to determine how to format your tag. Save the *index.html* file, and open your *index.js* file. You'll need to modify `makeMessage()` to handle this. The new function will emulate the apps you saw here by constructing several different types of NDEF messages. First, add a new local variable to read the HTML form element to find out which app the user wants to emulate. The rest of the local variables are the same names, but their values will be generated on the fly this time:

```javascript
makeMessage: function() {
    // get the app type that the user wants to emulate from the HTML form:
    var appType = parseInt(appPicker.value, 10),
        tnf,              // NDEF Type Name Format
```

```
recordType,       // NDEF Record Type
payload,          // content of the record
record,           // NDEF record object
message = [];     // NDEF Message to pass to writeTag()
```

The rest of the makeMessage() function will be totally changed. After the local variables, you're going to format a different NDEF message depending on which app you're emulating. Since the HTML form returns an integer from the option menu, you can use that result in a switch-case statement as follows. You can see that each case writes the same records as one of the previous apps. Case 1 creates a MIME media record containing the instructions for the Task Launcher app, then an Android Application Record to tell Android which app to launch:

```
switch (appType) {
    case 1: // like NFC Task Launcher
        // format the MIME media record:
        recordType = "x/nfctl";
        payload = "enZ:Foursquare;c:4a917563f964a520401a20e3";
        record = ndef.mimeMediaRecord(recordType, payload);
        message.push(record); // push the record onto the message

        // format the Android Application Record:
        tnf = ndef.TNF_EXTERNAL_TYPE;
        recordType = "android.com:pkg";
        payload = "com.jwsoft.nfcactionlauncher";
        record = ndef.record(tnf, recordType, [], payload);
        message.push(record); // push the record onto the message
        break;
```

Case 2 creates a Well-Known type record with the RTD set to URI. Since URIs have a standard format, the NDEF spec includes URI Identifier Codes to be used in place of some of the standard URI headers, to shorten the payload. For example, Table 4-2 shows the first few URI identifier codes.

Table 4-2. Some URI identifier codes

URI Identifier Code (UIC)	What it means
0x00	Nothing, used for custom headers
0x01	http://www.
0x02	https://www.
0x03	http://

The other URI headers you're used to, like *ftp://* and *mailto:* and *file:///*, are all included with their own numbers. For a complete list, see the URI Record Type Definition document, part of the NFC Specification on the NFC Forum site. It's also listed in Appendix A.

In order to add the UIC, you need to convert the URI string to an array of bytes and push the UIC on to the beginning of it. In Case 2, add 0x03, the UIC for *http://*:

```
case 2: // like Tagstand Writer
    // format the URI record as a Well-Known type:
    tnf = ndef.TNF_WELL_KNOWN;
    recordType = ndef.RTD_URI; // add the URI record type
    // convert to an array of bytes:
    payload = nfc.stringToBytes(
        "m.foursquare.com/venue/4a917563f964a520401a20e3");
    // add the URI identifier code for "http://":
    payload.unshift(0x03);
    record = ndef.record(tnf, recordType, [], payload);
    message.push(record); // push the record onto the message
    break;
```

Case 3 is special because it's creating a Smart Poster message. Smart Posters are unique among the Well-Known types in that they're records that contain NDEF messages. As you can see in the next example, you're constructing the payload of the Smart Poster record as an array of records. That array is the message.

In Chapter 5, you'll see how to extract a Smart Poster record by treating its content as a message, and extracting that message recursively:

```
case 3: // like NXP TagWriter
    // The payload of a Smart Poster record is an NDEF message
    // so create an array of two records like so:
    var smartPosterPayload = [
        ndef.uriRecord(
            "http://m.foursquare.com/venue/4a917563f964a520401a20e3"),
        ndef.textRecord("foursquare checkin"),
    ];

    // Create the Smart Poster record from the array:
    record = ndef.smartPoster(smartPosterPayload);
    // push the Smart Poster record onto the message:
    message.push(record);
    break;
```

Case 4 constructs a URI record and a text record that contains some binary data. As you saw in Case 2, you need to convert the URI to a byte array and push the URI Identifier Code on to the front of the array. In this case, since Samsung is using a custom URI header (*tectile://*), use the URI Identifier Code 0x00, which writes the URI exactly as written. TecTiles also writes a second record with TNF 01 (Well-Known type) and type "T."

Samsung is also using a proprietary token in the middle of the payload. You can determine this from reading a tag written with the TecTiles app with the NXP TagReader app. It's duplicated here so that the message is formatted just as the Samsung app wants it to be:

```
case 4: // like TecTiles
    // format the record as a Well-Known type
    tnf = ndef.TNF_WELL_KNOWN;
```

```
recordType = ndef.RTD_URI; // add the URI record type
var uri = "tectiles://www.samsung.com/tectiles";
payload = nfc.stringToBytes(uri);
var id = nfc.stringToBytes("0");
// URI identifier 0x00 because there's no ID for "tectile://":
payload.unshift(0x00);
record = ndef.record(tnf, recordType, id, payload);
message.push(record); // push the record onto the message

// text record with binary data
tnf = ndef.TNF_WELL_KNOWN;
recordType = ndef.RTD_TEXT;
payload = [];
// language code length
payload.push(2);
// language code
payload.push.apply(payload, nfc.stringToBytes("en"));
// Task Name
payload.push.apply(payload, nfc.stringToBytes("Task"));
// 4-byte token proprietary to TecTiles:
payload.push.apply(payload, [10, 31, 29, 19]);
// Application Name
payload.push.apply(payload, nfc.stringToBytes("Foursquare"));
// NULL terminator
payload.push(0);
// Activity to launch
payload.push.apply(payload, nfc.stringToBytes(
    "com.joelapenna.foursquared.MainActivity"));
// NULL terminator
payload.push(0);
// Application packageName
payload.push.apply(payload, nfc.stringToBytes(
    "com.joelapenna.foursquared"));
id = nfc.stringToBytes("1");
record = ndef.record(tnf, recordType, id, payload);
message.push(record); // push the record onto the message
break;
```

The TecTiles record is too large for certain tags, such as the Mifare
Ultralight, which has a limited capacity.

Case 5 constructs an Android Application Record to open Foursquare directly. It's just
like all the other Android Application Records you've made already. It's an External
TNF, with the record type android.com:pkg and the app name as the payload:

```
case 5: // like App Launcher NFC
    // format the Android Application Record:
    tnf = ndef.TNF_EXTERNAL_TYPE;
```

```
            recordType = "android.com:pkg";
            payload = "com.joelapenna.foursquared";
            record = ndef.record(tnf, recordType, [], payload);
            message.push(record); // push the record onto the message
            break;
        } // end of switch-case statement
```

Finally, finish off the `makeMessage()` function by setting the message to write and no-
tifying the user:

```
        app.messageToWrite = message;
        app.display("Tap an NFC tag to write data");
    }, // end of makeMessage()
```

With these changes you can save the *index.js* file and run the app (make sure you still
have the `writeTag()` function in your app from the previous example):

```
$ cordova run
```

When you do, you'll get a drop-down menu that lets you emulate any of the apps you
saw in Table 4-1. To use it, pick an app to emulate from the menu, then tap the phone
to a tag. Figure 4-5 shows the app.

The full source code can be found on GitHub (*http://bit.ly/4squareadv*).

*Figure 4-5. The Foursquare Check-In Advanced app; initial screen (left), showing op-
tions menu (center), and after writing to tag (right)*

PhoneGap-NFC NDEF Helper Functions, Summarized

As you can see, this app now covers multiple functions of the PhoneGap-NFC library by emulating various approaches to the same task. There are a few helper functions in the NDEF object it contains that can be used to write NDEF records. The main one is ndef.record(), which requires you to give it the TNF, record type, ID, and payload:

```
// Caller specifies the TNF and record type
record = ndef.record(tnf, recordType, id, payload);
// example:
record = ndef.record(ndef.TNF_EXTERNAL_TYPE, "android.com:pkg",
    [],"com.joelapenna.foursquared");
```

There's also a helper for MIME media records that takes just a MIME type and the payload:

```
// TNF: MIME media (02)
record = ndef.mimeMediaRecord(mimeType, payload);
// example:
record = ndef.mimeMediaRecord("text/json", '{"answer": 42}');
```

The URI helper builds a record using TNF 01, Well-Known, and record type "U" to send a URI as you saw in Case 3 of "Writing Different Record Types" on page 66. The helper will shorten your URI using a URI Identifier Code. In this example, *http://* will be written to the tag as 0x03 followed by *m.foursquare.com*:

```
// TNF: Well-Known Type(01), RTD: URI ("U")
record = ndef.uriRecord(uri);
// example:
record = ndef.uriRecord("http://m.foursquare.com/");
```

The text record helper makes text records using a Well-Known TNF and a text record type definition. If no language is specified, it defaults to English:

```
// TNF: Well-Known Type(01), RTD: Text ("T")
record = ndef.textRecord(text, language);
// example:
// defaults to English, since no language specified:
record = ndef.textRecord("How are you doing?");
```

The Smart Poster helper constructs a Smart Poster from other records:

```
//TNF: Well-Known Type (01), RTD: Smart Poster ("Sp")
record = ndef.smartPoster(ndefMessage);
// example:
record = ndef.smartPoster (
   // URI record:
   ndef.uriRecord("http://m.foursquare.com/venue/4a917563f964a520401a20e3"),
   // text record:
   ndef.textRecord("foursquare checkin")
);
```

There's also a helper you didn't see in this chapter, the empty record helper. This just makes an empty record for you to fill out:

```
// TNF: Empty (00)
record = ndef.emptyRecord();
// example:
record = ndef.emptyRecord();  // it's empty!
```

With these functions, you can construct all of the types of NDEF messages you'll see in the rest of this book.

Conclusion

We'll go further into NDEF records and messages in the following chapters. The key concepts to take away from this introduction, though, are as follows:

NFC-formatted *tags* contain NDEF *messages*. NDEF messages are composed of one or more NDEF *records*. You'll be tempted to talk about tags and messages and records interchangeably, but don't do it. Later in the book, you'll pass messages from device to device with no tags.

All NDEF records have a type. In the specs, its sometimes called Payload type, sometimes called Record type, other times just type. The type name format (TNF) categorizes the types broadly into a few areas and tells you how to interpret the type:

For TNF 01 (Well-Known)
    The NFC Forum Record Type Definition (RTD) specification tells you what types to use.

For TNF 02 (MIME)
    The MIME RFC (RFC 2046) tells you what types are valid.

For TNF 03 (URI)
    The URI RFC (RFC 3986) tells you how to make valid types.

For TNF 04 (External)
    The NFC Forum RTD specification tells you how to make your own types.

There are eight formal type name formats of NDEF messages, but most of the work gets done with just three: Well-Known, MIME media, and External. The Well-Known TNF includes a number of useful definitions for record types, including text messages, URIs, Smart Posters, and the various carriers needed for peer-to-peer handovers. You'll learn more about the peer-to-peer messages in Chapter 8. You'll see text messages and URIs used throughout this book. The MIME media TNF covers all Internet media types, and you can use it to make custom types as well, as you'll see in Chapter 6. The External TNF is used for records like the Android Application Record.

You won't see a lot of Smart Poster types in this book. As you saw in the Smart Poster case in "Writing Different Record Types" on page 66, the payload of a Smart Poster record is itself an NDEF message. So in order to read a Smart Poster, you first have to parse the message that encloses it, then you have to parse the message that it encloses. We feel this is redundant for most applications, and that it's better practice to simply use multiple records in an NDEF message.

There are multiple ways to achieve the same ends with NDEF messages. How that message is received depends on the operating system of the device that's receiving it. In the next chapter, you'll look at how Android offers you a few different ways to filter NDEF types to your application.

CHAPTER 5

Listening for NDEF Messages

Every well-designed application relies on good listening for relevant events, whether they're user input events, network events, or some other form. NFC applications are no different. NFC applications are always listening for NDEF messages, parsing and filtering the message type and contents, and taking action accordingly. In Chapter 4, you got an introduction on how to write NDEF messages using the PhoneGap-NFC plug-in, but we didn't dive deeply into the listening part.

There are two main ways to listen for NDEF messages: you can program your application to listen for them when it's the app in the foreground, or you can let the operating system of your device do the listening, and call your application when it sees a message that's relevant to your app. The PhoneGap-NFC plug-in offers several NFC events that you can program your app to listen for, and Android offers a *tag dispatch system* that allows you to tell the operating system which tags you're most interested in. NFC apps can take advantage of the tag dispatch system by writing *intent filters* in the Android Manifest that tell the operating system which tags to route to the app. They can also explicitly listen for some or all tags, overriding the intent filters of other apps using the *foreground dispatch system*. In this chapter, you'll learn a bit more about how to listen for and filter NDEF messages using PhoneGap-NFC's event listeners and Android's tag dispatch system.

PhoneGap-NFC's Event Listeners

Up until now, you haven't specified how Android should deal with tags, and you've used only one event listener, the `tagDiscoveredListener`. This event listener uses the foreground dispatch system to tell Android that you want your app to receive all NFC-related messages, and not to route them to other apps. It works well when you want everything to go through your app, and you've probably figured out already that some of the other apps you've seen, like TagWriter and TagInfo, also use the foreground dispatch system in this manner. When your app is in the foreground, it gets priority notification of all events, NFC and otherwise. That means it's up to you to decide what you want to listen for and what to ignore.

The PhoneGap-NFC plug-in offers you four different NFC-related event listeners:

Tag discovered listener
> Listens for all tags that are compatible with the reader hardware. This is the most general listener.

NDEF-formatable listener
> Listens for all compatible tags that can be formatted to receive NDEF messages.

NDEF listener
> Listens for any tags containing NDEF messages. If a legitimate NDEF message is received, this listener will generate an event.

MIME-type listener
> Listens only for those NDEF messages containing a MIME-type. This is the most specific of all the event listeners, and often the most useful. You can use the MIME-type listener to filter for messages containing a specific MIME-type. It will then ignore messages containing other MIME-types. You can also use it to filter for messages containing no type at all. You can't, however, register two MIME-type listeners for different types.

MIME Media-Types in NDEF

The word *type* has a lot of meanings when talking about NFC. If you're still confused, review "Type Name Format" on page 51 and "Payload Type" on page 51, which cover it in detail. Much of this chapter focuses on one particular type, the MIME media-type. *MIME* (originally *Multipurpose Internet Mail Extensions*) is an Internet standard originally designed to extend email to support various nontext media types. For a full list of MIME-types, see the Internet Assigned Numbers Authority (IANA) document on MIME types (*http://bit.ly/media-types*). The NFC Forum specification writers realized that they didn't need to re-invent a media type protocol, because MIME already did a pretty good job.

For NDEF records with TNF MIME media-type, you generally use one of the pre-existing MIME-types like `text/plain` as the record type to describe the contents of the payload. The NDEF specification says "The use of nonregistered media types is discouraged." We do it anyway. Why? MIME-types are an easy, convenient way to differentiate your NFC tags from other tags. When using the Hue lights in Chapter 6, for example, we define a MIME-type of `text/hue`. You also saw it in "NDEF in Practice" on page 56 when NFC Task Launcher used a type called `x/nfctl`. That's not a type you'll find in the general MIME specification.

> Android provides intent filters (see "Android's Tag Dispatch System" on page 89 further on in this chapter) that allow an application to register to listen for NFC tags it cares about. When the operating system encounters an NFC tag that your app is registered to listen for, it will launch your application and include the data from the NFC tag. NFC Task Launcher is likely registered to listen for the MIME-type x/nfctl. You'll do something similar when you get to Chapter 6.

You can register multiple listeners in the same app, and Android will generate only the most specific event if a given tag satisfies more than one listener. For example, a tag with a plain-text message on it could potentially trigger all of these listeners. It's a readable tag, it's NDEF-formatable, it's NDEF-formatted, and it has a legitimate MIME type (text/plain). However, since the MIME type is the most specific listener, that's the event that would be generated.

You can use multiple cascading listeners. For example, if you knew that most of your tags would be plain-text tags, you could have a specific MIME-type listener that captures them, then use an NDEF listener to capture all other NFC types, and an NDEF-formatable listener to search for empty tags and prompt the user to put something on them.

The next application shows this in action. In this app, you'll implement all four listeners, and use different tags to trigger each one.

An NDEF Reader Application

For this project, you need the following:

- An NFC-enabled Android phone
- At least four NFC tags (for best results across multiple devices, stick with the NFC Forum types; see "Device-to-Tag Type Matching" on page 19 for more on which tags work with which devices).

We also expect that you've gone through Chapter 3 and installed all the software needed to complete the examples in that chapter.

Start by making a new project using the cordova create command:

```
$ cordova create ~/NdefReader com.example.ndefreader NdefReader ❶
$ cd  ~/NdefReader ❷
$ cordova platform add android
$ cordova plugin add https://github.com/chariotsolutions/phonegap-nfc
```

❶　Windows users should type %userprofile%\NdefReader instead of ~/Ndef Reader.

❷ Windows users should type `/d %userprofile%\NdefReader` instead of `~/NdefReader`.

You can copy the *index.html* and *index.js* from the NFC Reader app as a base for this project:

```
$ cp ~/NfcReader/www/index.html ~/NdefReader/www/.
$ cp ~/NfcReader/www/js/index.js ~/NdefReader/www/js/.
```

The *index.html* for this project should look like this:

```
<!DOCTYPE html>

<html>
    <head>
        <title>NDEF Reader</title>
    </head>
    <body>
        <div class="app">
            <p>NDEF Reader</p>
            <div id="messageDiv"></div>
        </div>
        <script type="text/javascript" src="cordova.js"></script>
        <script type="text/javascript" src="js/index.js"></script>
        <script type="text/javascript">
          app.initialize();
        </script>
    </body>
</html>
```

Listening for Multiple Events

The *index.js* file starts with the same base as the NFC Reader app. The `initialize()` and `bindEvents()` functions will remain the same as well as the `display()` and `clear()` functions. The `onDeviceReady()` function will start the same, but you'll add three new listeners after the `addTagDiscoveredListener`. The new function will look like this:

```
/*
   this runs when the device is ready for user interaction:
*/
    onDeviceReady: function() {

      nfc.addTagDiscoveredListener(
         app.onNonNdef,         // tag successfully scanned
         function (status) {    // listener successfully initialized
            app.display("Listening for NFC tags.");
         },
         function (error) {     // listener fails to initialize
            app.display("NFC reader failed to initialize "
               + JSON.stringify(error));
         }
```

```
    );

    nfc.addNdefFormatableListener(
        app.onNonNdef,              // tag successfully scanned
        function (status) {         // listener successfully initialized
            app.display("Listening for NDEF Formatable tags.");
        },
        function (error) {          // listener fails to initialize
            app.display("NFC reader failed to initialize "
                + JSON.stringify(error));
        }
    );

    nfc.addNdefListener(
        app.onNfc,                  // tag successfully scanned
        function (status) {         // listener successfully initialized
            app.display("Listening for NDEF messages.");
        },
        function (error) {          // listener fails to initialize
            app.display("NFC reader failed to initialize "
                + JSON.stringify(error));
        }
    );

    nfc.addMimeTypeListener(
        "text/plain",
        app.onNfc,                  // tag successfully scanned
        function (status) {         // listener successfully initialized
            app.display("Listening for plain text MIME Types.");
        },
        function (error) {          // listener fails to initialize
            app.display("NFC reader failed to initialize "
                + JSON.stringify(error));
        }
    );

    app.display("Tap a tag to read data.");
},
```

As you can see, these listeners are all mostly the same in their structure. The only change is the message they display when they're successfully registered, and the callback function they invoke. Those that are likely to return an NDEF message call onNfc(), and those that are not call onNonNdef().

When the tag you read is not compatible with NDEF in any way, the listener doesn't return a tag. For example, you might read 13.56MHz RFID tags that are not even Mifare tags (Philips ICODE or Texas Instruments Tag-it); your reader can read its UID but nothing else. If you're using a device like the Nexus 4, which can't read Mifare Classic tags, you'll only be able to read the UID but no tag data. You need to handle these tags differently. The onNonNdef() handler takes care of this case.

The new onNfc() function will call clear() to clear the message div, then display the type of event that called it, and the details about the tag. The onNonNdef() function will read the tag UID and the tech types from the tag. Then add a showTag() function to show the tag details from onNfc():

```
/*
    Process NDEF tag data from the nfcEvent
*/
onNfc: function(nfcEvent) {
    app.clear();                    // clear the message div
    // display the event type:
    app.display(" Event Type: " + nfcEvent.type);
    app.showTag(nfcEvent.tag);    // display the tag details
},

/*
    Process non-NDEF tag data from the nfcEvent
    This includes
     * Non NDEF NFC Tags
     * NDEF-Formatable Tags
     * Mifare Classic Tags on Nexus 4, Samsung S4
     (because Broadcom doesn't support Mifare Classic)
*/
onNonNdef: function(nfcEvent) {
    app.clear();                    // clear the message div
    // display the event type:
    app.display("Event Type: " + nfcEvent.type);
    var tag = nfcEvent.tag;
    app.display("Tag ID: " + nfc.bytesToHexString(tag.id));
    app.display("Tech Types: ");
    for (var i = 0; i < tag.techTypes.length; i++) {
        app.display("  * " + tag.techTypes[i]);
    }
},

/*
    writes @tag to the message div:
*/

showTag: function(tag) {
    // display the tag properties:
    app.display("Tag ID: " + nfc.bytesToHexString(tag.id));
    app.display("Tag Type: " + tag.type);
    app.display("Max Size: " + tag.maxSize + " bytes");
    app.display("Is Writable: " + tag.isWritable);
    app.display("Can Make Read Only: " + tag.canMakeReadOnly);
},
```

That gives you enough to run the app. Save all your files and run the app as usual:

```
$ cordova run
```

Try this app with the Foursquare check-in tags you made for Chapter 4. Then try making a new tag, with a plain-text message. You can do this using NXP TagWriter. Tap "Create, write, and store," then "New," then "Plain Text," then enter a text message. Finally, tap "Next," then tap a new tag to the back of your device to write to it. Then re-open the NDEF Reader app you just wrote, and read this tag. It should read as an ndef-mime event, unlike the others. Figure 5-1 shows a few different results you should get from this app so far.

Figure 5-1. Results from the NDEF Reader app: a generic NDEF-formatted tag; a blank, but NDEF-formatable tag; and a text tag with MIME-type "text/plain"

You probably didn't get any new events of type "tag." That's because it's overridden by every other event listener. It's rare you'll run across a tag that's compatible with the NFC reader, but not at least NDEF-formatable. Certain non-Mifare RFID tags will show up this way (including Texas Instrument Tag-it HF tags, and one of Don's credit cards), but not much else. If you happen to write PhoneGap-NFC apps for BlackBerry 7, however, you'll see that all the eligible listeners will fire when a given tag comes into range, so you'll have to adapt your code for cross-platform use if you want BlackBerry users to get the same results as Android users. For more on cross-platform differences, see the PhoneGap-NFC plug-in README (*http://bit.ly/nfc-readme*) file.

Reading the NDEF Messages

Now that you've got an app that can read any type of compatible tag, you might as well extend it to give you the details of the NDEF messages on each tag it reads. Keep in mind NDEF messages are made of NDEF records, and when the record is a Smart Poster, the contents of the record is itself an NDEF message. In order to handle this, you'll need a showMessage() function that's called by showTag(), and a showRecord() function that's called by showMessage(). If the record is a Smart Poster, you'll need to call show Message() again. This is where recursion is your friend, as you'll see. Figure 5-2 shows you the flow of the whole program.

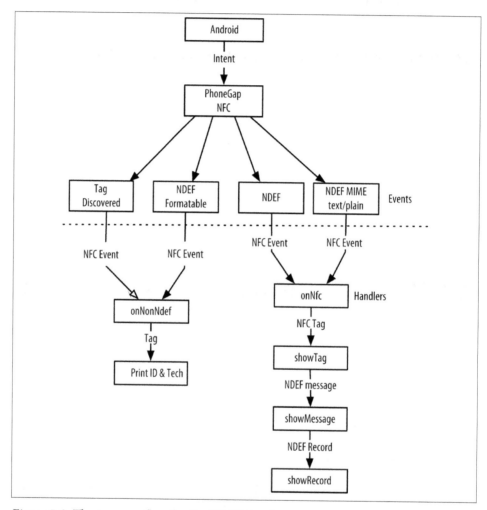

Figure 5-2. The program flow for the NDEF Reader app

Start by adding an if statement to the showTag() function that sends the NDEF message on the tag to the showMessage() function:

```
showTag: function(tag) {
    // display the tag properties:
```

```
app.display("Tag ID: " + nfc.bytesToHexString(tag.id));
app.display("Tag Type: " + tag.type);
app.display("Max Size: " + tag.maxSize + " bytes");
app.display("Is Writable: " + tag.isWritable);
app.display("Can Make Read Only: " + tag.canMakeReadOnly);

// if there is an NDEF message on the tag, display it:
var thisMessage = tag.ndefMessage;
if (thisMessage !== null) {
   // get and display the NDEF record count:
   app.display("Tag has NDEF message with " + thisMessage.length
      + " record" + (thisMessage.length === 1 ? ".":"s."));

   app.display("Message Contents: ");
   app.showMessage(thisMessage);
}
},
```

Next, add a function showMessage() to show the message. The message is just an array of records, so iterate over it to show each record using a second function, showRecord():

```
/*
   iterates over the records in an NDEF message to display them:
*/
showMessage: function(message) {
   for (var thisRecord in message) {
      // get the next record in the message array:
      var record = message[thisRecord];
      app.showRecord(record);          // show it
   }
},
/*
   writes @record to the message div:
*/
showRecord: function(record) {
   // display the TNF, Type, and ID:
   app.display(" ");
   app.display("TNF: " + record.tnf);
   app.display("Type: " + nfc.bytesToString(record.type));
   app.display("ID: " + nfc.bytesToString(record.id));

   // if the payload is a Smart Poster, it's an NDEF message.
   // read it and display it (recursion is your friend here):
   if (nfc.bytesToString(record.type) === "Sp") {
      var ndefMessage = ndef.decodeMessage(record.payload);
      app.showMessage(ndefMessage);

   // if the payload's not a Smart Poster, display it:
   } else {
      app.display("Payload: " + nfc.bytesToString(record.payload));
   }
}
};     // end of app
```

As you can see, showMessage() and showRecord() call each other recursively until all the contents of the tag are displayed.

Save these changes and run the app again. This app should read all compatible tags, and give you any NDEF messages on them. Besides showing the multiple NDEF event listeners, it's also a handy app for general tag reading. It's not the prettiest display of the records, because it's very bare-bones, with just enough code to extract the information. In a more fully developed app, you could add elements to the DOM of the *index.html* page for each message and record, so that you could indent the records in a message, and so forth.

Figure 5-3 shows a few example tags read with the NDEF Reader app. The full listing can be found on GitHub (*http://bit.ly/ndef-master*).

Figure 5-3. Results from the NDEF Reader app: a vCard tag (left), a plain-text message (center), and a tag with multiple records (right)

Filtering Tags Using Record Types

If you're making an app that needs to read multiple different types of messages, there are a number of ways to do it. You can separate them by TNF, but in most cases that won't tell you a whole lot about the message's purpose. Generally, the NFC Forum Record Type Definition will tell you more about a message. There are a few commonly used NFC RTDs that you'll see frequently: "U" for URI, "T" for text record, and "Sp" for Smart Poster. There are some external ones you've seen as well: android.com:pkg for an Android Application Record, for example. And of course, you can use any of the

Internet-standard MIME-types for your record type as well, the most common of which you'll encounter is text/plain. You can even make up your own types if you so choose. Next is a modified version of the NDEF Reader app's showRecord() function that filters records by type. This full source code can be found on GitHub (*http://bit.ly/ndef-master*):

```
showTag: function(tag) {
    // display the tag properties:
    app.display("Tag ID: " + nfc.bytesToHexString(tag.id));
    app.display("Tag Type: " +  tag.type);
    app.display("Max Size: " +  tag.maxSize + " bytes");
    app.display("Is Writable: " +  tag.isWritable);
    app.display("Can Make Read Only: " +  tag.canMakeReadOnly);

    // if there is an NDEF message on the tag, display it:
    var thisMessage = tag.ndefMessage;
    if (thisMessage !== null) {
        // get and display the NDEF record count:
        app.display("Tag has NDEF message with " + thisMessage.length
            + " record" + (thisMessage.length === 1 ? ".":"s."));

        var type =  nfc.bytesToString(thisMessage[0].type);
        switch (type) {
            case nfc.bytesToString(ndef.RTD_TEXT):
                app.display("Looks like a text record to me.");
                break;
            case nfc.bytesToString(ndef.RTD_URI):
                app.display("That's a URI right there");
                break;
            case nfc.bytesToString(ndef.RTD_SMART_POSTER):
                app.display("Golly!  That's a smart poster.");
                break;
            // add any custom types here,
            // such as MIME types or external types:
            case 'android.com:pkg':
                app.display("You've got yourself an AAR there.");
                break;
            default:
                app.display("I don't know what " +
                    type +
                    " is, must be a custom type");
                break;
        }

        app.display("Message Contents: ");
        app.showMessage(thisMessage);
    }
},
```

Filtering Using MIME-Types

Because MIME-type records are so useful, they get their own Type Name Format. They also get their own listener function in the NFC plug-in. Filtering by MIME-type is a quick way to make your app do what you want it to do with tags you care about, but ignore those tags that it doesn't care about. Other messages can then be handled by the operating system's tag dispatch system. As a demonstration of that, here's how to write a small app that reads text messages, but ignores other messages. This app uses the `MimeTypeListener` to do its work.

Start by making a new project using the `cordova create` command:

```
$ cordova create ~/MimeReader com.example.mimereader MimeReader ❶
$ cd  ~/MimeReader ❷
$ cordova platform add android
$ cordova plugin add https://github.com/chariotsolutions/phonegap-nfc
```

❶ Windows users should type %userprofile%\MimeReader instead of ~/Mime Reader.

❷ Windows users should type /d %userprofile%\MimeReader instead of ~/Mime Reader.

You can copy the *index.html* and *index.js* from the NFC Reader app as a base for this project again:

```
$ cp ~/NfcReader/www/index.html ~/MimeReader/www/.
$ cp ~/NfcReader/www/js/index.js ~/MimeReader/www/js/.
```

The *index.html* page is mostly the same (the only changes are cosmetic):

```
<!DOCTYPE html>

<html>
    <head>
        <title>NFC MIME Reader</title>
    </head>
    <body>
        <div class="app">
            <p>This app reads plain-text NFC tags.</p>
            Try tags with
            <ul>
                <li>TNF 03 with type "text/plain"</li>
                <li>TNF 01 with RTD "T"</li>
            </ul>
            <div id="messageDiv"></div>
        </div>
        <script type="text/javascript" src="cordova.js"></script>
        <script type="text/javascript" src="js/index.js"></script>
        <script type="text/javascript">
            app.initialize();
```

```
        </script>
    </body>
</html>
```

You only need to make three changes to the *index.js* to make this app. First, the onDeviceReady() function will get only one listener function like so:

```
onDeviceReady: function() {

    nfc.addMimeTypeListener(
        "text/plain",           // listen for plain-text messages
        app.onNfc,              // tag successfully scanned
        function (status) {     // listener successfully initialized
            app.display("Tap an NFC tag to begin");
        },
        function (error) {      // listener fails to initialize
            app.display("NFC reader failed to initialize " +
            JSON.stringify(error));
        }
    );
},
```

Second, you need to change the onNfc() function so that it reads the tag's message and extracts the payload of the record inside it. Since you're only listening for MIME media records, you know that the record in the message is a text record, so your checking can be fairly simple. You do need to extract the actual content from the language encoding that comes at the beginning of the payload, however. You can see how to do that, in the conditional statement that checks the first byte of the payload:

```
/*
    displays tag from @nfcEvent in message div:
*/

    onNfc: function(nfcEvent) {
        var tag = nfcEvent.tag,
            text = "",
            payload;

        app.clear();
        app.display("Read tag: " + nfc.bytesToHexString(tag.id));

        // get the playload from the first message
        payload = tag.ndefMessage[0].payload;

        if (payload[0] < 5) {
            // payload begins with a small integer, it's encoded text
            var languageCodeLength = payload[0];

            // chop off the language code and convert to string
            text = nfc.bytesToString(payload.slice(languageCodeLength + 1));

        } else {
```

```
        // assume it's text without language info
        text = nfc.bytesToString(payload);
    }

    app.display("Message: " + text);
},
```

Third and finally, you can delete the onNonNdef() function.

Try this app with some of the tags you've got formatted already. The plain-text ones should show up in this app, while the others will open whatever app corresponds to the message they carry. Since most of your tags are formatted for Foursquare, they should automatically open the Foursquare app. You can see the advantage to MIME-type filtering here in action: your app only gets events generated by tags with the appropriate MIME-type. Figure 5-4 shows the results of this app. The full source code can be found on GitHub (*http://bit.ly/mreader-master*).

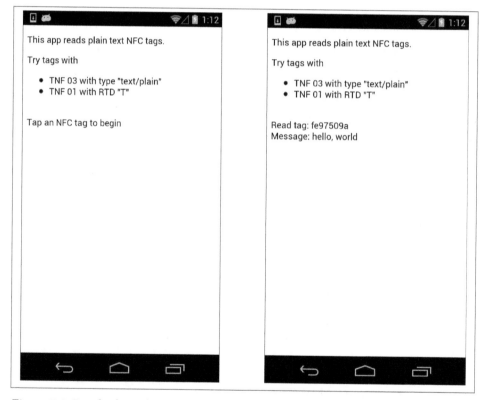

Figure 5-4. Results from the MimeReader app: waiting for tags (left) and reading a text tag with MIME type "text/plain" (right)

Android's Tag Dispatch System

Thus far, you've used Android's foreground dispatch system to capture all events; the PhoneGap-NFC plug-in uses this by default. In other words, your app that's in the foreground gets all the NFC events received, and decides which ones it's going to ignore and which ones it's going to deal with. But if your app isn't running, it doesn't get the message; that's not good interaction design.

Think about the ideal sequence of events when a user is interacting with a tag or another device: she sees the tag, taps her device to it, and the device takes action. She doesn't open an app or mess with any configuration. The phone's operating system should already be listening for tags, and then it should read the tag type and call the appropriate activity in the appropriate app. In order for this to happen, tag identification has to happen before your app is even opened. In fact, this is how Android's tag dispatch system normally works.

The tag dispatch system reads scanned tags, and depending on their TNF and record type, it opens the appropriate app. This is done using *intent filters*. When Android successfully reads the TNF and record type, it tries to map it to a known MIME type or URI pattern. From there, it generates an intent with this data. Then it scans its database of apps to see which app can handle this intent. If more than one app can handle it, Android presents the user with a chooser to decide what to do. Ideally, though, NDEF messages for your app should be distinctive enough that no other app is appropriate to handle them. Intent filters are declared in your app's *AndroidManifest.xml* file inside the <activity> element.

To configure your app to listen for a particular intent filter, you need to modify the app's *platforms/android/AndroidManifest.xml* file, and for one intent type, you also need to add a file to the *platforms/android/res/xml* directory. You can try out all of the combinations that follow with the NDEF Reader project to see what happens. Start with your app *not* running. When you tap the appropriate tag, the app should open. Take note of your tag types before you do, so you know which tags should trigger your app to open and which shouldn't.

Types of Intents

There are three possible intents that Android can generate in response to a tag, which we cover here.

TAG_DISCOVERED is the most general. This intent is generated for any tag the NFC reader recognizes that's not one of the known RFID or NFC tag types. If you're using any of the compatible RFID or NFC tag types, you generally won't see this intent.

Here's what the XML for this intent filter looks like:

```
<activity>

  ... other stuff in the activity element goes here

<intent-filter>
    <action android:name="android.nfc.action.TAG_DISCOVERED"/>
</intent-filter>
</activity>
```

TECH_DISCOVERED occurs when Android sees a compatible RFID or NFC tag. In order to use this intent, you have to declare a tech list of the types of tags for which you intend to listen. You declare the tech list in a separate file in the *platforms/android/res/xml* directory of your project. For example, if you plan to listen for Mifare Ultralight tags that are NDEF-formatable, you'd configure your intent filter to look for just those tag types. First you specify that you're using the action.TECH_DISCOVERED intent filter in the *AndroidManifest.xml*:

```
<activity>

  ... other stuff in the activity element goes here

<intent-filter>
    <action android:name="android.nfc.action.TECH_DISCOVERED"/>
</intent-filter>

<meta-data android:name="android.nfc.action.TECH_DISCOVERED"
    android:resource="@xml/nfc_tech_filter" />
</activity>
```

Then you'd make a file called *nfc_tech_filter.xml* in the *platforms/android/res/xml* folder like so:

```
<resources xmlns:xliff="urn:oasis:names:tc:xliff:document:1.2">
    <tech-list>
      <tech>android.nfc.tech.NdefFormatable</tech>
      <tech>android.nfc.tech.MifareUltralight</tech>
    </tech-list>
</resources>
```

Your tech list should specify only the types you want to filter for. The tag that it will filter for is the tag that matches all the specifications of the tech list. In this example, only tags that are Mifare Ultralight *and* NDEF-formatable will trigger this intent.

You can specify multiple tech lists so that you can scan for multiple combinations. For example, maybe you want tags that are either Mifare Ulralight and NDEF-formatable, NdefA and NDEF-formatable, or NdefB and NDEF-formatable. Your tech list file would look like this:

```
<resources xmlns:xliff="urn:oasis:names:tc:xliff:document:1.2">
    <tech-list>
```

```
    <tech>android.nfc.tech.NdefFormatable</tech>
    <tech>android.nfc.tech.MifareUlralight</tech>
  </tech-list>
  <tech-list>
    <tech>android.nfc.tech.NdefFormatable</tech>
    <tech>android.nfc.tech.NdefA</tech>
  </tech-list>
  <tech-list>
    <tech>android.nfc.tech.NdefFormatable</tech>
    <tech>android.nfc.tech.NdefB</tech>
  </tech-list>
</resources>
```

For reference, here's a tech list containing all the possible NFC-related tech types. This comes from the Android developer site's NFC Basics (*http://bit.ly/nfc-basics*) page. You can choose any subset you need from it:

```
<resources xmlns:xliff="urn:oasis:names:tc:xliff:document:1.2">
  <tech-list>
    <tech>android.nfc.tech.IsoDep</tech>
    <tech>android.nfc.tech.NfcA</tech>
    <tech>android.nfc.tech.NfcB</tech>
    <tech>android.nfc.tech.NfcF</tech>
    <tech>android.nfc.tech.NfcV</tech>
    <tech>android.nfc.tech.Ndef</tech>
    <tech>android.nfc.tech.NdefFormatable</tech>
    <tech>android.nfc.tech.MifareClassic</tech>
    <tech>android.nfc.tech.MifareUltralight</tech>
  </tech-list>
</resources>
```

NDEF_DISCOVERED is the third type of intent filter, and generally the most used. It's the most specific of the three. It looks for a tag that's NDEF-formatted, and can filter for a particular MIME-type or URL. Here's an NDEF_DISCOVERED intent that filters for the text/plain MIME-type:

```
<intent-filter>
  <action android:name="android.nfc.action.NDEF_DISCOVERED"/>
  <category android:name="android.intent.category.DEFAULT"/>
  <data android:mimeType="text/plain" />
</intent-filter>
```

In Android, tags with TNF 01 (Well-Known type) are not normally specified in an intent filter. However, there are a couple of exceptions built into the operating system. A record with a TNF 01 and an RTD of "T" (text) can be filtered using an NDEF_DISCOVERED intent filter set to look for mimeType="text/plain." So if you're looking for plain-text records, use TNF 01, RTD "T," then set your intent filter as shown previously. With this combination, text records will trigger an event whether you're filtering in the background or foreground.

The NDEF_DISCOVERED intent also lets you filter for MIME-types and URLs, and even URLs of a specific type. For example, remember all those tags you formatted in Chapter 4 that had the m.foursquare.com/venue URL embedded in them? Here's how you can filter for them:

```
<intent-filter>
    <action android:name="android.nfc.action.NDEF_DISCOVERED"/>
    <category android:name="android.intent.category.DEFAULT"/>
    <data android:scheme="http"
          android:host="m.foursquare.com"
          android:pathPrefix="/venue" />
</intent-filter>
```

Add this to the NDEF Reader app's *AndroidManifest.xml* file, then build and deploy the app using cordova run as usual. Then close it and tap one of the Foursquare tags to your device. You should see a chooser that asks you to choose between the NDEF Reader and the Foursquare app. Why? Because both of them filter for this URI pattern.

The more specific you can make your intent filter, the better chance there is that your app and only your app will answer to it. In light of this fact, it now makes more sense why the Samsung TecTiles app and the NFC Task Launcher app in Chapter 4 formatted their tags the way they did. Recall how they formatted their calls to Foursquare:

NFC Task Launcher (two NDEF records):

Record 1

- Record type: x/nfctl
- Payload: enZ:Foursquare;c:4a917563f964a520401a20e3

Record 2

- TNF: External
- Record type: android.com:pkg
- Payload: com.jwsoft.nfcactionlauncher

Samsung TecTiles:

Record 1

- TNF: Well-Known
- Record Type: U
- Payload: tectile://www/samsung.com/tectiles

Record 2
- TNF: Well-Known
- Record type: T
- Payload: ·enTask····Foursquare·com.joelapenna...

Both apps filter for a unique MIME-type or URI. NFC Task Launcher defines its own MIME-type (x/nfctl). The second record is an Android Application Record. This launches the NFC Task Launcher app and then calls Foursquare using the information contained in the payload of the first record. Samsung TecTiles defines a URI that's unique to their app (tectile://www/samsung.com/tectiles), so Android will open TecTiles. The TecTile task information for launching Foursquare is embedded in the second record.

Android Application Records

The *Android Application Record (AAR)* was introduced in Android version 4.0 (API version 14) as a way to give developers a surefire way to see to it that their apps were the ones that read a given tag. You've already seen Android Application Records in action; the NFC Task Launcher example uses an AAR. Android scans the whole NDEF message for an NDEF record containing an AAR as its record type, and if it finds one, it hands the intent to that app, overriding all other dispatch priorities. If you want to make absolutely sure your app is the one that gets a given intent, make sure the tag being read has an AAR that calls for your app. The only way to override AAR dispatch is to use the foreground dispatch system.

In the previous examples, it's likely that the second record for NFC Task Launcher was added after Android version 4.0. The first record is unique enough that the tag dispatch system should be able to filter for the app in question, but adding the AAR ensures that this will happen. Furthermore, if the application mentioned in the AAR is not installed, then Android will open the Play Store and ask to download the application.

Conclusion

By the end of this chapter, you should have a good understanding of how to listen for NDEF messages. You can use the foreground dispatch system if your app is already running, and use PhoneGap's event listeners to filter for the different events: tags discovered, NDEF-formatable tags, NDEF messages, or NDEF messages with specific MIME-types. You can also use the background dispatch system and let Android filter appropriate tag events to your app. You can filter for any recognizable tag using the action.TAG_DISCOVERED intent; you can filter for specific tag types using the action.TECH_DISCOVERED intent; or you can filter for specific MIME types, record types, or URI patterns using the `action.NDEF_DISCOVERED` intent. You can mix and match all of these to filter for a variety of tag types and content patterns as well.

Some applications of NFC might use multiple apps to achieve their end goals. In the next chapter, you'll build a full NFC-based application that uses the various elements you've learned already.

CHAPTER 6

An NFC Application in Practice

So far you've gotten an understanding of the differences between NFC and NDEF and an introduction to NDEF messages and records. You've also seen how Android's tag dispatch system can work in either the foreground or the background to filter tags by type and take action where appropriate. In this chapter, you'll use what you've learned to make a full application that can control the lights and music in your home from your mobile device. The application you're going to build is a classic. It's been done in so many forms and shown at so many tech conferences that it's a cliché by now. We'll call it the "Mood Setter" application.

The premise of the application is simple: you might want a different ambiance in your home for the various activities you do there. When you're cleaning the house, you probably want the lights nice and bright, and some cheery music on to keep you moving. When you're working at your desk concentrating, you might like quieter music, maybe something without words to distract you, and you don't need the whole place lit, just where you're working. At dinnertime, perhaps you want want a nice warm glow around the table and some soothing music in the background. Or perhaps you're just having a relaxing evening and want the lights down low and a little Barry White on the hi-fi. Who can resist that?

To make all that happen, you'll write the settings to NFC tags that are scattered around the house, and then use your device to read the tags and control the lights and the music. The lights in this application are the Philips Hue system (*https://www.meethue.com*). Hue is a lighting system that combines LED lamps with embedded ZigBee radios and a special Ethernet-to-ZigBee hub that controls the lights. The hub is running its own HTTP server, and the commands to set the lights are all JSON objects sent using a RESTful protocol. That means you can control the Hue lights using any device that can make an HTTP call. You'll play the music right on your device and stream it to your stereo using a Bluetooth speaker or receiver for the stereo. Figure 6-1 shows the hardware setup.

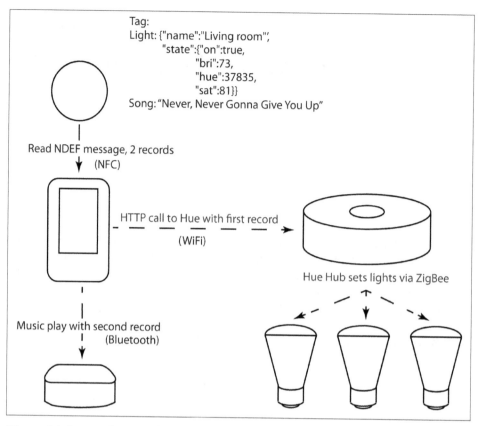

Figure 6-1. *System diagram for the Mood Setter application*

The Bluetooth receiver can be any audio device that receives Bluetooth audio. There are dozens on the market, some of which are combination amplifier-speaker devices with Bluetooth built-in, and others are simply receivers that convert Bluetooth audio to analog audio, so you can plug them into an existing receiver. You could even use a Bluetooth headset if you wanted to. We chose a Belkin Bluetooth Music Receiver (*http://bit.ly/belkin-bmr*) because it was inexpensive and could plug right into our existing stereo. You might also check out HomeSpot's NFC-enabled Bluetooth Audio Receiver (*http://bit.ly/homespot-receiver*), which allows you to pair your device with the receiver via NFC. We found both the Belkin and the HomeSpot worked adequately for this application. Once your device is paired with the audio receiver, go to the Android system settings, choose "Bluetooth," connect to the receiver, and you're ready to go.

We're pretty sure that every reader of this book isn't going to go out and buy a Philips Hue system, but we like the way Philips has implemented lighting control using web standards (HTTP, REST, and JSON) and an open radio protocol (the ZigBee LightLink lighting control protocol). The Hue system is a good example of how to handle messaging between applications using HTTP and JSON, so the concepts shown here can be generalized to many other web-based applications.

The User Interaction

There are a few actions you want the user to do with this app: set the brightness, hue, and saturation of your Hue lights, or turn them on or off; choose a song to play via Bluetooth, and play, stop, or pause it; and read or write NFC tags containing music and lighting data.

There are two main modes of operation for the app: read mode (in which it can read tags and change the lights and music automatically) and write mode (in which it can save its current settings to a tag). Regardless of which mode you're in, you want to be able to control the songs and lights.

When you tap your device to a tag in your house, if the app is in read mode, it will automatically change the lights and play the appropriate music, depending on what settings are embedded in the tag. If it's in write mode, it will automatically write the current settings to the tag.

The app interface has a mode button to switch from read to write mode and back; a pull-down menu to pick which light to control; controls for setting the brightness, saturation, and hue of the lights, and for turning them on or off; another pull-down menu for picking the song you want to play; and play/pause and stop controls.

The app's user interface is shown in Figure 6-2. It's divided into three sections: the tag mode section at the top, the lighting controls in the middle, and the music controls at the bottom. In the HTML, each of these has its own div. The message div you used in other apps is still present, but it could be removed once you're finished coding and testing the app.

When you change the lights, the app will keep a local copy of the Hue settings you've changed, so that it can write them to a tag when you bring a tag in proximity.

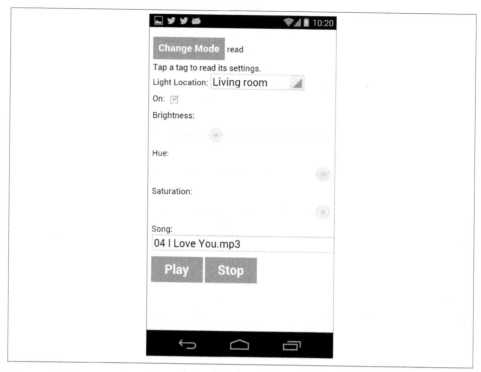

Figure 6-2. User interface for the Mood Setter application

Each tag you'll use to trigger lights and music will have an NDEF message with two records: the lighting data and the music data. The lighting data will be a custom MIME-type you'll make up, `text/hue`. Since it's a custom MIME-type, you'll be able to filter for it easily. The music tag will be a Well-Known type with a URI Record Type Definition. When your device reads the tag, it will check for a `text/hue` record, and if there's one there, it will make an HTTP call to the Hue hub and pass it along. If it discovers a URI on the tag, it will attempt to play the file as an audio file.

In order to write this app, you need to know a little about the Hue platform.

Getting to Know Hue, Getting to Know All About Hue

The Philips Hue lighting system is a well-implemented example of a web-enabled home appliance. It uses web standards for end-to-end communication so that app developers can extend its functionality without having to know about the hardware. Even if you're not interested in the Hue system itself, this section will help you to see how Internet-enabled appliances can be implemented in a way that makes them interoperable with the rest of the Web. We'll point out where the Hue's design choices are worth noting for other applications as we go.

The Hue system comes with three bulbs and an Ethernet-to-ZigBee hub, called the Bridge. Your device speaks to the Bridge using HTTP requests in a RESTful format. You can download the default app from Meet Hue (*http://www.meethue.com/*). You'll find instructions there for configuring your system as well (for further instructions, see Meet Hue's developer section (*http://developers.meethue.com/*)).

The first problem for any Internet-connected device that doesn't have its own screen is how to let the user know whether or not it's successfully connected to the network, and to any client devices used to control it. The Hue's Bridge connects to your home router using a wired Ethernet connection and uses DHCP to obtain an address, so there's no need to configure it for your particular WiFi network. Discovery is handled through a two-step interaction: first you open the app while it's on the same network as the Bridge, then you press the discovery button on the Bridge. For a few seconds after pressing the button, the Bridge will respond to discovery requests, which the app is sending. Assuming both actions happen within a few seconds of each other, the app discovers the Bridge and identifies itself. The Bridge then registers the app as one that has the right to control the lights.

It's worthwhile to compare the user experience of this discovery process with that of the HomeSpot NFC-enabled Bluetooth receiver. The HomeSpot receiver has an NFC tag inside containing the pairing details for its Bluetooth radio. The user pairs her NFC-enabled phone with it by tapping the phone to the receiver. Both this and the Hue discovery process rely on the fact that the user has to have physical control over both devices before they pair wirelessly. This is a common approach in networked appliances that have no screen for user interaction. You can find the IP address of your Hue hub by using the developers' broker page (*http://www.meethue.com/api/nupnp*). This page will look for any hub on your local area network that responds, then gives you the IP address. Note that the device you're browsing from must be on the same LAN as your hub when you do this. Once you've got the IP address, you can connect to it directly by browsing to `http://your.hub.ip.address/debug/clip.html`. You'll get a page that looks like Figure 6-3.

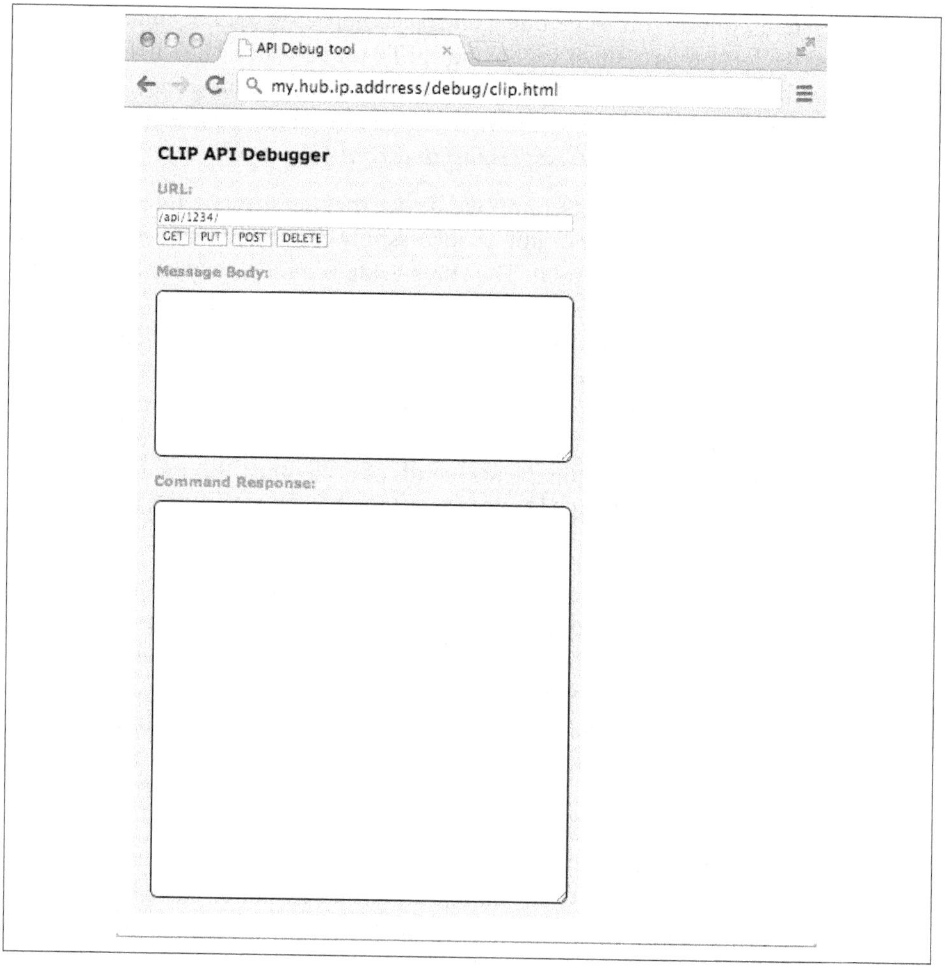

Figure 6-3. The Hue debug tool (this page is available from every Hue hub, as long as you know the hub's IP address)

Once you're connected to the Hue, you need to establish credentials for the app that you'll write. This is what the Hue app normally does, but since you're writing your own app, you'll need to do it yourself. There are a few steps to this process. First, enter the following into the URL field in the debug tool:

```
/api/
```

Then enter this into the body field, replacing yourAppName with your actual app name, press the link button, and click "POST:"

```
{"devicetype":"device type","username":"yourAppName"}
```

Your device type can be anything you want—for example, "Nexus 4" or "Galaxy SIII" or "My Magical Portal Window." Your username should be at least 10 characters long or you'll get an error. In the following application, you'll use the username "MoodSetterApp."

You should get a response like this:

```
[
    {
        "success": {
            "username": "MoodSetterApp"
        }
    }
]
```

Now that you've got a username registered with your Hue hub, you're ready to control it. To see it in action, enter the following into the debug tool:

```
/api/MoodSetterApp/
```

You'll get a response that describes all the lights on your hub in a JSON format.

The Hue Data Format

In order to know what you're going to write to the tag, you need to know the Hue's data format. The Hue data format is nicely designed to be both clear to read in JSON format, yet easy to parse in code. If you're developing your own Internet-enabled appliances, it's a worthwhile one to study. In Chapter 7, you'll develop an NFC-enabled door lock that uses a JSON data format for the same reason: readability from both the human and machine perspectives.

Philips has an excellent developer reference (*http://developers.meethue.com/*) that explains the whole API. For this app, what you need to know is that each light is described in a JSON object like so:

```
"1":
    {"state":
        {"on":true,"bri":65,"hue":44591,"sat":254,"xy":[0.1953,0.0959],
        "ct":500,"alert":"none","effect":"none","colormode":"hs","reachable":true},
    "type":"Extended color light",
    "name":"Living room",
    "modelid":"LCT001",
    "swversion":"65003148",
    "pointsymbol":
        {"1":"none","2":"none","3":"none","4":"none",
        "5":"none","6":"none","7":"none","8":"none"}
}
```

There's a lot there, but you're only going to modify a few of the properties. This is another aspect of the Hue data protocol worth copying: the device receiving the data (the Bridge) should accept any valid subset of the whole message, and if it can, take action.

For each light, you'll change four subproperties of the state property: the on property, the brightness, the hue, and the saturation. Here's a summary of the JSON you might write to change a light (without the comments, of course):

```
"1":                    // The light number
   {"state":            // the light's state, including:
      {"on":true,       // whether it's on or off
      "bri":65,         // the brightness (0 - 254)
      "hue":44591,      // the hue (0 - 65280 in the CIE colorspace)
      "sat":254},       // the saturation of the color (0 - 254)
   }
}
```

You might want to change the names of your lights to reflect where they're located in your house as well. To try this, enter the following in the debug tool:

URL:

```
/api/MoodSetterApp/lights/1/
```

Body:

```
{"name": "First Light"}
```

The response should be:

```
[
   {
      "success": {
         "/lights/1/name": "First Light"
      }
   }
]
```

And to change the state, try:

URL:

```
/api/MoodSetterApp/lights/1/state
```

Body:

```
{"on": true, "bri": 65, "hue": 44591, "sat": 254}
```

You should get a success message for every property you changed (another good general principle to note), and the light should now be a pleasant blue-lavender color.

You can't actually send the whole JSON object using the REST API at once. You have to set the state of a given light, then the name of a given light separately.

If you're not familiar with lighting color theory, the hue and saturation properties may be new to you. Philips uses a colorspace called the CIE, a map devised in 1931 by the International Commission on Illumination (CIE) to describe the color of light in a uniform way. Briefly, the CIE scheme maps color into two parts: the luminance and chromaticity. The luminance refers to the relative value of a color on a black-to-white scale, while the chromaticity refers to the relative value of the color. You can think of it this way: black, white, and gray all have the same chromaticity, but vary in their luminance. Figure 6-4 shows the CIE color space chromaticity diagram.

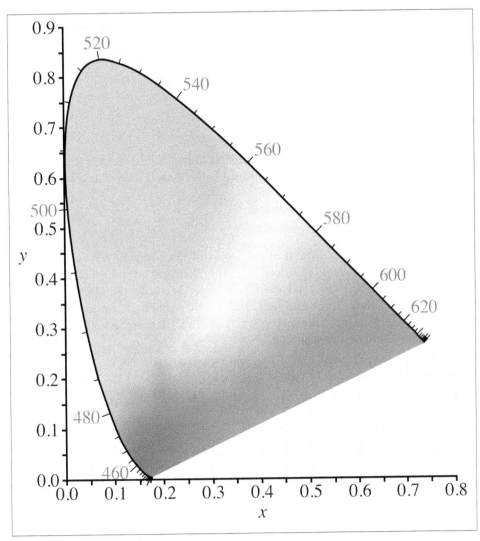

Figure 6-4. The CIE color diagram (image courtesy of Wikipedia)

As you change the hue of a lamp, you'll see it change around the CIE color space, moving from red at the low end, through all the other colors in the middle, and back to red. As you change the saturation, you'll see the color fade from a vibrant color to a paler tint.

For a Hue hub with three lights, the default package, you might send a JSON object like this:

```
{"1":
  {"state":
    {"on":true,"bri":65,"hue":44591,"sat":254}
  },
  "2":
  {"state":
    {"on":true,"bri":254,"hue":13122,"sat":211}
  },
  "3":
  {"state":
    {"on":true,"bri":255,"hue":14922,"sat":144}
  }
}
```

This JSON object will be the payload of the first of two NDEF records you'll write to the NFC tags used in this app. As mentioned before, you'll send it as a MIME type, text/hue.

The Hue's REST API

As you've probably noticed from the debug tool, the Hue's request API is RESTful. To get data, you use the format */api/MoodSetterApp/* then add on the specifics you want and make an HTTP GET request. For example, to get the state of light 1, it's */api/Mood-SetterApp/lights/1/state*. To change data, you use the same basic format with a PUT request. In the app you're building, you'll assemble a URL to make HTTP requests to the hub, one to PUT new data like so:

```
url: 'http://' + hub.ipaddress + '/api/' + hub.username
        + '/lights/' + lightId + '/state',
```

The other will GET data from the hub:

```
url: 'http://' + hub.ipaddress + '/api/' + hub.username,
```

Since the API is just REST URLs and JSON, you can simplify the app by using zepto.js, a slimmed-down version of the popular JQuery library. You'll see that in the HTML head in "The User Interface" on page 106.

The Android Shell

The other NDEF record will be a URI record with the full file path of the song you want to play. The file will then be played using PhoneGap's Media API. In order to simplify things, you should put all of the songs you want to use in one directory, or use the default directory for whatever music app you use on your device already.

The *Android Debug Bridge (ADB)*, which you've been using already, can do more than just show you log messages while you're debugging. You can also use it to access your Android device from the command line of your computer. To get to the shell, open a Terminal window on your computer while you've got the device attached via USB and type the following:

```
$ adb shell
```

You're now accessing the device directly, and you can do most of the things you expect from a shell: list files using `ls`, change directories using `cd`, make new directories using `mkdir`, and so forth. If you list your root directory, you should see a directory called `sdcard`. This is the default storage directory for user files on Android devices, so it's a good place to put your stuff.

You'll need some songs for this app, so create a new directory on your device for the songs you'll use. From Terminal, type:

```
$ adb shell
shell@android:/ $ mkdir sdcard/myMusic
shell@android:/ $ exit
```

Now that you've dropped out of the adb shell and you're back in your computer's shell, find some music on your computer that you want to transfer to the device, change to the directory it's in, and type:

```
$ adb push songName.mp3 /sdcard/myMusic/.
```

This will move the file from your machine to the device. You can log back into the device with `adb shell` to check that it's where you thought it was.

The PhoneGap Media API

To play music in this app, you're going to use PhoneGap's Media API, which allows you to both record and play back audio. For this app, you'll just use it for playback, but you can find the full documentation in the PhoneGap Guides (*http://docs.phonegap.com*), under "Media." The Media API is initialized by creating a new media playback object, like so:

```
var playBack = new Media(source, success, error, status);
```

The Media object's parameters allow you to control its behavior. The source URL can be a local file using the format *file:///path/to/filename*, or a remote URL using *http://example.com/path/to/filename*. The success, error, and status handlers are all optional. Success gets called after a Media object has completed the current play, record, or stop action. Error is called when there's a playback error, and status is called whenever you want to update the status of the playback. The playback status is useful for changing the behavior of control buttons, and for stopping and starting audio when your app is paused and resumed.

The Media object has the functions you'd expect from a Media object: you can start, stop, or pause playback; get the current position or the duration of the song; skip to a particular position; release the OS's audio resources; and start and stop recording. You'll see some of these functions used in the following code.

In order to use the Media API, you'll need to install two plug-ins: the Media plug-in itself and the Filesystem plug-in that you'll use to find files in a directory. Install them like so:

```
$ cordova plugin add \
  https://git-wip-us.apache.org/repos/asf/cordova-plugin-media.git
$ cordova plugin add \
  https://git-wip-us.apache.org/repos/asf/cordova-plugin-file.git
```

You'll also need to modify your app's *AndroidManifest.xml* to include the following permissions:

```
<uses-permission android:name="android.permission.RECORD_AUDIO" />
<uses-permission android:name="android.permission.MODIFY_AUDIO_SETTINGS" />
<uses-permission android:name="android.permission.WRITE_EXTERNAL_STORAGE" />
```

In addition, your app's *config.xml* (found in *platforms/android/res/xml/config.xml*) must contain the following plug-in:

```
<plugin name="Media" value="org.apache.cordova.AudioHandler" />
```

All of these XML settings will be added by default when you use the `cordova create` command, as you've been doing all along.

The User Interface

Now that you understand the new tools being used in this project, it's time to create the project and start writing some code.

To do this, you'll need the tools you saw in earlier chapters, and some new hardware:

- An NFC-enabled Android device
- The Android Software Developers Kit
- A text editor
- Cordova CLI installed on your machine
- Node.js and npm installed
- The minimized version of the Zepto jQuery library, available from Zepto JS (*http://zeptojs.com/*)
- An assortment of NFC Tags (for best results across multiple devices, stick with the NFC Forum types; see "Device-to-Tag Type Matching" on page 19 for more on which tags work with which devices)

- Philips Hue Lighting system
- A Bluetooth audio receiver, such as the Belkin Bluetooth Music Receiver or the HomeSpot NFC-enabled Bluetooth Audio Receiver

To get started, create a new project:

```
$ cordova create ~/MoodSetter com.example.moodsetter MoodSetter ❶
$ cd ~/MoodSetter ❷
$ cordova platform add android
$ cordova plugin add https://github.com/don/phonegap-nfc
$ cordova plugin add \
  https://git-wip-us.apache.org/repos/asf/cordova-plugin-media.git
$ cordova plugin add \
  https://git-wip-us.apache.org/repos/asf/cordova-plugin-file.git
```

❶ Windows users should type %userprofile%\MoodSetter instead of ~/Mood Setter.

❷ Windows users should type /d %userprofile%\MoodSetter instead of ~/Mood Setter.

Download the minimized version of the Zepto JS library and copy the *zepto.min.js* file to your *www/js* directory.

When the project's ready to go, open the *index.html* and the *index.js* files from the *www* directory.

Here's the HTML for the user interface, as shown in Figure 6-2. You're adding some CSS styling at the top this time, to make the buttons and sliders a bit easier to touch if you have big fingers:

```
<!DOCTYPE html>

<html>
  <head>
    <title>Mood Setter</title>
    <style>
    input {
        margin-top: 10px;
        margin-bottom: 10px;
    }
    input[type='range'] { /* finger sized sliders */
        display:block;
        width: 100%;
    }
    .button {
        display: inline-block;
        padding: 10px;
        min-width: 80px;
        margin-top: 10px;
        margin-bottom: 5px;
```

```
            text-align: center;
            background-color: #177bbd;
            color: #ffffff;
         }
         select {
            font-size: 1.25em;
         }
      </style>
   </head>
   <body>
      <div class="app">
         <div id="tagMode">
            <h3 id="modeButton" class="button">Change Mode</h3>
            <span id="modeValue"></span><br />
            <span id="tagModeMessage"></span>
         </div>

         <div id="lightControl">
            Light Location:
            <select id="lightNumber">
               <option value="1" >No Lights Found</option>
               <option value="2" >No Lights Found</option>
               <option value="3" >No Lights Found</option>
            </select><br />
            <label for="lightOn">On:</label>
               <input type="checkbox" id="lightOn"><br />
            Brightness: <input type="range" id="bri" min="0" max="254">
            Hue: <input type="range" id="hue"  min="0" max="65535">
            Saturation: <input type="range" id="sat" min="0" max="254">
         </div>

         <div id="songPicker">
            Song:
               <div>
                  <select id="songs">
                     <option>Loading Songs</option>
                  </select>
               </div>
               <div>
                  <h2 id="playButton" class="button">Play</h2>
                  <h2 id="stopButton" class="button">Stop</h2>
               </div>
         </div>

         <div id="messageDiv">No message</div>
      </div>
      <script type="text/javascript" src="js/zepto.min.js"></script>
      <script type="text/javascript" src="cordova.js"></script>
      <script type="text/javascript" src="js/index.js"></script>
      <script>
         app.initialize();
      </script>
```

```
    </body>
  </html>
```

There are four main sections to the app div:

- The mode div, which contains the mode button and reports the mode you're in
- The lightControl div, which contains all the controls for the lights
- The songPicker div, which lets you pick and control songs
- The message div, for general messages

All of the user controls have listeners that you'll see in the *index.js* file.

The names for the lighting controls in the HTML were chosen to match the names of the properties in the Hue's JSON format, as you've seen previously. The ranges for each of the objects are set using the ranges for those properties as specified in Philips' Hue specification. The initial values are set by querying the hub. The names of the lights in the lightNumber drop-down menu are changed dynamically when the hub is queried as well.

The Application Code

The main logic of the application will be in *index.js* as usual. The full source listing for this application can be found on GitHub (*http://bit.ly/moodsetter*). The JavaScript's going to start a bit differently than usual, however. Instead of starting with the app variable, start by making a variable to keep track of all the hub's properties as follows:

```
var hub = {                          // a copy of the hue settings
    lights: {},                      // states & names for the individual lights
    ipaddress: null,                 // IP address of the hue
    appTitle: "NFC Mood Setter",     // The App name
    username: "MoodSetterApp",       // the App's username
    currentLight: 1                  // the light you're currently setting
};
```

You'll use this object to store all the settings you need from the hub locally, as well as the app's title, your username, and the light that you're currently manipulating with the lighting controls in the user interface. There's more data in the full Hue JSON reply than you need, or that you can fit on a typical NFC tag, so you'll just take out the ones you need when you query the hub.

Next, start the app variable, beginning with a few parameters that will be used throughout:

```
var app = {
    mode: 'write',                            // the tag read/write mode
    mimeType: 'text/hue',                     // the NFC record MIME Type
    musicPath: 'file:///sdcard/myMusic/',     // path to your music
```

```
    songPlaying: null,        // media handle for the current song playing
    songTitle: null,          // title of the song
    musicState: 0,            // state of the song: playing stopped, etc.
    songUri: null,
```

Housekeeping Functions

After that, it's time for the usual housekeeping functions, initialize() and bindEvents(). As you can see here bindEvents() initializes listeners for all your user controls, as well as for pausing and resuming the app:

```
/*
    Application constructor
*/
initialize: function() {
    this.bindEvents();
    console.log("Starting Mood Setter app");
},

/*
    binds events that are required on startup to listeners.
*/
bindEvents: function() {
    document.addEventListener('deviceready', this.onDeviceReady, false);

    // hue faders from the UI: brightness, hue, saturation:
    bri.addEventListener('touchend', app.setBrightness, false);
    hue.addEventListener('touchend', app.setHue, false);
    sat.addEventListener('touchend', app.setSaturation, false);
    lightOn.addEventListener('change', app.setLightOn, false);
    lightNumber.addEventListener('change', app.getHueSettings, false);

    // buttons from the UI:
    modeButton.addEventListener('click', app.setMode, false);
    songs.addEventListener('change', app.onSongChange, false);
    playButton.addEventListener('touchstart', app.toggleAudio, false);
    stopButton.addEventListener('touchstart', app.stopAudio, false);

    // pause and resume functionality for the whole app:
    document.addEventListener('pause', this.onPause, false);
    document.addEventListener('resume', this.onResume, false);
},
```

In the onDeviceReady() handler, you're going to make the initial query to the Hue hub for settings using a function called findControllerAddress() that you'll write shortly. You'll also set the read/write mode of the app. You're also going to set up three NFC listeners. The first two will listen for any NFC-formatable or NDEF tag, so you can write to it in write mode. The third will listen for MIME-types, specifically for the text/hue type. Any tag with a record containing that MIME-type should contain data for you to set the lights, and ideally, a second record for playing music as well. In the MIME media handler, you'll need to differentiate between read and write mode. You'll see that later on.

The handler ends with a call to a new function, getSongs(), which you'll see shortly. It looks up the directory you assigned for music and populates the selector in the HTML with the names and URIs of the songs:

```
/*
    runs when the device is ready for user interaction.
*/
onDeviceReady: function() {
    app.clear();                      // clear any messages onscreen
    app.findControllerAddress();      // find address and get settings
    app.setMode();                    // set the read/write mode for tags

    // listen for NDEF Formatable tags (for write mode):
    nfc.addNdefFormatableListener(
        app.onWritableNfc,            // tag successfully scanned
        function (status) {           // listener successfully initialized
            console.log("Listening for NDEF-formatable tags.");
        },
        function (error) {            // listener fails to initialize
            app.display("NFC reader failed to initialize " +
                JSON.stringify(error));
        }
    );

    // listen for NDEF tags so you can overwrite MIME message onto them
    nfc.addNdefListener(
        app.onWritableNfc,            // NDEF type successfully found
        function() {                  // listener successfully initialized
            console.log("listening for Ndef tags");
        },
        function(error) {             // listener fails to initialize
            console.log("ERROR: " + JSON.stringify(error)); }
    );

    // listen for MIME media types of type 'text/hue' (for read or write)
    // Android calls the most specific listener, so text/hue tags end up here
    nfc.addMimeTypeListener(
        app.mimeType,                 // what type you're listening for
        app.onMimeMediaNfc,           // MIME type successfully found
        function() {                  // listener successfully initialized
            console.log("listening for mime media tags");
        },
        function(error) {             // listener fails to initialize
            console.log("ERROR: " + JSON.stringify(error)); }
    );

    app.getSongs();                   // load the drop-down menu with songs
},
```

After onDeviceReady(), add your old workhorse handlers, display() and clear(), for showing messages in the message div. They're the same as usual here:

```
/*
    appends @message to the message div:
*/
display: function(message) {
    var textNode = document.createTextNode(message),
        lineBreak = document.createElement("br");        // a line break

    messageDiv.appendChild(lineBreak);                   // add a line break
    messageDiv.appendChild(textNode);                    // add the message node
},

/*
    clears the message div:
*/
clear: function() {
    messageDiv.innerHTML = "";
},
```

Global Event Handlers

Next come your first event handlers, onPause(), onResume(), and the NFC event handlers. These are the only events your app will listen for that aren't generated directly by the user controls. They're pretty basic. The first two check the state of media playback, and either pause or resume it as appropriate:

```
/*
    This is called when the app is resumed
*/
onResume: function() {
    if (app.musicState === Media.MEDIA_PAUSED) {
        app.startAudio();
    }
},

/*
    runs when an NdefListener or NdefFormatableListener event occurs.
*/
onWritableNfc: function(nfcEvent) {
    if (app.mode === "write") {
        app.makeMessage();  // in write mode, write to the tag
    }
},
```

The NFC event handlers will do just that: handle NFC events. The onWritableNfc handler is the handler for both the NdefListener and the NdefFormatableListener. The formatable listener lets you write to any blank tag that can be formatted, and the more generic NdefListener lets you overwrite existing NFC tags with MIME media-types when you're in write mode. For example, if you had a tag that you'd used for a previous application, and that application used a MIME type that's not the one you're listening for in the MimeTypeListener, the NdefListener would catch it.

The `onMimeMediaNfc()` handler gets called only when one of your tags with the MIME-type `text/hue` shows up. If you're in read mode, it reads the tag and attempts to change the music and the lights. If you're in write mode, it overwrites the tag:

```
/*
    runs when an NdefListener or NdefFormatableListener event occurs.
*/
onWritableNfc: function(nfcEvent) {
    if (app.mode === "write") {
        app.makeMessage();  // in write mode, write to the tag
    }
},

/*
    runs when a MimeMedia event occurs.
*/
onMimeMediaNfc: function(nfcEvent) {
    var tag = nfcEvent.tag;

    if (app.mode === "read") {   // in read mode, read the tag
        // when app is launched by scanning text/hue tag
        // you need to add a delay so the call to get the
        // hub address can finish before you call the api.
        // if you have the address, delay 0, otherwise, delay 50:
        var timeout = hub.ipaddress ? 0 : 500;

        setTimeout(function() {
            app.readTag(tag);
        }, timeout);

    } else {                     // if you're in write mode
        app.makeMessage();  // in write mode, write to the tag
    }
},
```

Since tag actions depend on the mode you're in, you need a mode handler. This is the event handler for the mode button. You can see where it's initialized in `bindEvents()`, previously. It simply changes the `app.mode` variable, and the text of the tag mode div so the user knows what mode she's in:

```
/*
    Sets the tag read/write mode for the app.
*/
setMode: function() {
    if (app.mode === "write") {   // change to read mode
        app.mode = "read";
        tagModeMessage.innerHTML = "Tap a tag to read its settings.";
```

```
    } else {                              // change to write mode
        app.mode = "write";
        tagModeMessage.innerHTML = "Tap a tag to write current settings.";
    }
    modeValue.innerHTML = app.mode; // set text in the UI
},
```

Hub Communication Functions

Once the basic initialization housekeeping is done, you need to query the hub, get the settings you need, and copy them into the hub object. The querying is all done using the jQuery `ajax` function, from the Zepto JS library that you're using. The `findCon trollerAddress()` function shown here makes an Ajax query to Meet Hue's IP locator page (*http://www.meethue.com/api/nupnp*) to see if it returns any local hub IP addresses. If if finds one, it sets `hub.ipaddress`. If not, it prompts the user that no hub was found:

```
/*
    Find the Hue controller address and get its settings
*/
findControllerAddress: function() {
    $.ajax({
        url: 'http://www.meethue.com/api/nupnp',
        dataType: 'json',
        success: function(data) {
            // expecting a list with a property called internalipaddress:
            if (data[0]) {
                hub.ipaddress = data[0].internalipaddress;
                app.getHueSettings();     // copy the Hue settings locally
            } else {
                navigator.notification.alert(
                    "Couldn't find a Hue on your network");
            }
        },
        error: function(xhr, type){     // alert box with the error
            navigator.notification.alert(xhr.responseText +
                " (" + xhr.status + ")", null, "Error");
        }
    });
},
```

If you have a network that's not running DHCP, or your Hue and your Android device are running on different networks, you'll have to modify this program. Your Hue will need a public IP address, or you'll need to enable port forwarding on the router to which the Hue's connected. When you've got that done, enter the Hue's IP address for hub.ipaddress at the beginning of your program, and comment out the line in findControllerAddress() that reads

```
hub.ipaddress = data[0].internalipaddress;
```

Once you've made these changes, the app will always look for the hub at the fixed address you've given it.

After you've found the hub, you need to register your username and app name with it. The following functions, ensureAuthorized() and authorize(), take care of that. The first, ensureAuthorized(), just checks with the hub to see if your username and app name are registered with it. If it fails, it calls authorize() and attempts to get authorization. Both of these prompt the user when they fail, as you need to press the hub's link button to authorize a new user and app:

```
/*
    Checks that the username is authorized for this hub.
*/
ensureAuthorized: function() {
    var message;       // response from the hub

    // query the hub:
    $.ajax({
        type: 'GET',
        url: 'http://' + hub.ipaddress + '/api/' + hub.username,
        success: function(data){      // successful reply from the hub
            if (data[0].error) {
                // if not authorized, users gets an alert box
                if (data[0].error.type === 1) {
                    message = "Press link button on the hub.";
                } else {
                    message = data[0].error.description;
                }
                navigator.notification.alert(message,
                    app.authorize, "Not Authorized");
            }
        },
        error: function(xhr, type){     // error message from the hub
            navigator.notification.alert(xhr.responseText +
                " (" + xhr.status + ")", null, "Error");
        }
    });
},

/*
```

```
        Authorizes the username for this hub.
    */
    authorize: function() {
        var data = {                      // what you'll send to the hub:
            "devicetype": hub.appTitle,   // device type
            "username": hub.username      // username
        },
        message;                          // reply from the hub

        $.ajax({
            type: 'POST',
            url: 'http://' + hub.ipaddress + '/api',
            data: JSON.stringify(data),
            success: function(data){      // successful reply from the hub
                if (data[0].error) {
                    // if not authorized, users gets an alert box
                    if (data[0].error.type === 101) {
                        message = "Press link button on the hub, then tap OK.";
                    } else {
                        message = data[0].error.description;
                    }
                    navigator.notification.alert(message,
                        app.authorize, "Not Authorized");
                } else {                  // if authorized, give an alert box
                    navigator.notification.alert("Authorized user " +
                        hub.username);
                    app.getHueSettings();   // if authorized, get the settings
                }
            },
            error: function(xhr, type){   // error reply from the hub
                navigator.notification.alert(xhr.responseText +
                    " (" + xhr.status + ")", null, "Error");
            }
        });
    },
```

Once you're registered with the hub, you need to get the settings from it and copy them to your local hub object. Both findHueSettings() and authorize(), shown previously, call the function that follows. It doesn't copy all of the hub's settings, just the ones you need for setting on/off, brightness, hue, and saturation for the lights that the hub is controlling:

```
    /*
        Get the settings from the Hue and store a subset of them locally
        in hub.lights.  This is for both setting the controls, and for
        writing to tags:
    */
    getHueSettings: function() {
        // query the hub and get its current settings:

        $.ajax({
            type: 'GET',
```

```
            url: 'http://' + hub.ipaddress + '/api/' + hub.username,
            success: function(data) {
                if (!data.lights) {
                    // assume they need to authorize
                    app.ensureAuthorized();
                } else {
                    // the full settings take more than you want to
                    // fit on a tag, so just get the settings you want:
                    for (var thisLight in data.lights) {
                        hub.lights[thisLight] = {};
                        hub.lights[thisLight].name = data.lights[thisLight].name;
                        hub.lights[thisLight].state = {};
                        hub.lights[thisLight].state.on =
                            data.lights[thisLight].state.on;
                        hub.lights[thisLight].state.bri =
                            data.lights[thisLight].state.bri;
                        hub.lights[thisLight].state.hue =
                            data.lights[thisLight].state.hue;
                        hub.lights[thisLight].state.sat =
                            data.lights[thisLight].state.sat;
                    }
                    app.setControls();
                }
            }
        });
    },
```

The function you just wrote, which gets the settings, implies a complementary function to put new settings back to the Hue hub. You'll need such a function for whenever the user changes the lighting controls. So here's `putHueSettings()`, which takes a JSON object, converts it to a string, and sends it to the hub:

```
/*
    sends settings to the Hue hub.
*/
putHueSettings: function(settings, lightId) {
    // if no lightId is sent, assume the current light:
    if (!lightId) {
        lightId = hub.currentLight;
    }

    // if the light's not on, you can't set the other properties.
    // so delete the other properties before sending them.
    // if "on" is a property and it's false:
    if (settings.hasOwnProperty("on") && !settings.on) {
        // go through all the other properties:
        for (var prop in settings) {
            // if this property is not inherited:
            if (settings.hasOwnProperty(prop)
                && prop != "on") {        // and it's not the "on" property
                delete(settings[prop]); // delete it
            }
```

```
        }
    }

    // set the property for the light:
    $.ajax({
        type: 'PUT',
        url: 'http://' + hub.ipaddress + '/api/' + hub.username +
            '/lights/' + lightId + '/state',
        data: JSON.stringify(settings),
        success: function(data){
            if (data[0].error) {
                navigator.notification.alert(JSON.stringify(data),
                    null, "API Error");
            }
        },
        error: function(xhr, type){
            navigator.notification.alert(xhr.responseText + " (" +
                xhr.status + ")", null, "Error");
        }
    });
},
```

This function doesn't care what the settings are, nor does it bother to update the local hub object with the settings. It leaves all of that to the functions that call it. However, it handles one important error: the Hue won't let you set a given light's hue, brightness, and saturation if the light is off. So this function checks to see if the settings being sent contain an "on" property and if it's false. If so, then the function eliminates the other properties and just sends the "on" property (which is set to false).

Lighting User Interface Event Handlers

The next set of functions are the user interface control event handlers.

With the hub settings obtained by getHueSettings(), you can set the user interface controls to match the current settings of the lights they're controlling. At the end of a successful request, getHueSettings() calls the following function, setControls(), to update the value of the UI controls:

```
/*
    Set the value of the UI controls using the values from the Hue:
*/
setControls: function() {
    hub.currentLight = lightNumber.value;

    // set the names of the lights in the dropdown menu:
    // (in a more fully developed app, you might generalize this)
    lightNumber.options[0].innerHTML = hub.lights["1"].name;
    lightNumber.options[1].innerHTML = hub.lights["2"].name;
    lightNumber.options[2].innerHTML = hub.lights["3"].name;

    // set the state of the controls with the current choice:
```

```
        var thisLight = hub.lights[hub.currentLight];
        hue.value = thisLight.state.hue;
        bri.value = thisLight.state.bri;
        sat.value = thisLight.state.sat;
        lightOn.checked = thisLight.state.on;
    },
```

The user interface controls for the lighting are handled by a series of event handlers, each of which sets a specific property of the light. Figure 6-5 shows a detail of the lighting controls. The drop-down menu's event handler is `getHueSettings()`, which gets the current settings and updates the other controls.

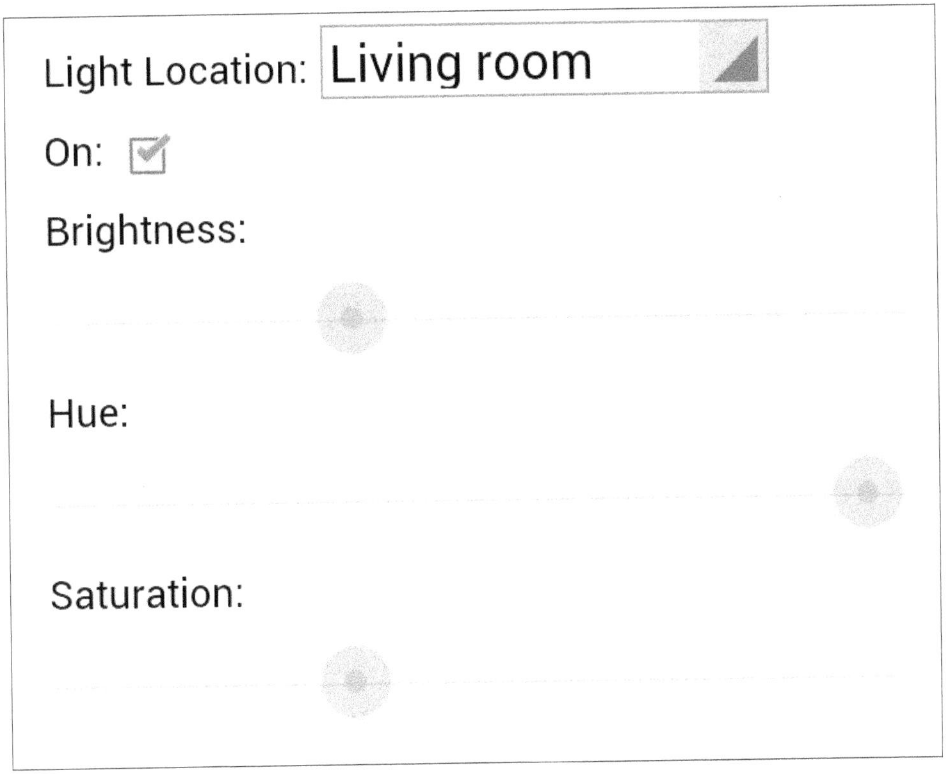

Figure 6-5. The lighting controls for the app

The on, brightness, hue, and saturation controls apply to whatever light is chosen in the Light Location drop-down menu. Each of the individual event handlers gets the value from the control, then sets that value in the local hue object. Finally, each handler uses the new setting to update the Hue hub:

```
/*
    These functions set the properties for a Hue light:
    Brightness, Hue, Saturation, and On State
```

```
*/
setBrightness: function() {
    // get the value from the UI control:
    var thisBrightness = parseInt(bri.value, 10);
    // get the property from hub object:
    var thisLight = hub.lights[hub.currentLight];
    // change the property in hub object:
    thisLight.state.bri = thisBrightness;
    // update Hue hub with the new value:
    app.putHueSettings({ "bri": thisBrightness });
},

setHue: function() {
    // get the value from the UI control:
    var thisHue = parseInt(hue.value, 10);
    // get the property from hub object:
    var thisLight = hub.lights[hub.currentLight];
    // change the property in hub object:
    thisLight.state.hue = thisHue;
    // update Hue hub with the new value:
    app.putHueSettings( { "hue": thisHue } );
},

setSaturation: function() {
    // get the value from the UI control:
    var thisSaturation = parseInt(bri.value, 10);
    // get the property from hub object:
    var thisLight = hub.lights[hub.currentLight];
    // change the property in hub object:
    thisLight.state.sat = thisSaturation;
    // update Hue hub with the new value:
    app.putHueSettings({ "sat": thisSaturation });
},

setLightOn: function() {
    // get the value from the UI control:
    var thisOn = lightOn.checked;
    // get the property from hub object:
    var thisLight = hub.lights[hub.currentLight];
    // change the property in hub object:
    thisLight.state.on = thisOn;
    // update Hue hub with the new value:
    app.putHueSettings( { "on": thisOn } );
},
```

These event handlers are the functions that ensure that the UI controls, the local hue object, and the remote Hue hub are in sync.

When you get to the tag-reading functionality, you'll need a function that takes all the lighting properties from the tag and writes them to the Hue hub. You can assume that this function is getting the states for all the lights passed to it as a parameter. Group that function with the previous functions:

```
/*
    Sets the state for all the lights. Assumes it's getting
    a JSON object like this:
    {
      "1": {"state": {"on":true,"bri":65,"hue":44591,"sat":254}},
      "2": {"state": {"on":true,"bri":254,"hue":13122,"sat":211}},
      "3": {"state": {"on":true,"bri":255,"hue":14922,"sat":144}}
    }
*/
setAllLights: function(settings) {
    for (var thisLight in settings) {
        app.putHueSettings(settings[thisLight].state, thisLight);
    }
},
```

Music User Interface Event Handlers

Now that the lighting user interface elements are taken care of, it's time to write the event handlers for the music playback. Figure 6-6 shows a detail of those controls.

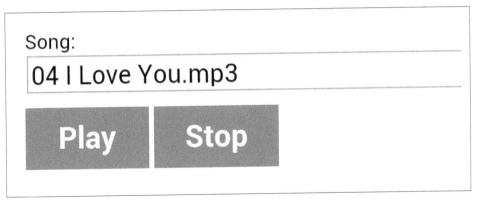

Figure 6-6. The music controls for the app

The first music event handler to write is the getSongs() handler. This handler is called in the onDeviceReady() handler. It uses PhoneGap's File API to read the directory listing of the music directory and get a list of all the song names and URIs to populate the music selector in the UI.

This function is heavily dependent on callbacks, so it helps to start reading it from the bottom. It starts by looking for the directory using resolveLocalFileSystemURI(), and when that succeeds, it calls foundDirectory(). That looks for the directory entries, and when it succeeds, it calls foundFiles() to fill the selector in the HTML. There's a common failure handler for all of these in case they fail: an alert box pops up with the cause of the failure.

```
/*
   gets a list of the songs in your music directory and
   populates an options list in the UI with them
*/
getSongs: function() {
  // failure handler for directoryReader.readEntries():
  var failure = function(error) {
    alert("Error: " + JSON.stringify(error));
  };

  // success handler for directoryReader.readEntries():
  var foundFiles = function(files) {
    if (files.length > 0) {
      // clear existing songs
      songs.innerHTML = "";
    } else {
      navigator.notification.alert(
        "Use `adb` to add songs to " + app.musicPath, {}, "No Music");
    }

    // once you have the list of files, put the valid ones in the selector:
    for (var i = 0; i < files.length; i++) {
      // if the filename is a valid file:
      if (files[i].isFile) {
        // create an option element:
        option = document.createElement("option");
        // value = song's filepath:
        option.value = files[i].fullPath;
        // label = song name:
        option.innerHTML = files[i].name;
        // select the first one and add it to the selector:
        if (i === 0) { option.selected = true; }
        songs.appendChild(option);
      }
    }
    app.onSongChange();        // update the current song
  };

  // success handler for window.resolveLocalFileSystemURI():
  var foundDirectory = function(directoryEntry) {
    var directoryReader = directoryEntry.createReader();
    directoryReader.readEntries(foundFiles, failure);
  };

  // failure handler for window.resolveLocalFileSystemURI():
  var missingDirectory = function(error) {
    navigator.notification.alert("Music directory " + app.musicPath +
      " does not exist", {}, "Music Directory");
  };

  // look for the music directory:
  window.resolveLocalFileSystemURI(app.musicPath,
```

```
        foundDirectory, missingDirectory);
    },
```

The function just shown and the event listener for the song picker call a function called onSongChange(), which changes the URI of the song. This, in turn, calls setSong(), which pulls the song name out of the URI it's handed, and sets up the conditions for playing a new song:

```
    /*
        changes the song URI and sets the new song:
    */
    onSongChange: function(event) {
        var uri = songs[songs.selectedIndex].value;
        app.setSong(uri);
    },

    /*
        sets the song URI
    */
    setSong: function(uri) {
        if (uri !== app.songUri) {
            app.stopAudio();             // stop whatever is playing
            app.songPlaying = null;      // clear the media object
            app.musicState = 0;          // clear the music state
            app.songUri = uri;           // saves the URI of the song
            // uses the filename for a title
            app.songTitle = uri.substring(uri.lastIndexOf('/')+1);
            $(songs).val(uri);           // ensure the UI matches selection
        }
    },
```

You'll see setSong() called directly without onSongChange() later, when you read a new song from an NFC tag.

The play/pause control is handled by a function called toggleAudio(), which checks the state of the media controller, and either starts playback, pauses it, or resumes it, as appropriate:

```
    /*
        toggles audio playback depending on current state of playback.
    */
    toggleAudio: function(event) {
        switch(app.musicState) {
            case undefined:              // if playback is undefined
            case Media.MEDIA_NONE:       // or if no media is playing
                app.startAudio();        // start playback
                break;
            case Media.MEDIA_STARTING:   // if media is starting
                state = "music starting";// no real change
                break;
            case Media.MEDIA_RUNNING:    // if playback is running
                app.pauseAudio();        // pause it
```

```
        break;
    case Media.MEDIA_PAUSED:    // if playback is paused
    case Media.MEDIA_STOPPED:   // or stopped
        app.playAudio();        // resume playback
        break;
    }
},
```

The startAudio() function is called by the play button, and you'll need it for when you read tags with valid song URIs on them as well. If there's no playback currently, this function will check to see if it's got a song name, and if so, start playback with it.

As you saw earlier, the Media API uses three callback functions: success, error, and status. All three of those are shown here as well. They don't do much, except for the status handler, which updates the playback status:

```
/*
    Start playing audio from your device
*/
startAudio: function() {
    var success = false;

    // attempt to instantiate a song:
    if (app.songPlaying === null) {
        // Create Media object from songUri
        if (app.songUri) {

            app.songPlaying = new Media(
                app.songUri,       // filepath of song to play
                app.audioSuccess,  // success callback
                app.audioError,    // error callback
                app.audioStatus    // update the status callback
            );
        } else {
            navigator.notification.alert("Pick a song!");
        }
    }

    // play the song:
    app.playAudio();
},

/*
    called when playback successfully initiated.
*/
audioSuccess: function() {
    console.log("Audio success");
},

/*
    displays an error if there's a problem with playback.
*/
```

```
audioError: function(error) {

    // Without timeout message is overwritten by "Currently Playing: ..."
    setTimeout(function() {
        app.display("Unable to play song.");
    }, 300);

},

/*
    updates the running audio status.
*/
audioStatus: function(status) {
    app.musicState = status;
},
```

The play, pause, and stop handlers are all very similar. They check to see that there's current media playback, take their action, update the button labels, and print the status and song name to the `message` div. Here they are:

```
/*
    resumes audio playback and changes state of the play button.
*/
playAudio: function() {
    if (app.songPlaying) {                    // if there's current playback
        app.songPlaying.play();               // play
        playButton.innerHTML = "Pause"; // update the play/pause button

        // clear the message div and display song name and status:
        app.clear();
        app.display("Currently playing: " + app.songTitle);
    }
},

/*
    pauses audio playback and changes state of the play button.
*/
pauseAudio: function() {
    if (app.songPlaying) {                    // if there's current playback
        app.songPlaying.pause();              // pause
        playButton.innerHTML = "Play";  // update the play/pause button

        // clear the message div and display song name and status:
        app.clear();
        app.display("Paused playing: " + app.songTitle);
    }
},

/*
    stops audio playback and changes state of the play button.
*/
stopAudio: function() {
```

```
        if (app.songPlaying) {              // if there's current playback
            app.songPlaying.stop();         // stop
            playButton.innerHTML = "Play";  // update the play/pause button

            // clear the message div and display song name and status:
            app.clear();
            app.display("Stopped playing: " + app.songTitle);
        }
    },
```

NFC Event Handlers

With hub communication, music, and user interface out of the way, you can write the
tag-reading and -writing functions. The first of these, readTag(), has the same structure
as similar functions for reading that you've written already. It will read the tag, extract
all the NDEF records in the NDEF message, and attempt to parse them. If it's got a URI
record, it will verify that the URI is a song's address, and attempt to play it. If it's got a
MIME record of type text/hue, it will assume the record contains the JSON-encoded
state for the lights, and attempt to send those settings to the hub:

```
/*
   reads an NDEF-formatted tag.
*/
readTag: function(thisTag) {
    var message = thisTag.ndefMessage,
        record,
        recordType,
        content;

    for (var thisRecord in message) {
        // get the next record in the message array:
        record = message[thisRecord];
        // parse the record:
        recordType = nfc.bytesToString(record.type);
        // if you've got a URI, use it to start a song:
        if (recordType === nfc.bytesToString(ndef.RTD_URI)) {

            content = ndef.uriHelper.decodePayload(record.payload);

            // make sure the song exists
            window.resolveLocalFileSystemURI(
                content,
                function() {
                    app.setSong(content);
                    app.startAudio();
                },
                function() {
                    navigator.notification.alert("Can't find " + content,
                        {}, "Missing Song");
                }
            );
```

```
        }
        // if you've got a hue JSON object, set the lights:
        if (recordType === 'text/hue') {
            // tag should be TNF_MIME_MEDIA with a type 'text/hue'
            // assume you get a JSON object as the payload
            // JSON object should have valid settings info for the hue
            // http://developers.meethue.com/1_lightsapi.html

            content = nfc.bytesToString(record.payload);
            content = JSON.parse(content);    // convert to JSON object

            app.setAllLights(content.lights); // use it to set lights
        }
    }
},
```

For write mode, you'll need to make an NDEF message with two NDEF records, one for the song and one for the lights. The lighting record should come first, so that it can trigger the MIME-type listener when you're in read mode. Since the hub object contains some properties that are not part of the Hue protocol, you'll need to extract the lights property and make a new object with just it. That'll be your first NDEF record. The second will be the song name.

Once you've got your NDEF record assembled, you can use the same writeTag() function you've used before to write the message to the tag. And once you're done with that, you've reached the end of the app!

```
/*
    makes an NDEF message and calls writeTag() to write it to a tag:
*/
makeMessage: function() {
    var message = [];

    // put the record in the message array:
    if (hub.lights !== {}) {
        var huePayload = JSON.stringify({"lights": hub.lights});
        var lightRecord = ndef.mimeMediaRecord(app.mimeType, huePayload);
        message.push(lightRecord);
    }
    if (app.songUri !== null) {
        var songRecord = ndef.uriRecord(app.songUri);
        message.push(songRecord);
    }

    //write the message:
    app.writeTag(message);
},

/*
    writes NDEF message @message to a tag:
```

```
    */
    writeTag: function(message) {
        // write the record to the tag:
        nfc.write(
            message,                        // write the record itself to the tag
            function () {                   // when complete, run this callback function:
                app.clear();                // clear the message div
                app.display("Wrote data to tag.");      // notify user in message div
                navigator.notification.vibrate(100);    // vibrate the device as well
            },
            function (reason) {         // runs if the write command fails
                navigator.notification.alert(reason,
                    function() {}, "There was a problem");
            }
        );
    }
};          // end of app
```

Again, the full source listing for this app can be found on GitHub (*http://bit.ly/mood setter*).

When you run the app, it will check whether it's registered with the Hue hub. If not, it will prompt you to press the link button in order to do so. Once it's contacted the hub, it will populate the Light Location drop-down. From there, you'll be able to change the lights and music independently of each other, and of the mode. If you're in write mode, bringing an NDEF formatable tag in range will automatically write your current settings to that tag. In read mode, the app will automatically read the tag for a song and a set of lighting settings.

You may find that you need to hold the tag close to the phone without moving for a second or so in order to get all the settings to work. Pulling away before the device has read the tag and acted on it will cause read errors. This is the most you've probably written to a tag before, and it shows you that the interaction between reading and writing and the actions they are meant to trigger can have effects on the physical interaction between user, device, and tag. The more you can write your program to keep them independent of each other, the better the interaction will be.

 If you decide to get fancy with the app and add your own styling through too much CSS, you may notice some performance effects on the interaction. We noticed that the Media API in particular was adversely affected by CSS stylings of the user interface. Solving those problems is beyond the scope of this book, but for more on this, look into hardware acceleration for CSS and PhoneGap.

Enabling Background Dispatch

Although your app will read tags just fine when it's in the foreground, you really want it to read text/hue MIME types even when it's in the background. You learned how to make this happen in Chapter 5. Open your *AndroidManifest.xml* file and add a new intent filter as follows:

```
<intent-filter>
    <action android:name="android.nfc.action.NDEF_DISCOVERED"/>
    <category android:name="android.intent.category.DEFAULT"/>
    <data android:mimeType="text/hue" />
</intent-filter>
```

Once you've updated the app, quit it, and try tapping a tag that's got a text/hue record on it. The app should launch automatically, change the lights, and play the music.

Conclusion

As you can see, the majority of making an NFC-enabled app isn't really about the NFC. The real NFC-related work is in thinking through how to format the data for the tag in a way that's most compatible with the rest of the functions of the app. In this case, you chose a Well-Known type record with a URI type definition because it made things easy for the Media API, and a MIME type record with a text/hue type because it made it easy to work with the Hue API. Once the user interface work was done, integrating the tag reading and writing was no different than in any of the sample apps you've built already. Keeping the NFC work encapsulated like this, and thinking through the protocols needed and the data structures to be used in advance will make writing NFC-enabled apps much easier for you as you move forward.

CHAPTER 7

Introduction to Arduino and NFC

As you've seen from Chapter 6, you can use NFC to initiate all kinds of action when you connect an NFC radio to devices that interface with the physical world. Although we relied on existing hardware in the previous chapter, we don't always have to do so. For example, imagine you wanted to make the Mood Setter application do more than control lights and music. Perhaps you'd like it to open or close the window blinds, lock the door, or even set off fireworks. All of these things are possible with a custom controller, a few electronic and mechanical components, and an NFC radio. Smartphones and tablets aren't the only devices that can use NFC. There are NFC modules on the market for microcontrollers as well. In this chapter, you'll get a brief introduction to NFC on the Arduino microcontroller platform.

Digital Meets Physical: Arduino

If you're interested in building new physical interfaces for electronic devices, you generally start with a microcontroller. Microcontrollers are the simple programmable computers at the heart of nearly every electronic device you own. The digital input and output pins of a microcontroller can read and generate electrical changes from sensors, or control other components like motors, lights, speakers, and more. The Arduino microcontroller platform makes it easy to begin developing your own microcontroller projects by combining a simple integrated development environment on the software side and a range of preassembled microcontroller interface boards on the hardware side.

Common Arduino projects include custom musical instruments, remote control pet feeders, environmental sensing projects, game controllers that afford different forms of action, and much more.

Both the Arduino software and hardware are open source. You can find the source code for the IDE, the source code for the firmware libraries, and the electrical schematics and board layout plans on the Arduino website (*http://www.arduino.cc*).

An Arduino is a general-purpose microcontroller. Its input and output pins are not dedicated to any specific application. Think of it like the CPU of your mobile phone: though it's programmable, it would be useless without the cellular radio, the screen controller, and the audio controller (not to mention the NFC controller). To make an Arduino useful, you need to connect it to more specific-purpose components, like communications radios, motor controllers, physical sensors, and so forth. The Arduino platform features a specification for add-on modules called shields that perform these various functions. For this chapter, you'll connect an Arduino Uno, the most common Arduino model, to an NFC radio shield.

Although microcontrollers are often used to introduce electronics development, you won't get much of that in this book. For the projects used here, you'll use mostly pre-built electronic modules that can be controlled from the Arduino or other microcontrollers using one of the methods outlined. You won't have to design or build your own circuits. You'll use shields and other pre-built modules for your electronic needs, so you can focus on the mechanics of using NFC in the Arduino environment.

Microcontrollers and Operating Systems

The processor at the heart of the Arduino is a very low-cost controller typical of many consumer appliances, from your coffeemaker to your alarm clock to your water heater. Even motion-activated light switches have a microcontroller on board. Bought in bulk, the processor at the heart of an Arduino costs around a dollar. The cost of the appliances in which a microcontroller is embedded lies in the support circuitry, the physical interface, the design, and the engineering that goes into making it easier to use.

Since these controllers are generally used for single-task applications, and since they are very limited in their processing power, they're typically run without the overhead of an operating system. The Arduino you'll use in this book can only run one program at a time, and that program runs until the microcontroller is unplugged. Until recently, the default in microcontroller programming was not to have an operating system. Learning to work simply, and to write programs that do one thing well, is a key skill for microcontroller programmers.

The cost of processing power is getting low enough that the cost of an operating system-capable processor is not that different from the most capable microcontrollers. The Raspberry Pi development board has made waves among microcontroller hobbyists because, at around the cost of an Arduino, it's capable of running a limited version of the Linux operating system. You can expect to see more and more embedded Linux development environments below $50 in the near future. You'll see more about NFC on embedded systems like the Raspberry Pi and the BeagleBone Black in Chapter 9.

Even when cost is ruled out, operating systems bring overhead to a project, however. Many sensors and actuators that interact with the physical world require the processor reading them to respond more quickly than a traditional operating system can. *Real-*

time operating systems (RTOS) feature some of the capabilities of regular operating systems, like multithreading, while preserving the responsiveness of a no-OS system. An RTOS generally lacks features like a filesystem or complex memory management, however. They also lack the conceptual simplicity of a system like Arduino. There is value in understanding both the embedded operating system approach and the single-program approach. Having shown you how to use NFC in an operating system context, we'll show you the no-OS approach in this chapter.

The Hardware Heart of NFC

At the heart of NFC communication is a radio controller. When reading passive targets like the tags you've used so far, the controller is the initiator. It generates the radio signal that the tag receives, then waits for a returned signal, as explained in Chapter 2. When communicating with active targets like a smartphone or tablet, the radio can be the initiator or the target. If it's the target, it listens for incoming radio signals and responds. The controller acts like a modem: it controls the transmission and reception of radio signals and converts those signals to data communications with its central processor.

One of the most popular NFC controllers on the market right now is the NXP PN532. It's common to a number of different NFC modules, and the PN53x family of controllers can be found in most of the NFC-enabled consumer devices on the market. There are several modules compatible with Arduino that use the PN532: the PN532 NFC/RFID controller breakout board v1.3 from Adafruit; the PN532 NFC/RFID Controller Shield for Arduino (also from Adafruit); and Seeed Studio's NFC Shield and NFC Shield v2.0. All of these modules are compatible with the NDEF libraries you'll use in this chapter.

In your Android device, the NFC controller is attached to the CPU's I/O pins, and communicates with it using similar protocols to the ones you'll use here. The NFC plug-in for PhoneGap serves the same purpose as the Arduino libraries you'll see here: it allows the central processor of your Android device to control the NFC chip on the device.

The Arduino Development Environment

To do the exercises introducing Arduino, you'll need the following:

- An Arduino Uno microcontroller, available from many outlets, including Arduino, Adafruit, Seeed Studio, and others
- The Arduino IDE (*http://bit.ly/arduino-software*)

The libraries and examples for this chapter have been tested thoroughly on the Uno, but not the Due or the Leonardo. They should work well on any Arduino derivative that uses the Atmega328 processor. For the other processors, it might work, but you're in uncharted territory.

Once you've downloaded and installed the Arduino IDE, open it and you'll get an editor window containing the following code:

```
void setup() {
  // put your setup code here, to run once:

}

void loop() {
  // put your main code here, to run repeatedly:

}
```

The Arduino programming framework is written in C++, and the code you write for Arduino is as well. The framework simplifies the more complex aspects of the language, however. There are two main functions to every Arduino program: setup() runs once when the processor powers up or is reset, and loop() runs repeatedly from the end of setup() until the processor is disconnected from power or reset. There are no callbacks, no multiple threading, just one single loop. You can call functions from the loop, though, as you'll see further on.

Here's your first running program for Arduino:

```
const int led = 13;        // give the LED pin number a name

void setup() {
  pinMode(led, OUTPUT);    // initialize pin 13 as an output
}

void loop() {
  digitalWrite(led, HIGH); // turn the LED on (HIGH is the voltage level)
  delay(1000);             // wait for a second
  digitalWrite(led, LOW);  // turn the LED off by making the voltage LOW
  delay(1000);             // wait for a second
}
```

After tying this in, pull down the Tools → Board menu and choose "Arduino Uno." In the Tools → Serial Port menu (or Tools → Port in later versions of Arduino) you'll see a list of serial ports. Unfortunately none of them will be named "Arduino," but you can find the name of your port by looking at the list, then plugging your Arduino Uno into a USB port (on Windows you'll be asked to install drivers; they're included in the IDE download) and looking at the list again. The new port in the list will be your Arduino

Uno. On OS X, you'll see two ports, one labeled */dev/cu.usbmodem-xxx* and another labeled */dev/tty.usbmodem-xxx*, with *xxx* being the board's serial number. Either one will work, as they're functionally the same port. For example, on a 2011-era MacBook Air running OS X 10.8, the ports are called */dev/tty.usbmodem621* or */dev/tty.usbmodem421*. On a Windows 7 or 8 machine, it's *COM3*. On Linux, it's usually */dev/ttyACM0*.

Pick your port, then click the "Upload" button on the toolbar, as shown in Figure 7-1.

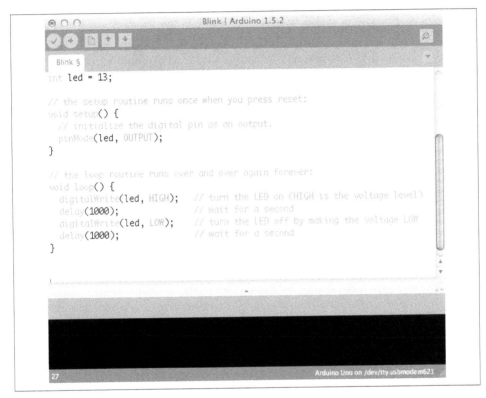

Figure 7-1. The Arduino IDE

This figure also illustrates the Toolbar buttons; from the left, they are Verify (compiles your code), Upload (compiles and uploads), New, Open, and Save. On the far right is the Serial Port Monitor. The selected board type and serial port appear on the bottom right of the window. The IDE will compile your code and upload it to the board. The board will reset and start running, and you'll see a blinking LED right next to the Arduino logo on the board (Figure 7-2). That LED is attached to one of the controller's I/O pins, digital pin 13.

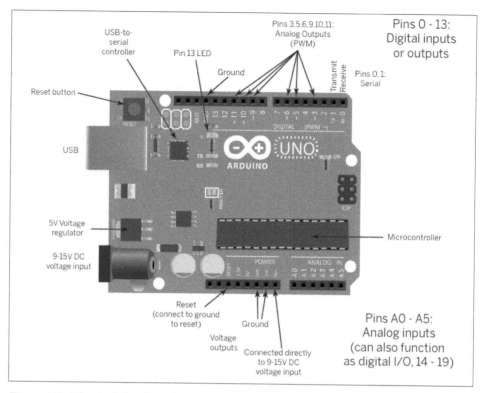

Figure 7-2. The Arduino Uno (image courtesy of Maker Media; adapted from Tom Igoe's "Making Things Talk" 2nd ed., originally drawn by Jody Culkin)

Arduino, like all microcontrollers, operates by reading or controlling the voltage on its I/O pins. The command `digitalRead()` returns a 1 or a 0 from a given pin, also called HIGH or LOW (referring to the voltage levels). The `digitalWrite()` command sets a given pin to HIGH or LOW. The Uno operates at 5 volts, so HIGH, or 1, refers to 5 volts, while LOW or 0 refers to 0 volts. Some of the I/O pins can operate in analog mode too: Analog pins A0 through A5 can read an analog voltage from 0 to 5 volts, with a resolution of about 0.05 volts (returns a range from 0 to 1,023). Digital pins 3, 5, 6, 9, 10, and 11 can "fake" a continuously changing analog output voltage by pulsing the pin with a duty cycle resolution of 256 steps.

In the previous code, the Arduino initializes digital pin 13 as an output pin, meaning it will drive voltage on that pin. In the loop, the processor sets the voltage to 5 volts (`digitalWrite(ledPin, HIGH)`), then to 0 volts (`digitalWrite(ledPin, LOW)`). In between, it does nothing for 1,000 milliseconds (`delay(1000)`). Because this is the only program running on the Arduino's processor, `delay()` really means the processor does nothing, so you won't see it used a whole lot.

The IDE creates a default directory for your sketches in your Documents directory called Arduino. For convenience, save this sketch there under the name Blink. You'll see more on this sketch directory later.

The core Arduino command reference can be found at Arduino's Language Reference page (*http://arduino.cc/en/Reference*). There are also dozens of examples of how to use the platform in the Learning section. You can also find these examples in the IDE, by choosing Examples from the File menu.

Serial Communication

In addition to the basic I/O functions, the Arduino can communicate using asynchronous serial over USB, as well as the I2C and SPI protocols used by the PN532 chip. You'll see serial-to-USB used a lot to send messages to and from your computer. It's also used to upload your compiled program (called a *sketch* in Arduino) to the Uno. Here's a sketch that reads input from your computer over the USB-to-serial connection and uses the input to control the output of the LED on pin 13:

```
const int led = 13;          // give the LED pin number a name

void setup() {
  Serial.begin(9600);        // open serial communication at 9600 bps
  pinMode(led, OUTPUT);      // make the LED pin an output
}

void loop() {
  if (Serial.available()) {
    char input = Serial.read();             // read a byte from the serial port
    if (input == 'H' || input == 'h') {     // if it's H or h
      digitalWrite(led, HIGH);              // turn the LED on
      Serial.println(input);                // echo what the user typed
    }
    else if (input == 'L' || input == 'l') {  // if it's L or l
      digitalWrite(led, LOW);               // turn the LED off
      Serial.println(input);                // echo what the user typed
    }
  }
}
```

The full source code can be found on GitHub (*http://bit.ly/serialled*).

Upload this sketch, then click the Serial Port Monitor on the right side of the toolbar and the Serial Monitor window will open. Type "H" or "h" and click "send" or hit Enter and the LED attached to pin 13 will turn on. Type "L" or "l" and it will turn off.

Once you understand digital in and out, analog in and out, and serial communication, you've got the basics of working with Arduino. Everything is controlled either by reading a voltage on an input pin, generating a voltage on an output pin, or sending digital communications using serial protocols. Serial protocols themselves are just timed series of voltage pulses on specific I/O pins.

For more information on developing projects with Arduino, see Massimo Banzi's *Getting Started with Arduino*, Tom Igoe's *Making Things Talk*, or Michael Margolis' *Arduino Bookbook*, among others. You'll also find thousands of Arduino example projects, sample code, libraries, and add-on modules on the Web.

SPI, I2C, UART?

The PN532 NFC chip at the heart of the shields mentioned here offers three different communications interfaces to the microcontroller that's controlling it. It can communicate using asynchronous serial communication using a universal asynchronous receiver-transmitter (UART). It can also use two forms of synchronous serial communication, Serial-Peripheral Interface (SPI) or Inter-Integrated Circuit communication (I2C). Asynchronous serial communication is commonly used between two computers that each have their own internal clock and can operate independently, while SPI and I2C are used for communication between a master computer and devices that rely on the master for direction. Asynchronous serial is always one-to-one communication, but I2C and SPI are bus protocols, meaning you can have several individually addressable devices sharing the same communications lines. Most programmable microcontrollers offer all three interfaces, and further differences between them are not relevant to this book.

Not all of the modules and shields for Arduino mentioned here provide all three interfaces, however. Adafruit's breakout board offers all three interfaces, but Adafruit's shield offers only SPI and I2C, while Seeed Studio's offers only SPI.

As of this writing, there are several Arduino libraries available for the PN532 controller, some of which use the SPI interface, and some of which use the I2C interface. The NDEF library used here is a wrapper around Seeed Studio's PN532 libraries, which offer either SPI or I2C functionality. You'll see how to include the appropriate version of the PN532 library as well as the NDEF library in this chapter.

Installing Arduino Libraries

The Arduino environment can be extended through the use of libraries, just like any programming platform. To use NFC with Arduino, you'll need a couple of libraries. Download the NDEF library from Don's GitHub repository (*https://github.com/don/ NDEF*). To install it as an Arduino library, click "Import Library…" in the Sketch menu, then choose the "Add Library…" submenu option. You can install the library from a ZIP file, or by choosing a directory and choosing "All Files." In either case, the IDE will import all the files from the ZIP or directory. Inside each library directory is a subdirectory called "Examples." After you import the library, these can be found in the File menu under "Examples," with a submenu for the library's name.

You'll also need an adapter library for the shield you're using. There are several different libraries for the PN532 chip, but in the examples that follow, you'll be using the PN532 libraries from Seeed Studio. These will work with both Seeed's shields and Adafruit's shield. You can download them from Seeed's GitHub repository (*http://bit.ly/seeed-github*). The Seeed Studio NFC libraries are separated into three different components: the *PN532* folder, the *PN532_I2C* folder, and the *PN532_SPI* folder. In order to get them to work with Arduino 1.5 and beyond, you should import each of these three folders as if they were separate libraries. That way they'll end up in the libraries folder properly, and when you compile your code, you'll save some memory, because you won't be adding the drivers for the communication protocol you don't need.

Other Libraries, and Library Namespace Collisions
Adafruit's NCFShield I2C library is also an excellent library for use with the PN532. You can download it from GitHub (*http://bit.ly/nfcshield_i2c*). Although the Adafruit library works only with the I2C interface, and therefore only works with the Adafruit shield, it is a very stable library, and takes a little less memory than the Seeed library. The Adafruit library doesn't work automatically with the NDEF library for Arduino, but can be made to do so with some slight modifications to the latter.

If you've experimented with some of the lower-level NFC libraries previously, and still have earlier versions of them in your libraries folder (like we did), you may get errors when you try to compile your code. If you do, remove any libraries related to the PN532 that you're not using from your Arduino libraries directory and restart the IDE. You can find the libraries directory inside your Arduino sketch directory.

For these examples, you'll need the following:

- An Arduino Uno microcontroller.
- The Arduino IDE.
- An NFC Shield (you can use Adafruit's PN532 NFC/RFID Controller Shield for Arduino (*http://bit.ly/pn532*) or Seeed Studio's NFC Shield (*http://bit.ly/seeed-sld80453p*) or NFC Shield v2.0 (*http://bit.ly/seeed-nfc-shield*))
- If you're using the Adafruit shield, you may want to get some Shield Stacking headers (*https://www.adafruit.com/products/85*) from Adafruit as well. You're going to have to do a little soldering to use this shield, but it's worth it.

- A few NFC tags (for this chapter, Mifare Classic are the most compatible with the Arduino libraries you're using, even though they won't work on some Android devices; see "Device-to-Tag Type Matching" on page 19 for more on which tags work with which devices).

- The Arduino IDE (*http://bit.ly/arduino-software*) version 1.5.3 or later.

- The Arduino NDEF library, available from Don Coleman's GitHub repository (*https://github.com/don/NDEF*).

- The SeeedStudio PN532 library (*http://bit.ly/seeed-github*).

The Adafruit shield comes without pin headers mounted, so you'll need to solder these on. It can be tricky to align these, but Adafruit's got a nice tutorial with pictures linked off the product page on how to do this. Plug your shield into your Arduino Uno (it will only fit one way), and you're ready to go.

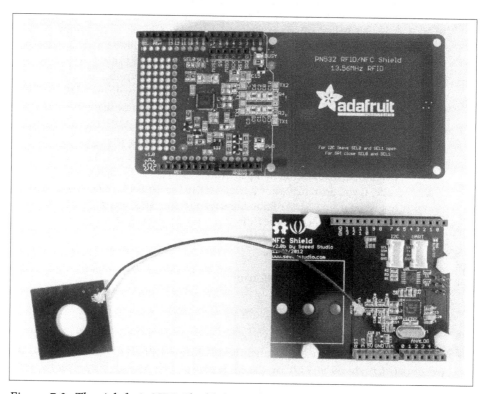

Figure 7-3. The Adafruit NFC Shield for Arduino (top) and the Seeed Studio NFC Shield for Arduino v2.0 (bottom)

The Arduino NDEF Library

The libraries you're using can be thought of as a stack. The PN532 adapter libraries provide the low-level commands to speak to the PN532 chip on the shield, one in SPI and the other in I2C. By themselves, they simply deliver the data from the tags as a string of bytes. In order to interpret those bytes, you need some helper libraries that describe the various tag protocols: Mifare Classic, Mifare Ultralight, and so forth, as described in Chapter 2. Above the tag type libraries is an NFC layer that removes the differentiation between tags and delivers a stream of bytes. Finally, above that, there's the NDEF library that reads the bytes passed on from the tag type libraries as a series of NDEF messages and records. Figure 7-4 shows the stack and the libraries' relationships to each other.

Without the NDEF library, you'd have to figure out byte-by-byte what's going on with the bytes coming in from your tags. With it, you can generally ignore what's going on at the lower levels, and concentrate on reading and writing NDEF messages as you've done previously.

Not all the tag type helper libraries have been written. So far, the NDEF library repository includes tag libraries for reading and writing to Mifare Classic tags and read capability for Type 2 (Mifare Ultralight), but not the others, so you'll need to use one of those two tag types, or be prepared to dive in and write your own tag descriptor library.

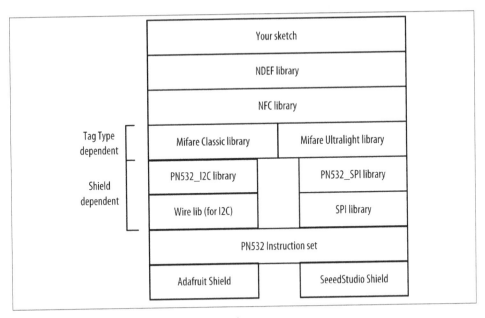

Figure 7-4. The Arduino NFC library stack

The NDEF library for Arduino contains some objects and concepts that should be familiar to you already:

NfcAdapter

This object is an instance of the lower level adapter library. It looks for tags for you.

NfcTag

This object contains metadata about the tag: UID, technology, and size.

NdefMessage

When you've read an NDEF-formatted tag, you'll get an NdefMessage, of course. This object handles the encoding and decoding of bytes to and from the NDEF format.

NdefRecord

This carries the payload and any record metadata, like the language, the TNF, the Type, and so forth.

The library has a number of helper functions for both reading messages and writing them. You won't use all of these functions, but most of them should seem familiar based on what you know of NDEF already. All the functions are listed by class in Table 7-1.

Table 7-1. NDEF for Arduino Library Functions

NfcAdapter functions	NfcTag functions	NdefMessage functions	NdefRecord functions
begin(void)	getUidLength()	getEncodedSize()	getEncodedSize()
tagPresent()	getUid()	encode()	getTypeLength()
read()	getUidString()	addRecord()	getPayloadLength()
write()	getTagType()	addMimeMediaRecord()	getIdLength()
	hasNdefMessage()	addTextRecord()	getTnf()
	getNdefMessage()	addUriRecord()	getPayload()
		addEmptyRecord()	getType()
		getRecordCount()	getId()
		getRecord()	setTnf()
			setType()
			setPayload()
			setId()

Reading NDEF in Arduino

The ReadTagExtended example that comes with the NDEF library shows many of the functions of the library and the workflow nicely. To see it, click the File menu, choose "Examples," then the "NDEF" submenu, then "ReadTagExtended." Upload it to your Arduino and try reading some of the tags you've already written.

You'll need to change the beginning of the sketch depending on which shield model you're using. If you're using an SPI-based shield like the Seeed Studio shields, your code should start like this:

```
#include <SPI.h>
#include <PN532_SPI.h>
#include <PN532.h>
#include <NfcAdapter.h>

PN532_SPI pn532spi(SPI, 10);
NfcAdapter nfc = NfcAdapter(pn532spi);
```

If you're using an I2C-based shield like the Adafruit shield, your code should start like this:

```
#include <Wire.h>
#include <PN532_I2C.h>
#include <PN532.h>
#include <NfcAdapter.h>

PN532_I2C pn532_i2c(Wire);
NfcAdapter nfc = NfcAdapter(pn532_i2c);
```

After that, everything will be identical, regardless of your shield type. The remainder of this chapter shows code for an I2C-based shield, so you should change the beginning as necessary if you're using an SPI-based shield.

As you can see from the following code, the program logic is similar to what you've seen before: first you check if a tag is present using `nfc.tagPresent()`. Since Arduino doesn't have event handlers, repeated polling is necessary for this. When you know there's a tag, you make a tag object and read the data into it using `NfcTag tag = nfc.read()`. Next you check if there's a message using `tag.getNdefMessage()`. If there's a message present, iterate over the records in the message and pull out the message attributes (TNF, type, payload, and ID):

```
#include <Wire.h>
#include <PN532_I2C.h>
#include <PN532.h>
#include <NfcAdapter.h>

PN532_I2C pn532_i2c(Wire);
NfcAdapter nfc = NfcAdapter(pn532_i2c);

void setup() {
  Serial.begin(9600);
  Serial.println("NDEF Reader");
  nfc.begin();
}

void loop() {
  Serial.println("\nScan a NFC tag\n");
```

```
if (nfc.tagPresent()) {
  NfcTag tag = nfc.read();
  Serial.println(tag.getTagType());
  Serial.print("UID: ");
  Serial.println(tag.getUidString());

  if (tag.hasNdefMessage()) { // every tag won't have a message
    NdefMessage message = tag.getNdefMessage();
    Serial.print("\nThis NFC Tag contains an NDEF Message with ");
    Serial.print(message.getRecordCount());
    Serial.print(" NDEF Record");
    if (message.getRecordCount() != 1) {
      // if there's more than one record, pluralize:
      Serial.print("s");
    }

    // cycle through the records, printing some info from each
    int recordCount = message.getRecordCount();
    for (int i = 0; i < recordCount; i++)
    {
      Serial.print("\nNDEF Record ");
      Serial.println(i+1);
      NdefRecord record = message.getRecord(i);

      Serial.print("  TNF: ");
      Serial.println(record.getTnf());
      Serial.print("  Type: ");
      Serial.println(record.getType()); // will be "" for TNF_EMPTY

      // The TNF and Type should be used to determine
      // how your application processes the payload
      // There's no generic processing for the payload.
      //  it's returned as a byte[]
      int payloadLength = record.getPayloadLength();
      byte payload[payloadLength];
      record.getPayload(payload);

      // Force the data into a String:
      String payloadAsString = "";
      for (int c = 0; c < payloadLength; c++) {
        payloadAsString += (char)payload[c];
      }
      Serial.print("  Payload (as String): ");
      Serial.println(payloadAsString);

      // id is probably blank and will return ""
      String uid = record.getId();
      if (uid != "") {
        Serial.print("  ID: ");Serial.println(uid);
      }
    }
```

```
    }
  }
  delay(3000);    // delay before next read
}
```

Upload this code then open the Serial Port Monitor by clicking the icon on the top right corner of the IDE window. When you run this with the tags from previous chapters, you should get output that looks something like this:

```
NDEF Reader
Found chip PN532
Firmware ver. 1.6

Scan a NFC tag

Mifare Classic
UID: A4 AF 77 5D

This NFC Tag contains an NDEF Message with 2 NDEF Records
NDEF Record 1
  TNF: 2
  Type: text/hue
  Payload (as String): {"lights":{"1":{"name":"Living room","state":
   {"on":true,"bri":223,
   "hue":47293,"sat":0}}

NDEF Record 2
  TNF: 1
  Type: U
  Payload (as String): /sdcard/myMusic/Forever.mp3
```

The `tagPresent` and `delay` functions are *blocking functions*. This means they stop the program until they complete; about 100 milliseconds for `tagPresent`, and as long as you set for delay. You should only call them when your controller needs to do nothing else. If you need to read physical inputs like pushbuttons or receive data via serial communications, prioritize those things, as you'll see in the application sketches that follow.

Writing NDEF in Arduino

Writing records to an NDEF message and sending it is also straightforward. The Write-TagMultipleRecords example gives you a good idea. To see it, click the File menu, choose "Examples," then the "NDEF" submenu, then "WriteTagMultipleRecords." Upload it to your Arduino and try writing to a tag, then reading it with your phone.

First, you set up an `NdefMessage` object, then you add records to it using the writing helper functions, such as `addTextRecord()`, `addUriRecord()`, or `addMimeMediaRe cord()`. Once the message is assembled, you send it using the `NfcAdapter write()` function, which will return success or failure:

```
#include <Wire.h>
#include <PN532_I2C.h>
#include <PN532.h>
#include <NfcAdapter.h>

PN532_I2C pn532_i2c(Wire);
NfcAdapter nfc = NfcAdapter(pn532_i2c);

void setup() {
    Serial.begin(9600);
    Serial.println("NDEF Writer");
    nfc.begin();
}

void loop() {
    Serial.println("\nPlace a formatted Mifare Classic NFC tag on the reader.");
    if (nfc.tagPresent()) {
        NdefMessage message = NdefMessage();
        message.addTextRecord("Hello, Arduino!");
        message.addUriRecord("http://arduino.cc");
        message.addTextRecord("Goodbye, Arduino!");
        boolean success = nfc.write(message);
        if (success) {
            Serial.println("Success. Try reading this tag with your phone.");
        } else {
            Serial.println("Write failed");
        }
    }
    delay(3000);
}
```

Once you've got a sense of the basic reading and writing functionality of the NDEF library, you're ready to build an application with it.

A Microcontroller NFC Application: Hotel Key Cards

If you've checked into a hotel in the last 10 years, chances are good you had an RFID-based room key card. This is an application that could easily be enhanced through the use of NFC, so as an example of embedded NFC, you'll build a simple NFC-based hotel room key card application. In this application, you'll write an NFC card writer sketch on an Arduino as well as an NFC card reader sketch. The latter will involve an extra piece of hardware: an electronically controlled door lock that you can use in a real door if you want. Because what's the fun of using a microcontroller if you can't make something physical happen?

The first half of this application you'll write is the tag writer in Arduino. You'll make a little box that sits behind the registration desk, attached to the desk computer. The clerk enters your name, room number, and how many nights you're staying, then inserts the card in the box. The tag writer sketch then writes this information to the tag as a MIME media record containing a JSON string.

The second half of the application that you'll write is the door lock controller. The Arduino will be attached to the door lock, and when it reads the card, it will check to see if the current time is in between check-in and checkout, and if the room number on the card corresponds to the room number of the door. If that's all correct, then the Arduino will open the door latch for three seconds so you can open the door.

Finally, you'll write a browser-based user interface to connect with the NFC tag writer so that the desk clerk can interact with the device in a familiar way.

While the first half of the application could be written on a mobile device using the methods you've learned already, the second half requires a controller because of the physical door lock. You also have to consider the physical context in which it's used. For example, a hotel guest is typically juggling a few items when she opens her room: suitcase, coat, purse or briefcase, and room key. You can't expect her to do more than tap or insert the key, and you've got to make sure the door locks behind her.

For this application, you'll need the same parts you needed for the preceding NFC examples. In addition, you'll need some new parts:

- A solderless breadboard or prototyping shield for Arduino. Here are a few options:
  — Arduino Proto Shield Rev3 (*http://bit.ly/17uFcHD*).
  — Adafruit Proto Shield for Arduino (*http://www.adafruit.com/products/51*).
  — A tiny breadboard (*http://www.adafruit.com/products/65*) (optional accompaniment to the previous two).
  — If you don't need everything mounted together, you can just use a half-size breadboard (*http://www.adafruit.com/products/64*).
- A solenoid-driven door lock, 12 volts or less. There are plenty of small solenoids that'll do the job. We used an Amico 0837L DC 12V 8W Open Frame Type Solenoid for Electric Door Lock (*http://amzn.to/1aEQe7S*) bought on Amazon, but you can also get solenoids from other retailers. Adafruit sells a similar lock-style solenoid (*http://www.adafruit.com/products/1512*) and Seeed Studio sells several models, so if you're ordering a shield from them, you can get a solenoid from them as well.
- A TIP120 Darlington transistor (*http://www.adafruit.com/products/976*).
- A 12V, 1000mA power supply (*http://www.adafruit.com/products/798*), with 2.1mm ID, 5.5mm OD, center-positive connector to power the solenoid circuit.
- jumper wires (*http://www.adafruit.com/products/759*) or 22AWG solid-core wire.
- Two LEDs (one red, one green). These are available from any electronics retailer, but for reference, check out Adafruit's red LED pack (*http://www.adafruit.com/products/299*) or green LED pack (*http://www.adafruit.com/products/298*).

- Two 220Ω resistors for the LEDs, which are available from any electronics retailer.
- The Time library (*http://bit.ly/time-library*) for Arduino by Michael Margolis.

If you plan to build and deploy both the NFC writer and the NFC reader/lock controller, you'll need two Arduinos and two NFC shields. However, you can learn the whole application with just one of each.

Figure 7-5 shows the system diagram for the application.

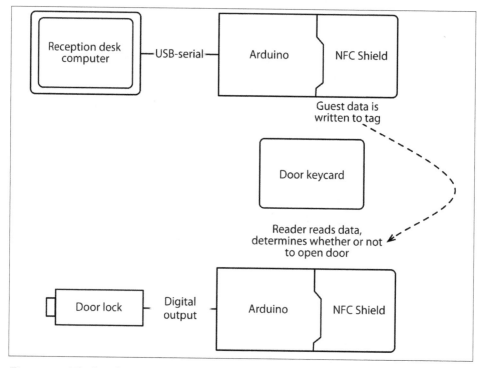

Figure 7-5. The hotel room key card application system diagram

The Interaction and Data Format

Both of the controllers in this application, the card writer and the reader/door lock control, should be as responsive as possible, so it's best to keep them as simple as possible. As you can see from the diagram, the writer will always be attached to a personal computer, which has a much richer physical interface. So you can leave the work of taking user input, working out the timestamps, and prompting the user to that computer. The microcontroller only needs to wait for a string of data, write it to the card, and report whether it succeeded or not. It won't care what the data is, it'll just write the text. To make things more compatible with other applications in this book, make the MIME media record a JSON string containing the basic details, like so:

```
{
  name: username,
  room: (room number),
  checkin: (checkin time in unix time),
  checkout: (checkout time in unix time),
}
```

The writer sketch will wait for a serial string ending in a } character, then look for a tag in its field. If it sees a tag, it will write the string to the tag as an NDEF message with one NDEF MIME media record. If it succeeds, it will turn on a green LED on pin 9, and if it fails, it will turn on a red LED on pin 8. It will check every three seconds, and turn off both LEDs.

The reader sketch needs to be a bit more complex, because it's a standalone device not attached to any other computer. It will need to keep time for itself, read and decode the tag data, check the current time against the check-in and checkout times, check the room number on the tag against its own number, and indicate to the user whether it read the tag, and control the lock appropriately.

The reader's main loop has to be very responsive, however. Its primary task is listening for tags. When it's not listening for tags, it should turn on an indicator LED, green or red, to indicate whether it got a good or bad read. If it's a good read, it should also hold the door lock open.

Because you're using JSON for the data exchange, you could add in other features as well. You could write a PhoneGap app for the guest, to display the room number and check-in and checkout times. You could write a series of room entry and exit times to the card. The advantage to this architecture is that it makes it trivial to add other information to the card and to applications on other physical devices that read it, while not affecting the most important device—the lock—at all.

Keeping Time

Unix and other POSIX operating systems keep time using the number of seconds since Thursday, January 1, 1970, not counting leap seconds. This format is called *Unix time*, or more correctly, *POSIX time*, and it's marked from midnight on January 1, 1970, which is called *Coordinated Universal Time* (UTC). This time format makes it easy to calculate differences between times, and allows you to compress time into a single long integer. If you haven't seen it before, get to know it. Most programming languages give you a way to convert to and from Unix time, so it's a handy univeral way to pass times around. For Arduino, there is a handy library for time keeping that you'll see later on.

One of the challenges you'll see in the examples that follow is that different libraries and platforms choose to denote this time in different scales. Date.valueOf(), the JavaScript standard for returning Unix time, returns the number of milliseconds since January 1, 1970, while various Arduino libraries return the number of seconds. So some conversion is needed, but they're *mostly* compatible.

If you'd like to see some dates and times in Unix time, open your browser's JavaScript console and type the following:

```
> var d = new Date("January 1, 2000");
> console.log(d);
> d = new Date("July 10, 1856");
> console.log(d);
> d = new Date("January 7, 1943");
> console.log(d.valueOf());
```

You'll notice that the dates after January 1, 1970, are positive, and before that date are negative. Try it with your own relevant dates.

The Arduino NDEF Writer Device

The circuit for the NDEF writer is shown in Figure 7-6. It plugs into the Arduino, and the circuit shown sits on top of the shield (which is not pictured). It contains two LEDs and the NDEF shield. Connect the solenoid circuit as shown. You should test the LEDs by using the previous Blink sketch; just change the output pin number from 13 to 8 or 9 and upload the code again. The LED should blink.

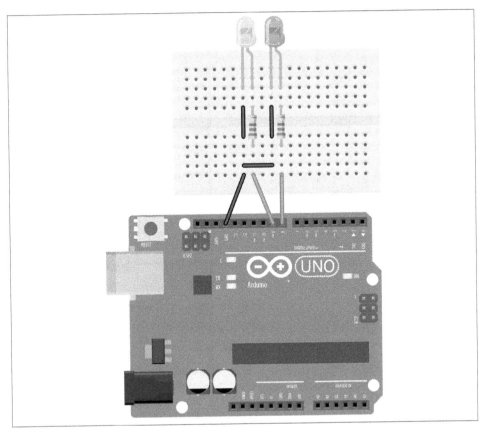

Figure 7-6. The circuit for the NFC reader door lock device

See Figure 7-7 for a picture of the NDEF writer in schematic view.

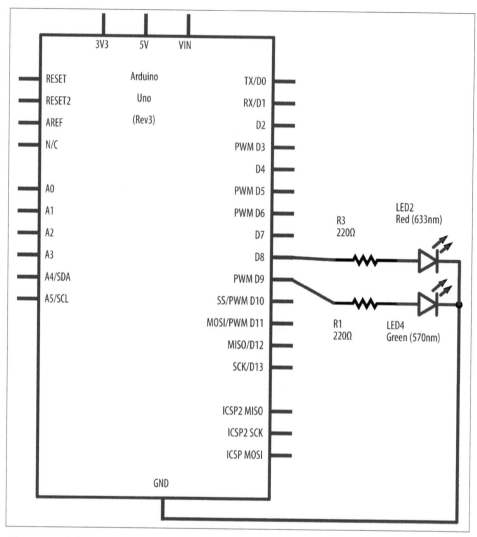

Figure 7-7. The NFC reader door lock device in schematic view

Start with the writer code, as it's simpler, and you've already got applications on your Android device that you can use to check it. Include the libraries you need and set up an NfcAdapter object. Then add some constants to name your output pins and a string for serial input, and a variable to track when you turn the indicator LEDs on, as you'll see in the following sketch. Then in the setup, initialize serial communications and the NfcAdapter object, and set the two indicator LED pins to be outputs.

```
// If you're using an SPI-based shield, change these to include the SPI library:
#include <Wire.h>
#include <PN532_I2C.h>
```

```
#include <PN532.h>
#include <NfcAdapter.h>
#include <Time.h>

PN532_I2C pn532_i2c(Wire);
NfcAdapter nfc = NfcAdapter(pn532_i2c);

const int greenLed = 9;        // pin for the green LED
const int redLed = 8;          // pin for the red LED

String inputString = "";       // string for input from serial port
long lightOnTime = 0;          // last time the LEDs were turned on, in ms

boolean readyToWrite = false;  // true when you are ready to write to NFC tag

void setup() {
  Serial.begin(9600);          // initialize serial communications
  nfc.begin();                 // initialize NfcAdapter
  pinMode(greenLed, OUTPUT);   // make pin 9 an output
  pinMode(redLed, OUTPUT);     // make pin 8 an output
}
```

The main function of the loop is to take input serially from a desktop app on a personal computer. When you've got the data, you'll call another function to look for a tag and write to it. Here is the main loop:

```
void loop() {
  // if there's incoming data, read it into a string:
  while (Serial.available() > 0) {
    char thisChar = Serial.read();
    // add incoming character to the end of inputString:
    inputString += thisChar;
    if (thisChar == '{') {
      // new message, reset buffer
      inputString = "{";
      readyToWrite = false;
    }
    else if (thisChar == '}') {
      // end of message, ready to write to tag
      Serial.println("Ready to write data to tag");
      readyToWrite = true;
    }
  }
  // keep looking for a tag to write to when
  // you've got a string to write:
  if (readyToWrite) {
    lookForTag();
  }

  if (millis() - lightOnTime > 3000 ) {   // check every three seconds
    digitalWrite(greenLed, LOW);          // turn off pin 9
    digitalWrite(redLed, LOW);            // turn off pin 8
```

```
        }
    }
```

The if statement at the end of the main loop uses the millis() function, which returns the number of milliseconds since the Arduino reset to check if three seconds have elapsed since you turned on the success or failure LED. If so, it turns them both off.

The lookForTag() function that's called when you have a full string looks for a tag and writes the input string to it. When there's a valid string to write, the main loop calls lookForTag() continuously until it succeeds. If lookForTag() succeeds in writing to the tag, it returns true. Otherwise, it returns false:

```
void lookForTag() {
    if (nfc.tagPresent()) {                   // if there's a tag present
        NdefMessage message;                  // make a new NDEF message
        // add the input string as a record:
        message.addMimeMediaRecord("text/hotelkey", inputString);
        boolean success = nfc.write(message); // attempt to write to the tag

        if (success) {
            // let the desktop app know you succeeded:
            Serial.println("Result: tag written.");
            digitalWrite(redLed, LOW);        // turn off the failure light if on
            digitalWrite(greenLed, HIGH);     // turn on the success light
            lightOnTime = millis();
            readyToWrite = false;             // clear write flag
        }
        else {
            // let the desktop app know you failed:
            Serial.println("Result: failed to write to tag");
            digitalWrite(greenLed, LOW);      // turn off the success light if on
            digitalWrite(redLed, HIGH);       // turn on the failure light
            lightOnTime = millis();
        }
    }
}
```

This function also sends a serial response whether it succeeded or failed to write to the tag, and both responses contain a common word, Result:. That's important, because it means a desktop application that's reading this response can parse for the line easily, whether the tag was written or not.

The full source code can be found on GitHub (*http://bit.ly/HotelTagWriter*).

That's the whole sketch. Save this, upload it to your Arduino, and test it by opening the Serial Port Monitor, placing a tag on the shield's antenna and typing in the following JSON object (you may want to type it into a text document beforehand and cut and paste, and feel free to set your own values for these):

```
{
    "name":"Nicky",
```

```
    "room":3327,
    "checkin":1357534800,
    "checkout":1373428800
}
```

When you enter the data, the green LED should turn on, and you should get the message "Result: tag written."

To test these tags, open any tag-reading app you have on your Android device, like NXP TagInfo, and try to read the tag. You should get a MIME media record with the same JSON string in it.

Your reader device doesn't have a user interface, other than the green and red LEDs. It relies on a desktop application that can read and write its serial protocol to provide an interface for the desk clerk. You wouldn't want the clerk to have to open the Arduino IDE and the Serial Port Monitor and type in a JSON string to write to the card. Instead, you'd write your desktop application to take input from the keyboard, convert it into a JSON string, and send it to the Arduino.

You could write a desktop interface in any programming environment that can access the serial ports of your computer. The clear serial communications protocol you established previously will help, namely that:

- Every message to the writer device should be a JSON string, ending in }
- Every response from the writer device will contain the word "Result:" to report success or failure in writing to a tag
- Every response from the writer ends in a new line (because you used `Serial.println()`)

You'll write a browser-based interface for this device in Node.js later on, but for now, move on to the reader device. You can see the writer device on a door in Figure 7-8. The dotted lines show where a control box and solenoid might be embedded in the door in a final version. The card would insert into a slot from the top or tap on the front of the reader as in most hotel rooms.

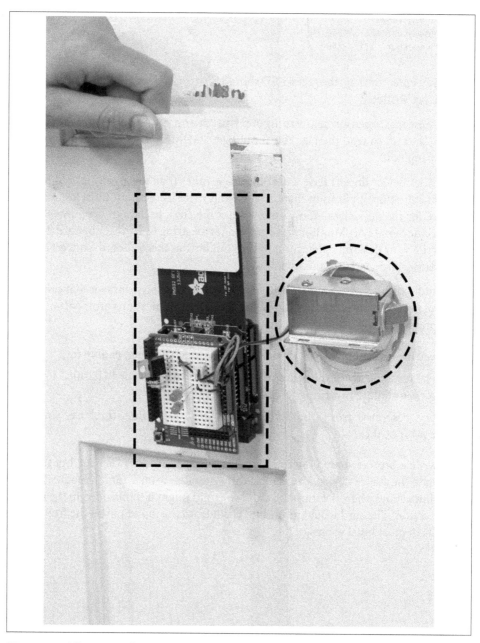

Figure 7-8. The writer device prototyped on a door

How Do You Make a Secure NDEF Record?

By now, you're probably thinking to yourself, "why would I use NDEF for hotel keys when anyone who's read this book could easily rewrite the tag and break into my hotel room?" Good question. You can encrypt the contents of a record any way you wish, as long as the reader's controller knows how to decrypt it. But if you want to provide authentication, the NFC Forum has defined the *Signature Record Type Definition* for handling situations like this. Version 1.0 is the currently adopted standard, and version 2.0 is a candidate specification. Details on both can be found on the NFC Forum Specifications page (*http://bit.ly/nfc-tech-specs*).

The Signature RTD sets a standard for developers to use when storing a public encryption key as part of an NDEF message. Using this standard, developers would include a signature record in every NDEF message that's used to verify the authenticity of the record that precedes it. The signature can contain a hash and certificate chain that's encrypted upon writing the tag, then decrypted by the reader. If the decrypted signature checks out, the reader knows the data is valid. If not, the reader knows to ignore the data. Both reader and writer would share the private key needed for accurate encryption and decryption.

The signature RTD specification doesn't mandate a particular public key cryptography infrastructure, but it supports various existing standards.

This specification is an authentication scheme, not an encryption scheme. The records other than the signature record would presumably still be readable by any reader, but they would not be verifiable. For greater security, you could design your application so that the writer encrypts the data itself, then includes a signature on the encrypted data. The reader would then first verify the signature, then decrypt the data using the same algorithm that the writer used to encrypt it.

The Arduino NDEF Reader and Door Lock Device

The NDEF reader device is a bit more complex than the writer. It has to interpret the JSON on the tags and take appropriate action. In order to do that, it has to not only read the tag, but parse the result. It has to know if you're at the right room number, and whether or not the current time is within the dates of your stay. To do this, it has to be able to tell time in Unix time. Michael Margolis's Time library for Arduino will help accomplish this. Originally written to interface with a *real-time clock* (RTC) chip like the Dallas Semiconductor DS1307 (*http://www.adafruit.com/products/264*) or the DS3231 (*http://www.adafruit.com/products/255*), this library can also keep time using the Arduino's internal clock. The latter is less accurate, but requires no extra hardware. It will do fine for this example.

The circuit for the reader is shown in Figure 7-9 with a solenoid lock (the NFC shield is not shown). It plugs into the Arduino and contains two LEDs, the NFC shield, and the solenoid circuit for the door lock part. Connect the solenoid circuit as shown. Note that, because the solenoid needs 12 volts and 667 milliamps to operate, you'll need to power the Arduino from the 12V power supply mentioned in the parts list. You should test the solenoid by using the previous Blink sketch; just change the output pin number from 13 to 7 and upload the code again. The solenoid should fire once a second. Note that the MOSFET transistor here can be swapped with a TIP120 Darlington transistor, as they have the same pinout.

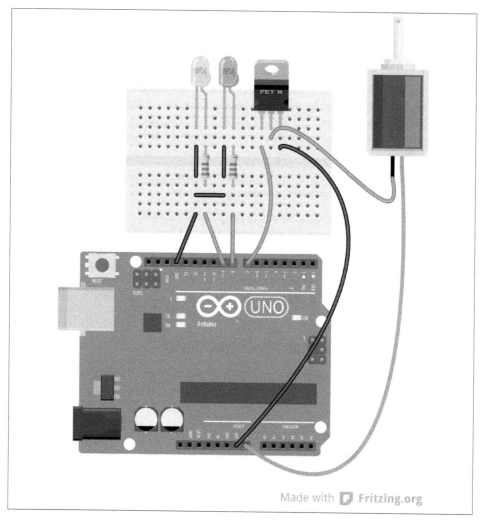

Figure 7-9. The circuit for the NFC reader device (breadboard view)

See Figure 7-10 for a picture of the same circuit in schematic view.

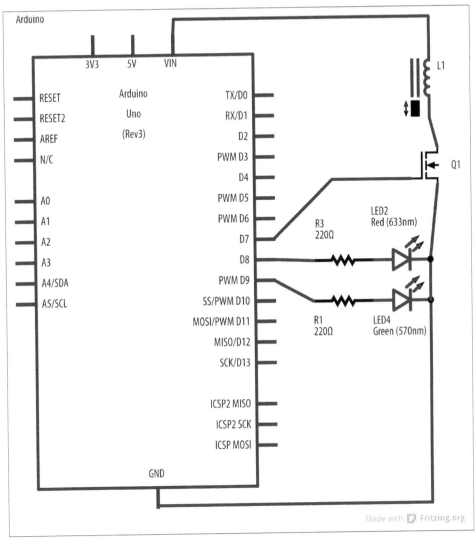

Figure 7-10. The circuit for the NFC reader device (schematic view)

As you did with the writer, start your Arduino sketch for the reader with library includes, constants, and global variables. In addition to instantiating the NfcAdapter, you also need to create an instance of the Time library. Use constants to give names to the output pins and the lock's room number, then add variables for the information from the card, like check-in time, checkout time, and whether or not your last card read was good:

```
// If you're using an SPI-based shield, change these to include the SPI library:
#include <Wire.h>
#include <PN532_I2C.h>
#include <PN532.h>
#include <NfcAdapter.h>
#include <Time.h>

PN532_I2C pn532_i2c(Wire);
NfcAdapter nfc = NfcAdapter(pn532_i2c);

const int lockPin = 7;           // pin that the solenoid door lock is on
const int greenLed = 9;          // pin for the green LED
const int redLed = 8;            // pin for the red LED
const long roomNumber = 3327;    // the room number

time_t checkin = 0;              // checkin time
time_t checkout = 0;             // checkout time
String cardName = "";            // name on the card
long cardRoomNumber = 0;         // room number on the card
long readTime = 0;               // last time you tried to read a card
boolean goodRead = false;
```

The setup() function initializes your output pins as usual, and initializes the nfcAdapter and serial communications. It also sets the time. Make sure to change the time values to reflect the current date:

```
void setup() {
  Serial.begin(9600);
  // set the clock to the date & time
  // hour (24-hour format), minute, second, day, month, year.
  // e.g. date shown here is Jan 9 2013, midnight:
  setTime(00, 00, 00, 1, 9, 2013);

  nfc.begin();                     // initialize the NFC reader
  pinMode(lockPin, OUTPUT);        // make the door lock pin an output
  digitalWrite(lockPin, LOW);      // set it low to lock the door
  pinMode(greenLed, OUTPUT);       // make pin 9 an output
  pinMode(redLed, OUTPUT);         // make pin 10 an output

  Serial.println(F("\nHotel NDEF Reader")); ❶
  Serial.print(F("Current Hotel Time is "));
  Serial.println(formatTime(now()));
  Serial.print(F("This is the lock for room "));
  Serial.println(roomNumber);
}
```

❶ The Serial.print(F()); notation writes these constant strings to flash memory to preserve program memory.

The loop checks how many milliseconds have passed since the last card read, using the millis() function, that returns how many milliseconds since the Arduino was reset. If it's less than 3 seconds (3,000ms), then the lock and indicator LEDs are turned on or off, as appropriate, depending on the state of the last card read.

If more than three seconds have passed since the last card read (good or bad read), the loop calls a function to listen for tags:

```
void loop() {
  if (millis() - readTime < 3000) {    // less than three seconds since last tag
    digitalWrite(greenLed, goodRead);   // green LED lights for a good read
    digitalWrite(lockPin, goodRead);    // lock opens if you get a good read
    digitalWrite(redLed, !goodRead);    // red LED lights if you don't
  }
  else {                                // after three seconds, lock again
    digitalWrite(greenLed, LOW);        // turn off green LED
    digitalWrite(redLed, LOW);          // turn off red LED
    digitalWrite(lockPin, LOW);         // lock door
    goodRead = listenForTag();          // listen for tags
  }
}
```

The listenForTag() function does just that: listens for tags using the NfcAdapter's tagPresent() function. If a tag shows up, and it if has an NDEF message, a for loop cycles through the records, reading them one by one. In this case, there will be only one record. Once you know the record's length, you can set up a byte array to hold it, and copy the record into the array using getPayload(). Once you've converted the byte array into a String, you need to go through it and get the relevant parts out so that you can determine the guest name, room number, check-in date, and checkout date. That's handled by a method called parsePayload(), which you'll see further down:

```
boolean listenForTag() {
  boolean unlockDoor = false;
  resetValues();

  if (nfc.tagPresent()) {          // if there's a tag present
    readTime = millis();           // timestamp the last time you saw a card
    NfcTag tag = nfc.read();
    if (tag.hasNdefMessage()) {    // every tag won't have a message
      NdefMessage message = tag.getNdefMessage();
      NdefRecord record = message.getRecord(0);

      if (record.getTnf() == TNF_MIME_MEDIA &&
        record.getType() == "text/hotelkey") {
        // Get the length of the payload:
        int payloadLength = record.getPayloadLength();
        byte payload[payloadLength];   // make a byte array to hold the payload
        record.getPayload(payload);

        // convert the payload to a String
        String json = "";
        for (int c=0; c< payloadLength; c++) {
          json += (char)payload[c];
```

```
    }
    parsePayload(json);        // parse the payload

    // check if you can let them in or not:
    unlockDoor = isValidKey();
      }
    }
  }
  return unlockDoor;
}
```

To parse the payload for the relevant data, you need to iterate over the record and look for the key/value pairs from the JSON object it contains. Start by finding the position of the opening and closing brackets. Within that, the key-value pairs are separated by commas, with a colon in the middle of each one. So if you know the position of the current comma, the last one, and the colon in between, you can extract each key/value pair. There is no comma after the last pair, so when you can't find another comma, you're on the last one:

```
void parsePayload(String data) {
  // you only care about what's between the brackets, so:
  int openingBracket = data.indexOf('{');
  int closingBracket = data.indexOf('}');
  // your individual data is between two commas:
  int lastComma = openingBracket;
  int comma = 0;
  // parse the data until the last comma:
  while (comma != -1){
    String key, value;
    int colon = data.indexOf(':', lastComma); // get the next colon
    comma = data.indexOf(',', colon);          // get the next comma
    // key is between the last comma and the colon:
    key = data.substring(lastComma+1, colon);

    // if there are no more commas:
    if (comma == -1) {    // value is between colon and closing:
      value = data.substring(colon+1, closingBracket);
    }
    else {                // value is between colon and next comma:
      value = data.substring(colon+1, comma);
    }
```

Once you've got the key/value pairs, you need to throw away the quotation marks. A quick way to do that is to convert them to spaces using String.replace(), then trim the whitespace from the string using String.trim():

```
// now to get rid of the quotation marks:
key.replace("\"", " ");       // replace any " around the key with spaces
key.trim();                   // trim away the spaces
value.replace("\"", " ");     // replace any " around the value with spaces
value.trim();                 // trim away the spaces
```

```
    // now, look for the possible data you care about:
    setValue(key, value);
    lastComma = comma;
  }
}
```

Once you've got the key/value pair, make a function called `setValue()` to check which pair it is and set the appropriate global variable. The name value needs to be kept as a string, the room number as an integer, and the check-in and checkout are of type `time_t` (which is just a 32-bit integer) for comparison to the current time. The `String` class has a handy function for parsing these strings into integers:

```
void setValue(String thisKey, String thisValue) {
  if (thisKey == "checkout"){
    checkout = thisValue.toInt();
  }
  else if (thisKey == "checkin") {
    checkin = thisValue.toInt();
  }
  else if (thisKey == "name") {
    cardName = thisValue;
  }
  else if (thisKey == "room") {
    cardRoomNumber = thisValue.toInt();
  }
}
```

The next function you need for this sketch is the `isValidKey()` function, which is called from the `listenForTags()` function. This takes the check-in time (called `arrival` in the function's parameters), and the departure (called `departure`) and compares them to the current time. If you're within the guest's window of stay, this function returns true. Otherwise, it returns false:

```
boolean isValidKey() {
  boolean result = false;

  if (cardRoomNumber == roomNumber) {
    if (now() <= checkin) {
      Serial.println("You haven't checked in yet.");
      Serial.println("Current time " + formatTime(now()));
      Serial.println("Your arrival " + formatTime(checkin));
    }
    else if ((now() >= checkin) && (now() <= checkout)) {
      Serial.println("Welcome back to your room, " + cardName + ".");
      result = true;
    }
    else if (now() >= checkout) {
      Serial.println("Thanks for staying with us! You've checked out.");
      Serial.println("Current time " + formatTime(now()));
      Serial.println("Your departure " + formatTime(checkout));
    }
```

```
    }
    else {
      Serial.print("This card can't unlock room ");
      Serial.print(roomNumber);
      Serial.println(".");
    }
    return result;
  }
```

There are plenty of serial messages in this function, but they are just for debugging purposes, since the actual device has no serial interface. If you want to save memory, you could comment out all of these serial messages once you know the sketch works. The only part that matters for the physical user interface is the part that sets the result to true or false. Here is the simplified version without the serial messages:

```
boolean isValidKey() {
  boolean result = false;

  if (cardRoomNumber == roomNumber) {
    if ((now() >= checkin) && (now() <= checkout))  {
      result = true;
    }
  }
  return result;
}
```

There is one other utility function to this sketch that takes a time variable and formats it as a string for printing. Again, if you're looking to minimize the code, this function and the calls to it could be commented out once you know the sketch works properly:

```
String formatTime(time_t time) {
  TimeElements elements;
  breakTime(time, elements);
  String formatted = "";
  formatted += elements.Month;
  formatted += "/";
  formatted += elements.Day;
  formatted += "/";
  formatted += elements.Year + 1970;
  formatted += " ";
  formatted += elements.Hour;
  formatted += ":";
  formatted += elements.Minute;
  return formatted;
}
```

The full source code can be found on GitHub (*http://bit.ly/hoteltagreader*).

You set the time back in the setup function, and so long as the time you set is between the times you wrote to the tag, the lock will open. Upload this sketch three times, changing the setTime() parameters in the setup function each time, and see what happens. Pick times that are before, in between, and after the check-in and checkout dates.

If you used the sample JSON shown at the end of the Tag Writer example, your check-in is January 7, 2013, and your checkout is July 10, 2013.

A Browser Interface for the Arduino NDEF Writer Device

As you can see, it's not easy to type the guest's record into the Serial Port Monitor as a JSON object. What you need is a desktop application that can send messages through the serial port to the tag writer device. It would be nice if you could simply write an HTML page to take form input and send it out the serial port.

Most desktop programming languages provide an external library to access the hardware ports of your computer. However, web browsers generally don't provide that functionality to protect devices attached to your computer from damage wrought by code from external websites. But when the server application that's serving the pages is resident on your computer, you can access the hardware ports relatively safely.

Node.js bears a lot of conceptual similarity to PhoneGap. Both are tools that allow you to run JavaScript applications in an operating system rather than just a browser. Both allow you to write your applications in JavaScript and HTML while still taking advantage of the functionality afforded by native libraries. Node.js is a JavaScript interpreter engine running as a native application on OS X, Windows, and Linux. It can be expanded through various libraries to do what any native application on your computer can do, including access to the serial ports, the A/V hardware, and more. In order to benefit from the rich input of HTML, you can use Node.js to write a server program in JavaScript that runs on your computer, serving the user interface to your browser and reading and sending data from the serial port as well.

If you've been through the earlier chapters, you've already installed Node.js. You used its package manager (npm) to install the Cordova-CLI tool. Now you're going to use it to write the user interface for the tag reader device.

You'll need two external libraries to Node.js, a web framework called express.js and a serialport library called node-serialport. Express.js lets you construct web server applications with a RESTful structure. Each element of a URI can be used to determine the functionality of your program. Serialport lets you read from and write to your computer's serial ports.

Node.js Application Specification: package.json

Node and npm use a file called *package.json* to describe the dependencies of a given node application. This file describes the application, its dependencies, and the engines it relies on. This file lives in the application's directory. The package manager uses it to install all the libraries in a subdirectory for the application before you start it. Thanks to this, you can just distribute the source code for your application and the web interface files (HTML, JavaScript, CSS, images, etc.).

For the application you're about to build, the *package.json* looks like this:

```
{
  "name": "HotelNodeApp",
  "version": "0.1.0",
  "description" : "A browser-to-serial application",
  "keywords": "serial, node-serialport",
  "author": {
   "name":"Tom Igoe"
  },
  "dependencies": {
    "serialport": "1.1.x",
    "express": "3.x"
  },
  "engines": {
    "node": "0.10.x",
    "npm": "1.2.x"
  }
}
```

The most important part of the package file in this case is that it lists the minimum version of Node.js and npm that you need, and the library dependencies and their versions. You also need a version number in the format that node uses, as shown here.

Make a directory for this application and save this there as *package.json*. The other files you'll need are your main source file, which you'll call *index.js*, and an *index.html* file that you'll use to create the user interface. The rest will be installed by the node package manager, npm.

The Client-Side Code

The *index.html* file for this application is fairly simple. There's a form with the fields you need to enter: name, room number, number of days you're staying. The check-in time is calculated automatically by a script in the document head, and filled into a hidden field in the form. You can see the browser view in Figure 7-11. Here is the HTML:

```
<!DOCTYPE html>
<html>
    <head>
    <script type="text/javascript">

      function tick() {
        var now = Date(),
          clock = document.getElementById("clock"),
          checkin = document.getElementById("checkin");
        clock.innerHTML = now.toString();
        checkin.value = now;
      }

    </script>
    </head>
```

```
<body onload="setInterval(tick, 1000);">
<form action="/submit" method="post">
    Name: <input type="text" name="name"><br />
    Room: <input type="text" name="room"><br />
    Checkin time: <span id="clock"></span><br>
    <input type="hidden" name="checkin" id="checkin" >
    Number of days: <input type="text" name="days"><br />
    <input type="submit" value="submit">
</form>
</body>
</html>
```

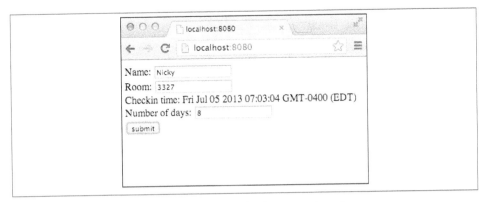

Figure 7-11. The browser view of the hotel check-in user interface

The Server-Side Code

The server-side JavaScript, *index.js*, starts by declaring a number of variables. It instantiates the serialport library and the express library, then creates an HTTP server using express to handle the request routes. It opens the serial port using the third token from the command-line invocation (you'll invoke this from the command line by typing node index.js portname where portname is the path to your serial port—more on that later). The last two variables are for maintaining a local copy of the hotel record and for any incoming messages from the Arduino via the serial port:

```
var serialport = require("serialport"),       // include the serialport library
    SerialPort = serialport.SerialPort,       // make a local instance of serial
    express = require('express'),             // make an instance of express
    app = express(),                          // start Express framework
    server = require('http').createServer(app), // start an HTTP server
    portName = process.argv[2],               // third token of the command line
    record = {},                              // NDEF record to send
    deviceMessage = "";                       // messages from the writer device
```

Next, you're going to tell express.js that you want to use its body parser middleware. This will make it easy to parse the body of the HTTP requests you get from the page. Following that, you start the server (note that it's running on port 8080, not the normal port 80 for HTTP servers) and open the serialport, and let the user know on the command line:

```
// use the bodyParser middleware for express:
app.use(express.bodyParser());
server.listen(8080);                    // listen for incoming requests on the server
console.log("Listening for new clients on port 8080");

var myPort = new SerialPort(portName, {     // open the serial port
  // look for newline at the end of each data packet:
  parser: serialport.parsers.readline("\n")
});
// print the port you're listening on:
console.log("opening serial port: " + portName);
```

The parser invoked in this serial port instantiation allows you to tell the serial port when to generate an event. It's easiest to read incoming serial data from the serial port if the port generates an event for each incoming line of text, so the parser looks for the newline character, \n.

The rest of the program consists of three event handlers: one to handle incoming serial data, and two to handle incoming HTTP requests. The serial data handler looks for a new line of incoming serial data, and if that line contains the term Result:, it copies it to one of the global variables, deviceMessage:

```
// listen for new serial data:
myPort.on('data', function (data) {
  // for debugging, you should see this in the terminal window:
  if (data.search("Result:") != -1) {
    deviceMessage = data;
  }
  console.log("Received: " + data);
});
```

The next two handlers are functions from express.js for handling HTTP GET and POST requests. The app.get() returns the *index.html* page for any GET request. So *http://localhost.com:8080*, *http://localhost.com:8080/index.html*, *http://localhost.com:8080/foo*, or anything else you put in the browser will return the index page:

```
// respond to web GET requests with the index.html page:
app.get('/*', function (request, response) {
  response.sendfile(__dirname + '/index.html');
});
```

The form in the index page makes a POST request that's handled by the final handler, app.post(). There are two parts to this handler. In the first part, you extract the elements from the form and put them into the record variable. The time conversions at the end of this section are done because JavaScript's Date object handles time in milliseconds, while the Time library for Arduino handles it in seconds, as you saw in the previous

Arduino example. Once all the necessary parts of the record are extracted from the form or calculated, the handler sends the record out the serial port:

```
// take anything that begins with /submit:
app.post('/submit', function (request, response) {
  record.name = request.body.name;    // get the name from the body
  record.room = request.body.room;    // get the room number from the body
  var days = request.body.days;       // get the number of days from the body
  var today = new Date(request.body.checkin);  // get the time from the body
  // calculate the checkout timeStamp:
  var departure = new Date(today.valueOf() + (days * 86400000));
  // convert to unix time in seconds:
  record.checkin = Math.round(today.valueOf()/1000);
  record.checkout = Math.round(departure.valueOf()/1000);
  // send it out the serial port:
  myPort.write(JSON.stringify(record) + "\n");
```

The Arduino NFC writer device attached to the serial port needs time to read the data, then write it to a tag before it will respond. So the second part of the app.post() handler is a bit of a hack to account for that. It sends the beginning of an HTTP response, including enough of the HTML page to tell the client what's going on and to give her a link back to the form. Then it keeps the connection open for three seconds using setTimeout(), waiting for a response from the serial port so that it can include the NFC writer device's response. If there's no response in that time, it closes the port:

```
// write the HTML head back to the browser:
response.writeHead(200, {'Content-Type': 'text/html'});
// send the data:
response.write("<p><a href=\"/\">Return to form</a></p>");
response.write("Sent the following to the writer device:<br>");
response.write(JSON.stringify(record) + "<p>");

// wait 3 seconds before closing the connection, so that
// you can get a response from the writer:
setTimeout(function() {
  // if you got a response from the writer, send it too:
  if (deviceMessage != "") {
    response.write("response from writer device: " + deviceMessage + "<p>");
    deviceMessage = "";
  } else {
    response.write("no tag present");
  }
  // send the link back to the index and close the link:
  response.end();
}, 3000);     // end of setTimeout()
});            // end of app.post()
```

If you were developing a full UI, you might have some client-side JavaScript to receive that JSON string and present it in a more readable way. But for now, this should illustrate the principles.

The full source code can be found on GitHub (*http://bit.ly/hotel-node-app*).

That's all of the application code. Once you've saved the *index.js* file, you need to import the libraries. To do that, change directories to the application's directory on the command line if you're not already there. You should have three files in this directory:

- *package.json*
- *index.html*
- *index.js*

To import the libraries, type:

```
$ npm install
```

You should see several lines of response, starting with a series of npm GET requests for the appropriate files, and ending in two compile summaries that look like this:

```
express@3.3.3 node_modules/express
├── methods@0.0.1
├── fresh@0.1.0
├── range-parser@0.0.4
├── cookie-signature@1.0.1
├── buffer-crc32@0.2.1
├── cookie@0.1.0
├── debug@0.7.2
├── mkdirp@0.3.5
├── send@0.1.2 (mime@1.2.9)
├── commander@1.2.0 (keypress@0.1.0)
└── connect@2.8.3 (uid2@0.0.2, pause@0.0.1, qs@0.6.5, bytes@0.2.0, ...)

serialport@1.1.1 node_modules/serialport
├── bindings@1.1.0
├── sf@0.1.6
├── async@0.1.18
└── optimist@0.3.7 (wordwrap@0.0.2)
```

If you see the words NOT OK, heed them. It means that something has gone wrong, and if you scroll back through the npm responses, you'll find the problem. The most common errors are not using the latest version of node or npm or the libraries (which you can fix by updating your *package.json* with the version numbers of the latest), not having a network connection, or an incompatibility with one of the libraries and your operating system. In the latter case, check the issues list or forums for the library in question for solutions.

Node-serialport and OS X

On OS X 10.8.x (Mountain Lion) and beyond, you may have trouble installing node-serialport. You need to install the XCode command line tools. Apple doesn't make these handy utilities easy to find, but you can download them with a login from the Apple developer site (*https://developer.apple.com/xcode/*). You should be able to do this with a regular Apple login, and not need a paid developer license.

Once you've installed the libraries, there will be a new subdirectory in your application's directory called `node_modules`. That's where the libraries live. Now you're ready to test the app.

First, make sure you've uploaded the tag writer sketch from "Writing NDEF in Arduino" on page 145 onto your Arduino using the Arduino IDE. Note the name of your Arduino's serial port. Then on the command line, type:

```
$ node index.js portname
```

For `portname`, use the name of your serial port, as you learned in "The Arduino Development Environment" on page 133. You should get a response like this:

```
Listening for new clients on port 8080
opening serial port: /dev/tty.usbmodem621
```

Now open a browser to *http://localhost:8080* and you should get the page shown in Figure 7-11. When you place a tag on the writer device and enter your information, you should get a return page with something like Figure 7-12.

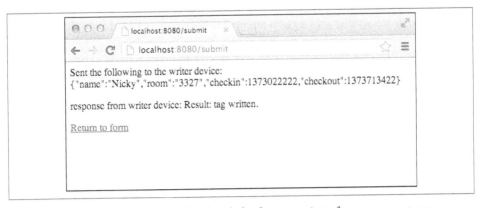

Figure 7-12. The browser view of the hotel check-in user interface response page

Conclusion

Now that you've finished the UI, you've got a hotel registration system built, from check-in to door lock. Congratulations! Here's a review of all the components:

There are two physical devices, built on Arduino Unos with NFC shields (you probably just recycled the same Uno and shield in your case). The first is an NFC writer that accepts a JSON string serially and writes it to a tag. This device is attached to a laptop or desktop computer, which is running the node application you just wrote. The check-in user interface, provided in the brower by the node application, takes the guest's name, room number, autogenerated time and date, and the number of days the guest is staying, and generates the JSON string for the writer.

The second physical device is the door lock. When the guest taps a tag to the device, it checks the room number and check-in and checkout times on the tag and the current time to see if it should open the door or not. If all is in order, the solenoid lock on the door opens.

This opens up the possible uses for NFC to a wide range of physical situations. As you can see, the concepts for using NFC on a microcontroller are the same as they are for mobile or desktop contexts. Even though microcontroller programming environments might be more limited than what an operating system affords, they still offer the same basic capabilities: reading and writing tags and interpreting NDEF messages and records. They can also provide the ability to sense and control the physical world in ways a traditional computer or mobile device might not be able to do directly.

Given a wider range of computing devices for NFC applications, you have to consider the strengths and limitations of each, and choose your tools appropriately. For example, while the microcontroller was a good choice for the door lock in this application, you could have done the registration application entirely with a tablet device, or with a USB-based NFC reader that you'll see later on. When you do need to build a custom physical interface, you should determine the minimum physical interaction necessary and try to design and program your device for maximum responsiveness and clarity in the given situation. Small details like limiting your use of blocking functions and providing LED feedback for every physical event make a big difference in the perceived reliability of the device.

In the next chapter, you'll move beyond simply reading and writing tags into a feature that really differentiates NFC from RFID: peer-to-peer communication between devices.

CHAPTER 8

Peer-to-Peer Exchange

All the examples you've seen in this book so far have used a passive tag as an intermediary to carry NDEF data. This is a big change for RFID, as it introduces a common data format that covers a range of different tag types (though not all RFID tag types). The other major difference between RFID and NFC is the latter's ability to make *peer-to-peer* exchanges. These exchanges are between two active devices directly. Prior to NFC, RFID was not used in a peer-to-peer context. In this chapter, you'll see examples of how to program peer-to-peer (P2P) exchanges.

In each P2P exchange, there is a target and an initiator, both of which are active devices. This means that when you send a target an NDEF message via P2P, the target can manipulate the data that you send it, and send you something back in response. You can also copy information from a tag, store it on a device, and transfer it to another device or another tag. P2P offers a range of interesting possibilities.

Peer-to-peer exchanges rest on yet another NFC protocol, the *Simple NDEF Exchange Protocol* (SNEP). SNEP is a request-and-response protocol: the initiator sends a request about the kind of data it would like to exchange, and the target responds with the requested data. SNEP rests on the NFC Forum's *Logical Link Control Protocol* (LLCP). Although you won't have to wrestle with SNEP and LLCP directly if you're writing application code, it's helpful to know where they sit in the NFC architecture, because it helps explain how P2P differs from tag reading and writing. As you can see from Figure 8-1, SNEP and LLCP fit in around the same area as the various RFID tag formats: data packetization and transport in peer-to-peer exchanges are dependent on SNEP and LLCP just as they are dependent on tag formats in reader-to-tag exchanges. That layer is a crucial link between the device controllers and the NDEF layer.

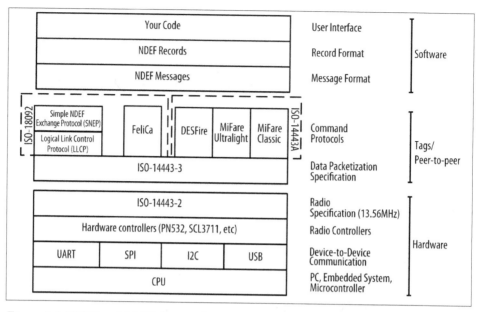

Figure 8-1. SNEP and LLCP fit into the NFC architecture as a data-link layer, performing a similar function to the tag formats

SNEP and LLCP don't define how peer-to-peer exchanges should be handled by an operating system or presented to a user. Each operating system implements SNEP and LLCP in its own way. Android's current implementation is called Android Beam (prior to Android 4.0, Android had an implementation called the NDEF Push Protocol, or NPP). Using Beam, when you want to exchange data between two Android devices, you touch them back to back, and the "Touch to beam" interface appears. When you tap on the sending device, it initiates a P2P exchange with the receiving device and the data is sent as an NDEF message or series of messages. Beam is designed to let you operate at the upper layers of the stack shown in Figure 8-1. It handles the peer-to-peer logical link exchanges and hands NDEF messages off to the dispatch system mentioned in Chapter 5 and Chapter 6.

When you enable NFC, Beam keeps the NFC radio active and looking for connections from other devices or tags. You've already seen in Chapter 5 that when a tag comes close and there's no foreground app to handle it, the tag dispatch system handles it. Beam handles peer-to-peer similarly. If the NFC radio on your device detects another radio, Android brings up the "Touch to beam" interface, no matter what app is running. Figure 8-2 shows this interface. If your app implements the P2P sharing functions (the NDEF Push Protocol in the Android Java framework), then whatever data you choose to share will be sent to the target phone. If not, then Android will send the URI of your app. If the target has the app, it will open. If not, Android will open the Google Play app store to locate it.

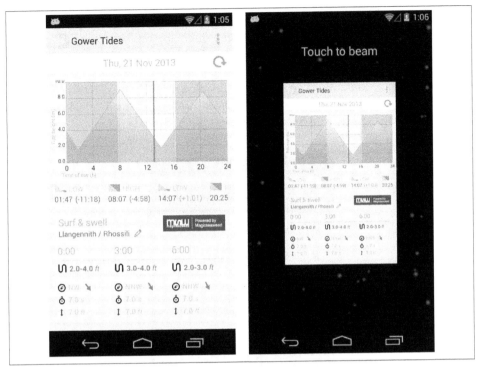

Figure 8-2. "Touch to beam" interface on Android (Gower Tides app, left, and the app being beamed, right)

This is where Android Beam differs from previous implementations of peer-to-peer on Android, and from its implementation on other operating systems. This default can be annoying in some cases, but it can be turned off by adding the following line to your *AndroidManifest.xml* file right after the opening <application> tag:

```
<application android:debuggable="true" android:hardwareAccelerated="true"
    android:icon="@drawable/icon" android:label="@string/app_name">
    <meta-data android:name="android.nfc.disable_beam_default"
        android:value="true" />
    <activity android:configChanges=
        "orientation|keyboardHidden|keyboard|screenSize|
        locale" android:label="@string/app_name" android:name="P2P"
        android:theme="@android:style/Theme.Black.NoTitleBar">
```

Sending Peer-to-Peer Messages in PhoneGap

The best way to understand P2P is to try it out. You'll need two NFC-enabled Android devices for this. To see the default behavior, you don't even need to write another app. You can use NXP TagInfo, or the NDEF Reader app you wrote in Chapter 5. Open either of these apps on your target device, then open any other app on your initiator device. Bring the two devices together back-to-back, and tap the initiator device's screen. On the target, you should get the URI of the foreground app on the initiator. Figure 8-3 shows the result of beaming an app called Gower Tides from the initiator device to the NXP TagInfo app. When an app that doesn't implement P2P is beamed, Android Beam will pass a message containing two records by default: a record with a TNF 01 containing a URI for the app on the Play Store, and a second record with a TNF 04 containing the app's Android Application Record (AAR).

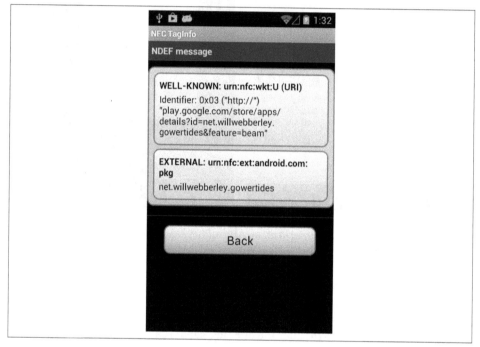

Figure 8-3. The default message sent from Gower Tides using Android Beam; this app does not implement peer-to-peer, but Android Beam sends an NDEF message for it

When you want to override this behavior and send your own NDEF messages in Android, you can either set an NDEF Push message or set a Beam push URI. There are methods for both in Android, with callback options for both. In the PhoneGap-NFC plug-in, NDEF push is simplified to `nfc.share()`, and URI Beam is simplified to `nfc.handover()`. When you share a message, it gets pushed, and when the target receives the message successfully, you get a success callback.

The next app uses some of the NDEF messages you've written to tags before so that you can see how Android behaves differently when receiving messages via P2P instead of reading them from tags. In most cases, you'll see there's no difference. You can also use this app to send your own custom messages via P2P to see how they behave.

To do this, you'll need the tools you saw in earlier chapters:

- Two NFC-enabled Android devices
- The Android Software Developers Kit
- A text editor
- Cordova CLI installed on your machine
- Node.js and npm installed as well

To get started, create a new project:

```
$ cordova create ~/P2P com.example.p2p P2P ❶
$ cd ~/P2P ❷
$ cordova platform add  android
$ cordova plugin add https://github.com/don/phonegap-nfc
```

❶   Windows users should type %userprofile%\P2P instead of ~/P2P.

❷   Windows users should type /d %userprofile%\P2P instead of ~/P2P.

When the project is ready to go, open the *index.html* and the *index.js* files from the *www* directory.

The *index.html* page has a simple form for entering a new NDEF record and a drop-down menu that lets you choose one of several pre-made records. You'll populate the menu from the *index.js* file later:

```
<!DOCTYPE html>

<html>
   <head>
      <title>PhoneGap NFC P2P</title>
   </head>
   <body>
      <h2>PhoneGap NFC P2P</h2>
      <div class="app">
         <div id="messageDiv"></div>
         <form>
            <select id="sampleField"></select><br />
            <input type="hidden" id="kindField" /><br/>
            <div id="typeDiv">
              Type:<br/>
              <input type="text" id="typeField" value="" size="30" />
            </div>
            Payload:<br/>
            <textarea id="payloadField" rows="10" cols="30"></textarea>
            <br/>
```

```
      </form>
    </div>
  <script type="text/javascript" src="cordova.js"></script>
  <script type="text/javascript" src="js/index.js"></script>
  <script type="text/javascript">
    app.initialize();
  </script>
  </body>
</html>
```

The *index.js* starts with an array called `data` that holds several JSON-encoded NDEF records. You'll recognize most of these from past examples. They'll be sent as various different record types:

```
var data = [
    {
        name: "Text Record",
        kind: "text",
        data: "hello, world"
    },
    {
        name: "URI Record",
        kind: "uri",
        data: "http://oreilly.com"
    },
    {
        name: "Address",
        kind: "mime",
        type: 'text/x-vCard',
        data: 'BEGIN:VCARD\n' +
            'VERSION:2.1\n' +
            'N:Coleman;Don;;;\n' +
            'FN:Don Coleman\n' +
            'ORG:Chariot Solutions;\n' +
            'URL:http://chariotsolutions.com\n' +
            'TEL;WORK:215-555-1212\n' +
            'EMAIL;WORK:don@example.com\n' +
            'END:VCARD'
    },
    {
        name: "Hue Settings",
        kind: "mime",
        type: 'text/hue',
        data: JSON.stringify({
        "1":
            {"state":
                {"on":true,"bri":65,"hue":44591,"sat":254}
            },
        "2":
            {"state":
                {"on":true,"bri":254,"hue":13122,"sat":211}
            },
```

```
       "3":
          {"state":
             {"on":true,"bri":255,"hue":14922,"sat":144}
          }
       })
    },
    {
       name: "Android Application Record",
       kind: "external",
       type: "android.com:pkg",
       data: "com.joelapenna.foursquared"
    },
    {
       name: "Empty",
       kind: "empty",
       data: ""
    }
];
```

The main app comes next. The first few functions will look very familiar. There's an initialize(), a bindEvents(), and an onDeviceReady() to set things up:

```
var app = {
  /*
     Application constructor
   */
  initialize: function() {
    this.bindEvents();
    console.log("Starting P2P app");
  },
  /*
     bind any events that are required on startup to listeners:
  */
  bindEvents: function() {
    document.addEventListener('deviceready', this.onDeviceReady, false);
    sampleField.addEventListener('change', app.showSampleData, false);
    // modify the form so it doesn't generate a submit event:
    document.forms[0].onsubmit = function(evt) {
      evt.preventDefault();        // don't submit
      payloadField.focus();        // put the payload field in focus
    };
    // if either type or payload is changed, update the share:
    typeField.onchange = app.shareMessage;
    payloadField.onchange = app.shareMessage;
  },

  /*
     this runs when the device is ready for user interaction:
  */
  onDeviceReady: function() {
    var option;

    // populate the sampleField from the data array
```

```
    sampleField.innerHTML = "";
    for (var i = 0; i < data.length; i++) {
        option = document.createElement("option");   // make an option element
        option.value = i;                            // give it this number
        option.innerHTML = data[i].name;             // get the data object
        if (i === 0) {                               // select the first element
            option.selected = true;
        }
        sampleField.appendChild(option);             // add this to sampleField
    }

    app.showSampleData();
},
```

Next come the P2P functions. `shareMessage()` looks for the data record currently in the form, formats it as an NDEF message, and uses `nfc.share()` to share it via P2P:

```
/*
    Share the message from the form via peer-to-peer:
*/
shareMessage: function () {
    // get the MIME-type, and payload from the form
    // and create a new record:
    var payloadType = typeField.value,
        payloadData = payloadField.value,
        kind = kindField.value,
        record;

    app.clear();                        // clear the message div
    app.display("Publishing message");  // display the notification

    // use a different ndef helper to format the message
    // depending on the kind:
    switch (kind) {
        case "text":
            record = ndef.textRecord(payloadData);
            break;
        case "uri":
            record = ndef.uriRecord(payloadData);
            break;
        case "mime":
            record = ndef.mimeMediaRecord(payloadType, payloadData);
            break;
        case "external":
            record = ndef.record(ndef.TNF_EXTERNAL_TYPE, payloadType, [], ...);
            break;
        case "empty":
            record = ndef.emptyRecord();
            break;
        default:
            alert("ERROR: can't build record");
    }
```

```
        console.log(JSON.stringify(record));

        // share the message:
        nfc.share(
            [record],                   // NDEF message to share
            function () {               // success callback
                navigator.notification.vibrate(100);
                app.display("Success! Message sent to peer.");
            },
            function (reason) {         // failure callback
                app.display("Failed to share message " + reason);
            });
    },
```

When a message is successfully received on the target, the success callback is called on the initiator, and you get the message "Success! Message sent to peer." You can use this callback to trigger other behaviors as well.

The nfc.share() function has two optional callbacks, for success and failure. The success function gets called only when the target device has acknowledged that it got the message. This can be a useful way to tell the initiator when the target's ready for something new.

The unshareMessage() function turns off sharing once the data's been shared. In this app, it's not used, but it's shown here so you can see what it might look like:

```
    /*
        Stop sharing:
    */
    unshareMessage: function () {
        // stop sharing this message:
        nfc.unshare(
            function () {                           // success callback
                navigator.notification.vibrate(100);
                app.clear();
                app.display("message is no longer shared");
            },
            function (reason) {                     // failure callback
                app.display("Failed to unshare message " + reason);
            });
    },
```

There is just one UI-related function. When the drop-down menu changes, it calls showSampleData() to get the appropriate date element and fill it into the form fields:

```
    /*
        Get data from the data array and put it in the form fields:
    */
    showSampleData: function() {
        // get the type and payload from the form
        var index = sampleField.value,
            record = data[index];
```

```
        // fill form with the data from the record:
        kindField.value = record.kind;
        typeField.value = record.type;
        payloadField.value = record.data;

        // hide type for kinds that don't need it
        if (typeof record.type === 'string') {
            typeDiv.style.display = "";
        } else {
            typeDiv.style.display = "none";
        }

        app.shareMessage();
    },
```

Last, but not least, comes the familiar `display()` and `clear()` functions for writing to the message div:

```
    /*
       appends @message to the message div:
    */
    display: function(message) {
        var label = document.createTextNode(message),
            lineBreak = document.createElement("br");
        messageDiv.appendChild(lineBreak);        // add a line break
        messageDiv.appendChild(label);            // add the text
    },
    /*
       clears the message div:
    */
    clear: function() {
        messageDiv.innerHTML = "";
    },
};      // end of app
```

You only need to run this app on one of the two devices. When you run it, you'll get the interface shown in Figure 8-4. You can pick any of the items in the drop-down menu as your data to share, or make up your own. To share the message, pick any of the pre-made records, or make one yourself, then touch the device running this app back-to-back with your second device. If Foursquare and the Mood Setter app are on the second device, then they will open when you share the records corresponding to those apps. The address record will trigger Android to ask you to save the record in your contacts.

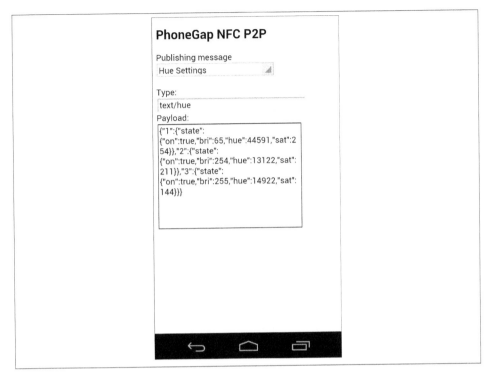

Figure 8-4. Your first peer-to-peer app

Receiving Peer-to-Peer Messages in PhoneGap

Receiving P2P messages is just like receiving tag-based messages. You simply need to add one or more of the NFC event listeners you learned about in Chapter 5. When the foreground app receives an NDEF message via push, it treats it just like it would a tag-based message.

To add receive capability to the app you just wrote, you'll need to add an event listener. You've got at least two different types of NDEF messages you're sending (MIME type or external type), so if you want to catch them both with one listener, you need an NdefListner. Add the following to the onDeviceReady() function:

```
nfc.addNdefListener(
    app.onNfc,                  // nfcEvent received
    function (status) {         // listener successfully initialized
       app.displayMessage("Listening for NDEF messages.");
    },
    function (error) {          // listener fails to initialize
       app.displayMessage("NFC reader failed to initialize "
           + JSON.stringify(error));
    }
);
```

Then add a function called `onNfc()` to handle this event. You can add this anywhere you like within the app variable. This is a very truncated example, but if you want something more detailed, there are good functions to display messages in the NDEF Reader example from Chapter 5:

```
/*
displays info from @nfcEvent in message div:
*/
onNfc: function(nfcEvent) {
    // if there is an NDEF message on the tag, display it:
    var thisTag = nfcEvent.tag,
        thisMessage = thisTag.ndefMessage,
        tagData = "";

    // display the tag properties:
    tagData = "Tag ID: " + nfc.bytesToHexString(thisTag.id) + "<br />"
        + "Tag Type: " +  thisTag.type + "<br />"
        + "Max Size: " +  thisTag.maxSize + " bytes<br />"
        + "Is Writable: " +  thisTag.isWritable + "<br />"
        + "Can Make Read Only: " +  thisTag.canMakeReadOnly + "<br />";

    if (thisMessage !== null) {
        // get and display the NDEF record count:
        tagData += "<p>Tag has NDEF message with " + thisMessage.length
            + " records.</p>";
    }

    app.displayMessage(tagData);
},
```

Save this file and run it. When you share messages from one device to the other, the new code will listen for those messages and display information about them as well.

The full source code can be found on GitHub (*http://bit.ly/master-p2p*).

You may have noticed that we left the tag type display and tag UID display in the code from Chapter 5 as well. But since there are no physical tags used in this exchange, you get a whole series of empty results:

```
Tag ID: 00
Tag Type: android.ndef.unknown
Max Size: 0 bytes
Is Writable: false
Can Make Read Only: false
```

The tags are replaced as a datalink layer by the LLCP and SNEP layers, as explained previously, so the tag ID, type, size, and other metadata are meaningless in peer-to-peer exchanges. But that doesn't matter to your application because it still gets the NDEF messages it's looking for. You could restructure this app to remove the tag metadata functionality and do no damage to it.

The fact that P2P messages show up exactly like tag messages is useful because it means you can design applications where the interaction is the same whether touching a tag or another device.

Handover

Peer-to-peer sharing works great with short messages, but when you want to transfer something larger, like an audio file or a photo, it's not so great. You have to hold the devices together while the exchange happens, so if you've got a large message to transfer, you could be stuck holding the devices together for a long time. This is inconvenient.

The NFC *Connection Handover Specification* is designed to handle this type of situation. When a handover message is received, the NFC library checks the operating system it's running on to see if there's a better transfer medium, like Bluetooth or WiFi, and attempts to transfer the data over that medium instead.

Handover works like this: the initiator sends an NDEF message that starts with a *Handover Request Record* (TNF: Well-Known type, RTD: Handover Request ("Hr")), followed by a number of *Alternative Carrier Records* (TNF: Well-Known type, RTD: Alternative Carrier ("ac")). The alternative carrier records are all the different transport media that the initiator has available: Bluetooth, WiFi, or whatever else it has. The payload of this record is the MAC address of the alternative carrier.

The target, when it gets this message, replies with a *Handover Selector Record* (TNF: Well-Known type, RTD: ("Hs")) and a set of its own alternative carrier records. These are generally listed in order of the target's preference. The initiator then chooses an alternative carrier, and sends back a *handover carrier* message (TNF: Well-Known type, RTD: ("Hc")) with the alternative carrier. The target then replies with a handover carrier message that contains the configuration data and/or credentials for that carrier, so that the data can be transferred without Bluetooth pairing, WiFi login, or other negotiations.

The negotiation to set up a handover involves a few exchanges, as you can see. In order for the handover to be successful, you have to maintain contact until those exchanges are done and the handover is complete, or the transfer will fail.

When it works, handover is magical. There's no pairing to be done, no passwords to be exchanged. Even if your devices' Bluetooth or WiFi radios are not on, the NFC stack will ask the operating system to turn them on and make the exchange. There's even facility in the handover protocol for targets and initiators to state the power of the alternative carrier to preserve battery life.

There are some potential issues with handover, however. If your alternative carrier is being used for something else, it can fail. For example, if you're streaming audio over Bluetooth, and you try to send a file over it, you'll encounter significantly slower transfer speeds, and the transfer will sometimes fail. If your devices go out of carrier range, the transfer will also fail.

As mentioned previously, every platform implements peer-to-peer in its own way. For example, Beam Android to BB10 works, but there is an extra step to accept the remote device's pairing request. SNEP is potentially cross-platform and is supposed to simplify pairings regardless of operating system, but until everyone has implemented it, there are bound to be quirks.

Static Handover

The NFC Forum provided for a way to manage data exchange between NFC-enabled devices and non-NFC-enabled devices using handover as well. If the non-NFC device has a passive NFC tag attached, and the tag contains a Handover Selector Record with the associated configuration data in the message, then the NFC device will attempt to begin communication with the non-NFC device over the alternative carrier. For example, imagine you wanted to exchange data from an Android NFC-enabled device to an Apple iPhone. If the iPhone has an NFC tag stuck to it with its Bluetooth or WiFi configuration data in a Handover Select Message, then the Android device can get the configuration data via NFC and try to connect.

This isn't a perfect method, as it depends on the non-NFC device to have its alternative carrier open and ready for business. If it's not, the connection will fail, or the iPhone user will have to explicitly enable the connection. By the time you've gone through the trouble to enable the connection manually, it might simply be easier to start by trying to exchange your data over Bluetooth or WiFi between the two devices, and skip the static handover request. The ideal use case might be an iPhone or iPad-driven kiosk communicating to a user's NFC-enabled device.

Sending Handover Messages in PhoneGap

In the PhoneGap-NFC plug-in, Android's Beam URI methods, which manage handover, are simplified to `nfc.handover()`. Its API is similar to `nfc.share()`, but it shares a file instead of an NDEF Message. The following example shows how to use it. You can either choose a file to send, or take a photo and send that. To do this, you'll need the same tools:

- Two NFC-enabled Android devices
- The Android Software Developers Kit
- A text editor
- Cordova CLI installed on your machine
- Node.js and npm installed

To get started, create a new project:

```
$ cordova create ~/FileSender com.example.filesender FileSender ❶
$ cd ~/FileSender ❷
$ cordova platform add android
$ cordova plugin add https://github.com/don/phonegap-nfc
$ cordova plugin add https://github.com/don/cordova-filechooser
```

❶   Windows users should type `%userprofile%\FileSender` instead of `~/File Sender`.

❷   Windows users should type `/d %userprofile%\FileSender` instead of `~/File Sender`.

You're using an extra plug-in here, *filechooser*, because the PhoneGap File API is clumsy to work with, as you may have noticed in Chapter 6. The filechooser plug-in simplifies the process of choosing a file by using Android's native file chooser UI to return a URI you can use.

The *index.html* has a few elements in addition to the usual `message` div: a button for taking a picture, a button for choosing a file, and a div for displaying the picture you take:

```html
<!DOCTYPE html>

<html>
  <head>
    <title>File Sender</title>
  </head>

  <body>
    <h1 id="cameraButton">Take Picture</h1>
    <h1 id="filePicker">Choose File</h1>

    <div id="messageDiv"></div>
    <div id="photoDiv"></div>
    <script type="text/javascript" src="cordova.js"></script>
    <script type="text/javascript" src="js/index.js"></script>
    <script type="text/javascript">
      app.initialize();
    </script>
  </body>
</html>
```

The *index.js* file starts in the usual way, by binding event handlers to the UI elements:

```
var app = {
  /*
  Application constructor
  */
  initialize: function() {
    this.bindEvents();
    console.log("Starting File Sender app");
  },

  /*
  binds events that are required on startup to listeners.
  */
  bindEvents: function() {
    // bind events to the UI elements:
    document.addEventListener('deviceready', this.onDeviceReady, false);
  },

  /*
  runs when the device is ready for user interaction.
  */
  onDeviceReady: function() {
    cameraButton.addEventListener('touchstart', app.takePicture, false);
    filePicker.addEventListener('touchstart', app.chooseFile, false);
  },
```

The event handlers for the `filePicker` button and the camera button open the appropriate Android UI for both, and return the URI of the file you choose, or the image file you create. The `takePicture()` handler also sets the camera settings for taking the picture. You can learn more about the camera capture API from the PhoneGap documentation page (*http://docs.phonegap.com/*) under "Camera":

```
  /*
  brings up the file chooser UI:
  */
  chooseFile: function() {
    fileChooser.open(
      app.onFileSystemSuccess,    // success handler
      app.failure                 // failure handler
    );
  },

  /*
  Brings up the camera app:
  */
  takePicture: function () {
    navigator.camera.getPicture(
      app.onCameraSuccess,        // camera capture success handler
      app.failure,                // failure handler
      {                           // image capture options
        quality: 75,
```

```
              destinationType: Camera.DestinationType.FILE_URL,
              sourceType: Camera.PictureSourceType.CAMERA,
              targetWidth: 300,
              targetHeight: 300,
              correctOrientation: true,
              saveToPhotoAlbum: false
          }
      );
  },
```

Once either handler succeeds, it calls its respective success handler. The onFileSuc cess() handler doesn't do much beyond calling shareMessage(). The onCameraSuc cess() handler displays the camera image on the page before calling shareMessage(). They share the same failure() handler:

```
/*
When you get a good picture, share it:
*/
onCameraSuccess: function (imageURI) {
    var img = document.createElement("img");
    img.src = imageURI;              // add the URI as the img src
    photoDiv.innerHTML = "";         // clear old image
    photoDiv.appendChild(img);       // add the image element to the photoDiv
    app.display(imageURI);           // show the URI
    app.shareMessage(imageURI);      // share the image
},

/*
When you get a good file, share it:
*/
onFileSystemSuccess: function (fileURI) {
    photoDiv.innerHTML = "";
    app.display(fileURI);
    app.shareMessage(fileURI);
},

/*
When you fail to get a file or photo, cry:
*/
failure: function (evt) {
    console.log(evt.target.error.code);
},
```

Here's the part you've been waiting for: shareMessage(). It's almost identical to the function of the same name in the last example. This version takes the URI of the file as a parameter, and it also does a check to see if the URI contains spaces (%20 when escaped for a URI). This is because the Android Beam API has a bug in it that prevents you from sending URIs with spaces in them, even when escaped. In a more fully developed version of this app, you'd make a local copy of the file and rename it without spaces, then send the copy. But for now, you'll have to settle for sending files with no spaces:

```
/*
Share the URI from the file or photo via P2P:
*/
shareMessage: function (uri) {
   // Android Beam API has a bug that prevents sending files
   // with spaces in the URI:
   if (uri.search("%20") > 0) {
      app.clear();
      app.display("Sorry. Can't beam a URI with spaces. Android Beam Bug");
      return;
   }

   app.clear();
   app.display("Ready to beam " + uri);
   app.display("Place your device back to back with another device to beam.")
   // beam the file:
   nfc.handover(
      uri,
      function () {                      // success callback
         navigator.notification.vibrate(100);
         // you know when the beam is sent and the other device received
         // the request but you don't know if the beam completes or fails
         app.display("Success! Beam sent.");
         app.unshareMessage();       // unshare the file when complete
      },
      function (reason) {               // failure callback
         app.clear();
         app.display("Failed to share file " + reason);
      }
   );
},
```

Because there's a `shareMessage()` handler, there has to be an `unshareMessage()` handler. It's the same as in the previous application. Following it are `display()`, `clear()`, and `clearAll()`, to clear the photo div as well:

```
/*
Turns off sharing
*/
unshareMessage: function () {
   // stop beaming:
   nfc.stopHandover(
      function () {                      // success callback
         navigator.notification.vibrate(100);
         app.display("File is no longer shared");
         setTimeout(app.clearAll, 5000);   // clear the screen after 5 seconds
      },
      function (reason) {            // failure callback
         app.display("Failed to unshare file " + reason);
      }
   );
},
```

```
/*
appends @message to the message div:
*/
display: function(message) {
    var label = document.createTextNode(message),
    lineBreak = document.createElement("br");
    messageDiv.appendChild(lineBreak);      // add a line break
    messageDiv.appendChild(label);          // add the text
},

/*
clears the message div:
*/
clear: function() {
    messageDiv.innerHTML = "";
},

clearAll: function() {
    app.clear();
    photoDiv.innerHTML = "";
}
};      // end of app
```

The full source code can be found on GitHub (*http://bit.ly/master-filesender*).

When you run this, you'll see that you get a success message well before the Beam is done. That message comes after the initial handover request is made and acknowledged (Figure 8-5). If you hold until you see that, the transfer generally goes through just fine. If you have trouble sending files using handover, make sure your Bluetooth connection (or other alternate carrier) is not doing something else at the time.

Handover isn't just for large file transfer. It can be used as a convenient way to pair devices. For example, HomeSpot makes an NFC-enabled Bluetooth audio receiver that you tap your device to in order to complete Bluetooth pairing. After that, your device streams audio to the receiver. We used this as one of the devices to test the project in Chapter 6. This method of pairing could be used by many different consumer devices as a way to turn your phone or tablet into a remote control. In addition to pairing, you could include the URI to download the controller app in the initial handover request.

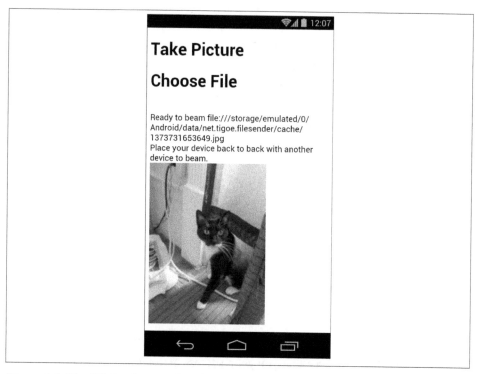

Figure 8-5. The FileSender app that demonstrates handover

Peer-to-Peer Using Arduino

While Peer-to-Peer is possible on Arduino using the NFC shields mentioned in Chapter 7, it has complications. As of this writing, there are no libraries that abstract the SNEP and LLCP layers sufficiently to allow you to focus only on the NDEF exchange. The most promising work on peer-to-peer for Arduino to date has been done by Michael Weir, and can be found on GitHub (*http://bit.ly/embed-pn532*). While this library is functional, it lacks the abstraction usually provided by an Arduino-style API, and requires more in-depth knowledge of C than most libraries. Explaining the code in this library in its current state is beyond the scope of this book. It could theoretically serve as the base for a simpler library, however.

Seeed Studio has done some work to integrate the NDEF library seen in Chapter 7 with Weir's work. Their work can be found on GitHub (*http://bit.ly/nfc-dev*) as well. There is still more work to be done to fully abstract SNEP and LLCP, but this work is looking promising, and is worth following.

Thus far, both of the peer-to-peer options work only over SPI, so the Adafruit shield needs modification to work with these libraries. You need to solder a jumper across the SEL0 and SEL1 pads on the shield to make this work. You also need to add jumpers from the MISO, MOSI, SS, and SCK headers on the shield to the pins you choose for SPI initialization in the Weir or SeeedStudio libraries.

At this time, handover is not supported using any of the libraries we've used with Arduino. Handover would require an additional Bluetooth shield or module or a WiFi shield to work as the alternate carrier, and a library would have to be written to integrate both NFC and either Bluetooth or WiFi. This could easily push the limits of the Arduino Uno's available program memory, but might be possible on the Arduino Due.

Card Emulation

In addition to reading and writing tags and communicating in peer-to-peer mode, NFC devices are also able to operate in *tag emulation* mode. In this mode, your NFC device responds to other NFC devices exactly as if it were an NFC tag. It means that your device performs just like a contactless smart card, from the reading device's perspective.

This has some useful applications. When your device performs like a smart card, the reader device can verify the data on your card (or card emulator) by ensuring not only that the data is authenticated, but that the card ID associated with the data is accurate. For example, if your bank account number is on the card, and the card has the same UID as the card issued by your bank, then an ATM or cash register can make a reliable transaction. Tag emulation is designed to make financial transactions like this, or like ticketing, reliable over NFC. This is the technology behind Google Wallet and other systems that let your phone act like a cash card or credit card.

In order to make tag emulation secure, banks and other clients using this technology need to know that the system is secure. So the NFC forum has specified that NFC readers include a *secure element* or *secure access module* in their hardware. This is just a simple processor that's attached to the NFC controller. The secure element can be programmed to verify a code sent by the reader using public key encryption and decryption. Because the secure element of a reader/writer (or of a smart card) is capable of running small programs on its own (called applets or taglets), it can even generate new hashes on the fly. If you have full control over the hardware, of course you can configure the secure module any way you wish.

Part of the thinking behind card emulation is that, by having your NFC device emulate the various smart cards you might have in your wallet (credit card, employee ID/access card, transit card, etc.), you could eliminate the need to carry all those cards. While this works in theory, it's more difficult in practice. It means that several stakeholders have to participate with your mobile phone manufacturer, who makes your phone, and your mobile service provider, who provisions the software on your phone. Your bank, your employer's security system vendor, and your public transit operator all need access to the secure element of your phone's NFC reader in order to emulate their cards. While this is technically possible, it's no simple feat politically.

Access to the secure element is generally limited by the hardware vendor, often in agreement with the software or firmware vendor. The standard distribution of Android presents no API for accessing the secure element of the NFC-enabled devices on which Google has licensed Android to run. It is possible to get access to the secure element by making the right agreement with the various stakeholders—if you're American Express and you decide to implement phone-based transactions, then Google and Samsung will be happy to work with you. If you're a two-person crafts store in Peoria, Illinois, you might be waiting a while.

Since Android is open source, you can find modified distributions of it that open access to the NFC secure element. Access is dependent on both the operating system and the particular hardware module your device is running, though, so there's not a universal solution.

The NXP PN532 module on the Adafruit and Seeed Studio shields has a secure element as well, and it is configurable. As of this writing, however, no Arduino libraries have been written to simplify custom programming of the PN532's Secure Access Module (SAM). The libraries mentioned in this book simply put the SAM into normal operation mode for the reader to act as a reader/writer, not to perform card emulation.

Conclusion

NFC peer-to-peer exchanges add a valuable component to NFC that simple RFID can't offer: the ability to send NDEF messages directly from one device to another. Because of the complexity of the exchange, it's mostly limited to devices running an operating system at the moment, like Android, BlackBerry, or Windows Phone devices. Hopefully, the state of P2P on Arduino and other simpler microcontrollers will improve in the near future. Meanwhile, the final chapter of this book will give you a taste of what's currently possible using embedded devices running Linux and the NFC libraries available for it.

CHAPTER 9

NFC on Embedded Systems

So far, we've seen the possibilities that NFC offers for mobile applications and physical interaction applications. There are other embedded device platforms besides Android, of course, and there are other physical interaction platforms besides Arduino. The most interesting at the moment are the embedded Linux systems like Texas Instruments' BeagleBone and the Raspberry Pi project, supported by Broadcom. Both of these platforms provide the capability of running a Linux distribution on an ARM processor with a development board that's less than $50. Both afford access to the physical input and output pins of the CPU as well. This makes them really fertile ground for projects that bridge the gap between the two platforms you've already seen. In this chapter, you'll get an overview of the current state of NFC on these platforms, and get a brief introduction to programming NFC apps for them in Node.js.

Just as you saw with Arduino, the state of NFC tools on embedded Linux is somewhat less fully developed than the PhoneGap-NFC plug-in, or even than the standard APIs for Android, BlackBerry, or Windows Phone. The available libraries are generally lower level, providing access to the information at the lower end of the NFC stack. But there is a lot of interest in NFC from embedded developers, so the tools are developing quickly.

 This chapter is not for those who are intimidated by the command line. You'll see lots of CLI installs, configurations, and build instructions. If you haven't spent a lot of time with CLI-based compilers and package managers, you may find some unfamiliar terms. You've gotten a small taste of that through Cordova CLI, but in this chapter you'll get a whole lot more. Although we've done our best to explain it all, you may need other reference material if you're new to Linux programming tools.

Introduction to Embedded Linux Devices and Package Managers

Texas Instruments' Beagle boards, BeagleBone, BeagleBone Black, and BeagleBoard MX, based on TI's ARM AM335x, AM35x, and AM37x processors, are embedded Linux boards designed for hobbyist projects. They're compact, inexpensive, and the hardware designs are all available openly on the Web (*http://beagleboard.org/*). They also come with a customized version of the Ångström Linux distribution for embedded development, but can run Ubuntu, Android, and other distributions as well. For the examples that follow, we recommend the BeagleBone Black.

The Raspberry Pi Foundation's boards, model A and model B, are based on an ARM processor by Broadcom. Unlike the BeagleBone, the designs for the Pi are not open to the general public, but installation and purchase information can be found on the foundation's website (*http://www.raspberrypi.org/*). The Pi models run a custom version of the Debian Linux distribution called Raspbian. For the examples in this book, we used Adafruit's version of Raspbian called Occidentalis. Like the BeagleBoard boards, the Pi can run other embedded Linux distributions. The model A shipped after the model B and is the stripped-down version: one USB port, no Ethernet, half the memory. For best results, you want a model B.

Other than the sites listed previously, you can find material for getting started with the Raspberry Pi or the BeagleBone Black at Adafruit's tutorials site (*http://learn.adafruit.com*). The books Getting Started with Raspberry Pi by Matt Richardson and Shawn Wallace, and Getting Started with BeagleBone by Matt Richardson, are also good introductions.

Network, USB, and NFC

There are three important things you need for your workflow in this chapter:

- Terminal access to your board (you can do this via a serial terminal session or an SSH terminal session)
- Internet access for your board (you'll need this to download packages, and for SSH)
- A USB port on your board for the NFC adapter

The hardware features of the various Pi and BeagleBone models will affect how you get these things. Here's what you need to consider:

- Neither Raspberry Pi nor BeagleBone have built-in WiFi. You'll need a USB-to-WiFi adapter if you can't connect via wired Ethernet.
- Raspberry Pi model A, BeagleBone, and BeagleBone Black have only one USB port. That means no WiFi USB adapter while you use the USB NFC Adapter.

- Raspberry Pi model A has no wired Ethernet port. So you need WiFi if you're going to connect it to the Internet. The model A is the only one of the boards mentioned that can't be simultaneously on the Internet and using an NFC adapter.

- Raspberry Pi (both models) does not have a built-in USB-to-serial interface. It requires a 3.3V USB-to-serial adapter to connect serially to your computer. Both BeagleBone models have USB-to-serial built into the USB mini-B connector.

- Raspberry Pi's default setup interface is via keyboard and screen. You'll need a monitor, HDMI cable, and keyboard if you follow the defaults. However, you can set it up with a USB-to-serial adapter instead, if you have one. You can also do it from the command line, with a little more work. See "Raspberry Pi Peculiarities" on page 202 for more details.

- Raspberry Pi is generally easier to set up software for for NFC, but more complex for hardware. In our testing, we found the Raspberry Pi and the BeagleBone Black to be roughly equivalent in terms of ease of use, performance, and price, especially when factoring in necessary externalities like cables and power supplies.

The various embedded Linux boards on the market offer different hardware features and processors and they use different Linux distributions. But there are a few features they share in common. All of them are networkable, of course, and they'll all give you a command-line interface, though it's not always the simplest thing to get to right out of the box. They all support standard hardware interfaces like USB and UART serial. Most importantly, they can all run software that's written for Linux, as long as they have the necessary storage space, memory, and hardware components. There are also a handful of programming languages that most of them support as well. All of them will support C++ at least, which is why many of the packages you've used have a C++ core, even if you didn't use it. In order to facilitate code development, all mainstream operating systems, even the basic Linux distributions you'll use here, support package management systems as well. You won't be writing your own C++ code in this chapter, but you will be installing and compiling a lot of it using a few different tools.

Software developers rely on libraries and tools developed by their colleagues and predecessors to do their work, and different software projects have different *dependencies*. A project that allows you to use a USB-based NFC reader as you'll see here will depend on other software libraries that support USB communication, among others. Good developers assume nothing and list all their dependencies, of course, but the job of managing that is made easier by automated build and install tools called *package management systems*. You've already been using one of them in this book, the node package manager, or npm. Cordova isn't really a package manager, it's more of an automated project-building tool, but is moving toward having a package manager with Cordova CLI's plug-in tools. Tools like APT, opkg, npm, and even the app stores consumers use every day, like Apple's Mac App Store and the Google Play store for Android, are all package managers. The difference between more consumer-facing app stores and the ones developers use is that the latter generally install source code and compile it on your machine, while the former download and install pre-compiled binaries.

Package management systems for Linux, Unix, and other POSIX operating systems make the process of installing and compiling software libraries more or less the same regardless of what flavor of the operating system you're using. The file structures and APIs for all such operating systems are similar enough that the same code prepared for Linux on the Raspberry Pi will work (more or less) the same on Mac OS X, for example. As a result, we're going to give you examples in this chapter in generic command-line Linux terms, and assume that you can make them work on your embedded Linux board. We've tested them on the Raspberry Pi and the BeagleBone Black, and we'll note any particularities for those two platforms as needed.

 You won't see any instructions for Mac OS X or Windows in this chapter. Although it's possible to build these tools for those platforms, the focus here is on the embedded world.

For the remainder of this chapter, you'll need the following:

- BeagleBone, Raspberry Pi, or other embedded Linux board
- 1 amp or greater power supply for your board
- SLC3711 Contactless USB Smart Card Reader (*http://bit.ly/1fBYLhm*) (we'll refer to this as an NFC adapter from here on)
- A few Mifare Classic NFC tags (for this chapter, Mifare Classic are the most compatible with the Linux libraries you're using, even though they won't work on some Android devices; see "Device-to-Tag Type Matching" on page 19 for more on which tags work with which devices)
- A text editor

Optional but useful:

- A USB WiFi adapter for your board (Adafruit's Miniature WiFi (802.11b/g/n) Module (*http://www.adafruit.com/products/814*) works well)
- A USB A-to-A extender for your NFC adapter
- A USB to TTL Serial Cable - Debug/Console Cable (*http://www.adafruit.com/products/954*) (make sure you get one that operates at 3.3 volts, not 5 volts)

The NFC reader mentioned here and the optional WiFi adapter both consume more current than the boards can draw from your computer's USB port. When you try to read tags while your board's powered from your computer's USB port, you'll get a lot of misreads. You should power your board from a separate power supply that can supply at least one amp of current, preferably two amps.

Since the setup for each board is idiosyncratic and sometimes complex, we'll skip it here. You should follow your board's particular instructions for setup and connection to the Internet, and familiarize yourself with logging into the command line. The rest of this chapter will assume you can get to the command line of your board on your own, and that you can connect to the Internet through your board.

The USB Smart Card reader mentioned here is an NFC reader with a USB interface. It's running the same NXP PN53x chip that's in the shields you used in Chapter 7. The antenna on it is weak, so you may find that it has trouble reading tags unless positioned carefully. We found that a USB extender cable was helpful in working with this reader, so you could get the reader near the tags easier.

NFC on Embedded Linux: The Overview

Since there are no embedded Linux boards on the market at the moment with built-in NFC, you'll need a separate NFC controller. You could use the PN532 shields, but they're not designed to interface with the BeagleBone or the Pi, so a USB-based module is easier to use. For this chapter, we chose the Identive SLC3711 Contactless USB Smart Card Reader (*http://bit.ly/1fBYLhm*). It works with many of the libraries we examined because it's got a PN532 NFC controller as its heart.

There are a handful of NFC libraries available, in varying states of completeness. The best one as of this writing is *libnfc*, available from NFC Tools (*http://nfc-tools.org/*). Libnfc is a low-level library for NFC. It supports the control protocols ISO14443A and -B (used by most of the tag types), ISO-18092 (the protocol used for peer-to-peer) and JIS-X-6319-4 (used by FeliCa smart cards).

Libnfc's roadmap for the project is quite helpful in understanding how it's developed, and where it's headed. It can be found on the libnfc Roadmap page (*http://bit.ly/libnfc-roadmap*). The layered abstraction model is based on NFC's abstraction model, and leaves a lot of room for the project to increase in compatibility with other readers and in higher level functionality.

There are a few useful subprojects based on libnfc, including *libfreefare*, which adds an API for reading from and writing to Mifare tags. Libfreefare is available on the NFC Tools site. There is also an implementation of LLCP for libnfc (*http://bit.ly/llcp-libnfc*). Libfreefare only offers limited support for NFC Forum tag types. It's fully compatible with Mifare Classic tags, but as of this writing, it doesn't offer support for all four NFC forum tag types. Its architecture could support them, however, when an enterprising programmer submits a patch to add that support.

Libnfc is cross-platform and will run on Windows, OS X, and other POSIX systems, including the various Linux distributions. You'll see how it works on the Raspberry Pi and BeagleBone, but it should work fine on other embedded Linux boards as well.

We've built a Node.js library that uses libnfc and libfreefare to read to and write from Mifare Classic tags. At this point, like libfreefare, it does not offer support for the NFC Forum tag types (though patches are welcome). You'll see this later on, but first, you need to install libnfc and libfreefare, and learn a little bit more about them.

Housekeeping Details

Before you install any NFC-specific tools, there are some housekeeping tasks you should take care of first. These are necessary tasks that you might overlook if you do them midstream, but if you do them at the start, things will go much smoother.

Get Comfortable with Your Editing Workflow

You're going to be writing a lot of text that needs to live on your board, so you should use an editor that you're comfortable with. If you like working in nano or vi, both of which are Linux-based editors available on the Pi and the BeagleBone, you're all set. If you prefer a graphic editor on your personal computer though, you'll need a way to move files from your computer to your embedded board. Any SFTP/FTP client will do the job, or you can use scp from the command line. If you have a workflow for writing files on a remote web server, that same workflow should work for this too.

Know Your Package Manager

There are two major differences you'll encounter between the Raspberry Pi, which is running a variant of the Debian Linux distribution, and the BeagleBone Black, which is running a variant of Ångström. The first difference is that the BeagleBone runs as the administrator, known as root, by default. The Pi's default user is called pi. In order to do many administrative tasks, you need to have administrator privileges. By running as root, you get these automatically. If you're not running as root, you can get administrative privileges using the sudo command. The first time in a session that you use sudo, you will have to enter the root password, but after that, everything will be done as if you are an administrator. Whenever you type sudo before a command, you're asking to execute that command as an administrator (or super-user, hence sudo: "su do"). Wherever you see sudo in the commands that follow, assume that this command needs to be run as an administrator.

Change your default password, whether you're running as root on the BeagleBone Black, or whether you're running as pi on the Raspberry Pi. Keeping your password unique and secure is just good operating system hygiene.

The second difference is that they use different package managers. The Pi uses APT, the advanced package tool. The BeagleBone uses the opkg package manager. The two are similar in many ways, but have different commands for some things. The most common commands you'll use are listed in Table 9-1 for comparison.

Table 9-1. APT versus opkg: common functions

APT function	opkg function	Description
`apt-get update`	`opkg update`	Update list of available packages
`apt-get upgrade`	`opkg upgrade`	Upgrade all installed packages to the latest version
`apt-cache search <pattern>`	`opkg search <pattern>`	Full text search of available packages
`apt-get install <package>`	`opkg install <package>`	Install a package
`apt-get remove <package>`	`opkg remove <package>`	Remove a package
`dpkg --get-selections`	`opkg list-installed`	List installed packages

The first step before using any package manager is to make sure it has the most updated set of available packages. To do this for Raspberry Pi, run the following command:

```
$ sudo apt-get update
```

For BeagleBone Black, run the following:

```
$ opkg update
```

Set the Date and Time

Make sure your board has the correct date and time. Without the date set correctly, some installers will not function correctly. The Raspberry Pi will set its clock automatically if it has a network connection, but a BeagleBone won't. To check the time that the board thinks it is, type `date`. To set it, make sure you're connected to a network, and type:

```
$ ntpdate -b -s -u pool.ntp.org
```

This is a one-time update, which will sync your board's clock with the network time servers at the Network Time Protocol (*http://ntp.org*). The Raspberry Pi will periodically sync to an NTP server by default. The BeagleBone won't, but for good instructions on how to do this on the BeagleBone, see Derek Molloy's page on setting the BeagleBone clock (*http://bit.ly/1bEappq*). Pi users who want to use `ntpdate` will have to `sudo apt-get install ntpdate` first.

Make a Downloads Directory

Next, make a directory in your home folder to store your downloads:

```
$ cd ~
$ mkdir downloads
$ cd downloads
```

You'll do the rest of this installation in this directory or its subdirectories.

There are a few tools for compiling and installing that are used in most of the libraries you'll install, so it's best to make sure they are all there. When you install using `apt-get` (on Pi) or `opkg` (on BeagleBone), the package manager will inform you if you've already got the latest package, so there's no harm in trying to install these even if they are there.

For Raspberry Pi, use the following:

```
$ sudo apt-get install autoconf automake libtool libusb-1.0-0-dev
```

And for BeagleBone Black, use this:

```
$ opkg install autoconf automake libtool libusb-1.0-dev
```

BeagleBone Peculiarities

You might have trouble with HTTPS requests from Git on the BeagleBone. To avoid this, make sure your board has the proper SSL certificates installed, and that Git is configured as follows.

You need to set up your Git config file to look for SSL certificates, like so:

```
$ opkg install ca-certificates
```

If you get a response telling you that this package is already installed, that's OK. Next you need to tell Git where to find SSL certificates:

```
$ git config --global http.sslCAinfo /etc/ssl/certs/ca-certificates.crt
```

Raspberry Pi Peculiarities

The Raspberry Pi setup installations require you to have an HDMI cable and a keyboard to set the board up for the first time, but you can avoid this in a couple ways. One way is connect to the serial port of your board to open a terminal connection. You can connect to the serial port with a 3.3V USB-to-serial cable like the USB to TTL Serial Cable - Debug/Console Cable (*http://www.adafruit.com/products/954*) available from Adafruit. The other way to connect is to connect to your board through an SSH connection. If you don't want to buy a cable, you can connect your Pi to your local network and find it in the following way. On the command line, type the following:

```
$ for i in 192.168.1.{1..254}; do ping -c 1 -W 3 $i & > /dev/null; done
$ netstat -nr -f inet | grep -i "b8:27"
```

If your router doesn't have the address 192.168.1.1, change the address here to the first three octets of your router.

The first command will query all the devices on your local network. The second will give you a list of all the devices that replied and that have MAC addresses that begin with the prefix B8:27. The Pi boards should all have MAC addresses starting with this prefix. If there's a device on your network with that prefix, chances are it's your Pi. Copy the IP address associated with it and type:

```
$ ssh pi@ip-address
```

When you get a login prompt, login with the username pi and the default password raspberry.

Installing Node.js on the Raspberry Pi

The BeagleBone Black comes with Node.js pre-installed, but the Pi doesn't. You'll need to manually install it using the following steps. Make sure your Pi has Internet access first, then:

```
$ cd ~/downloads
$ curl -O http://nodejs.org/dist/v0.10.12/node-v0.10.12-linux-arm-pi.tar.gz ❶
$ cd /usr/local
$ sudo tar xzf ~/downloads/node-v0.10.12-linux-arm-pi.tar.gz ❷
$ cd bin
$ sudo ln -s ../node-v0.10.12-linux-arm-pi/bin/node ❸
$ sudo ln -s ../node-v0.10.12-linux-arm-pi/bin/npm
```

❶ Download node.

❷ Install it in */usr/local*.

❸ Make symlinks (aliases) to node and npm so you can call them from the command line easily.

Once you have Node installed for Pi, you're ready to go with the rest of the chapter.

Installing the Tools for NFC

To install the libraries for the projects in this chapter, you'll need to make sure your board has Internet access. You'll also need a few software libraries:

- libusb compatibility library
- libnfc

- libfreefare
- ndef-mifare-classic-js
- ndef-js

These libraries all depend on each other, so the order in which you install them is important, as you'll see. Once they're all installed, you'll be able to read from and write to your NFC reader. The installation details are similar on the BeagleBone and the Raspberry Pi, and the differences are noted.

Since you know that the NFC adapter you're using connects via USB, you might not be surprised to learn that libnfc and libfreefare depend on a USB library, libusb. Installing these libraries starts with libusb.

Installing the Libusb Compatibility Library

Download `libusb-compat-0.1.5.tar.bz2` from libusb (*http://www.libusb.org/*), uncompress it, and install it like so:

```
$ cd ~/downloads
$ wget http://sourceforge.net/projects/libusb/files/\
    libusb-compat-0.1/libusb-compat-0.1.5/libusb-compat-0.1.5.tar.bz2
$ tar xjf libusb-compat-0.1.5.tar.bz2
$ cd libusb-compat-0.1.5
$ ./configure
$ make
$ make install ❶
```

❶   Raspberry Pi users need to use `sudo make install` here.

Installing libnfc

Next, you're going to download and install libnfc:

```
$ cd ~/downloads
$ git clone https://code.google.com/p/libnfc/
$ cd libnfc
$ autoreconf -vis
$ export PKG_CONFIG_PATH=/usr/local/lib/pkgconfig ❶
$ ./configure
$ make
$ make install ❷
```

❶   BeagleBone users will need to do this, but not Pi users; libfreefare's configure tool needs to know where libnfc was installed.

❷   Raspberry Pi users need to use `sudo make install` here.

Raspberry Pi

libnfc is installed to *usr/local/lib*; running ldconfig will update configuration so the linker can find the libraries when required:

```
$ sudo ldconfig
```

There's a little post-install configuration you need to do for libnfc. Create a new file:

```
$ sudo nano /etc/modprobe.d/blacklist-libnfc.conf
```

And add to the file:

```
blacklist pn533
blacklist nfc
```

Press Ctrl-X then press Y to save and exit nano. Then copy the PN53x rules file from the libnfc distribution as follows:

```
$ sudo cp contrib/udev/42-pn53x.rules /lib/udev/rules.d/
```

BeagleBone Black

As with the Pi, there's a little post-install configuration you need to do for libnfc. Create a new file:

```
$ nano /etc/modprobe.d/nfc.conf
```

And add to it:

```
install pn533 /bin/true
install nfc /bin/true
```

Press Ctrl-X then press Y to save and exit nano.

Testing the Installation on Raspberry Pi or BeagleBone

At this point, you've got libnfc working on your board. Plug in your NFC reader and test that it shows up and is available with the nfc-list command, which will produce the following output:

```
$ nfc-list

nfc-list uses libnfc libnfc-1.7.0-rc7-40-gbb5b712
NFC device: SCM Micro / SCL3711-NFC&RW opened
```

If you get a result like this, your reader is working, and you're ready to move on.

Installing libfreefare

Now that you have libnfc installed, download and install libfreefare:

```
$ cd ~/downloads
$ git clone https://code.google.com/p/libfreefare/
```

```
$ cd libfreefare
$ autoreconf -vis
$ ./configure
$ make
$ make install ❶
$ sudo ldconfig ❷
```

❶   Raspberry Pi users need to use `sudo make install` here.

❷   BeagleBone Black users can skip this step.

Now that you've installed all the necessary packages, the following examples should run
identically on the Raspberry Pi or the BeagleBone unless specifically stated otherwise.

If you're simply interested in developing applications that read and write NDEF in
JavaScript or another scripting language, you probably don't want to know too many of
the details about libnfc and libfreefare. They provide a C/C++ API to the NFC reader,
and that's it. The next section covers some of the highlights of both. Following that is
an introduction to a Node.js library for reading and writing NDEF from Mifare Classic
tags, so if you're only interested in the high-level details, skip down to "NDEF Reading
and Writing in Node.js" on page 208.

Libnfc and Libfreefare Command Line Tools

Libnfc provides some command line tools which you can find in the *utils/* directory.
These give you the tools to do a lot of low-level NFC tasks:

nfc-anticol	nfc-emulate-uid
nfc-read-forum-tag3	nfc-dep-initiator
nfc-list	nfc-relay
nfc-dep-target	nfc-mfclassic
nfc-relay-picc	nfc-emulate-forum-tag2
nfc-mfsetuid	nfc-scan-device
nfc-emulate-forum-tag4	nfc-multralight

The most interesting tool of the lot is `nfc-mfclassic` (*http://bit.ly/185A8Ij*), which will
read a tag and dump the contents to a file. It gives you the raw byte stream from the tag,
not differentiating between what's content and what's metadata at all. Plug in NFC reader
and place it close to a Mifare Classic tag. The command works like this, producing the
following output:

```
$ nfc-mfclassic r b dump.mfd

NFC reader: SCM Micro / SCL3711-NFC&RW opened
Found MIFARE Classic card:
ISO/IEC 14443A (106 kbps) target:
```

```
ATQA (SENS_RES): 00  04
   UID (NFCID1): 2d  10  18  07
   SAK (SEL_RES): 08
Guessing size: seems to be a 1024-byte card
Reading out 64 blocks |...................................|
Done, 64 of 64 blocks read.
Writing data to file: dump.mfd ...Done.
```

The arguments for nfc-classic are:

r

Read a protected Mifare Classic tag

b

Use key b, the Mifare encryption scheme that NDEF uses

dump.mfd
The output file in which to dump the contents

 The antenna on the SLC3711 reader responds best if you hold the tag about a centimeter away from the tag. You may find it easier to work with the reader if you have a USB A-to-female-A extender cable.

This and all the libnfc utilities are relatively low-level tools. Libfreefare provides some slightly higher level tools. It can read, write, and format Mifare Classic, Ultralight, and DESFire tags. It can read and write NDEF messages to these tags as well. The examples for libfreefare, written in C, can be found in the *examples/* subdirectory of the *libfreefare* directory:

```
mifare-classic-format            mifare-desfire-ev1-configure-random-uid

mifare-classic-read-ndef         mifare-desfire-format

mifare-classic-write-ndef        mifare-desfire-info

mifare-desfire-access            mifare-desfire-read-ndef

mifare-desfire-create-ndef       mifare-desfire-write-ndef

mifare-desfire-ev1-configure-ats mifare-ultralight-info
```

As an example, here's the `mifare-classic-format` command in action:

```
$ mifare-classic-format

Found Mifare Classic 1k with UID 6b57ee65. Format [yN] y
Formatting 16 sectors [...4...8...12...16] done.
```

One of the handy things you can do with libfreefare is to copy a tag. To do this, you read a tag, dump the results to a file on your board, and then write the file to another tag. Here's how to write it to a file called *ndef.bin*:

```
$ mifare-classic-read-ndef -o ndef.bin
```

When the tag is written successfully, you can look at it with the xxd command. You may recognize the NDEF message from a previous chapter:

```
$ xxd ndef.bin

0000000: d101 3055 036d 2e66 6f75 7273 7175 6172   ..0U.m.foursquar
0000010: 652e 636f 6d2f 7665 6e75 652f 3461 3931   e.com/venue/4a91
0000020: 3735 3633 6639 3634 6135 3230 3430 3161   7563f964a520401a
0000030: 3230 6533                                 20e3
```

Once you've got a file, you can write the message to another tag like so:

```
$ mifare-classic-write-ndef -i ndef.bin
```

Libfreefare provides the basis for the highest level tool in this chapter, the mifare-classic-js and ndef-js packages for Node.js.

NDEF Reading and Writing in Node.js

In order to give you a high-level tool to read and write NDEF messages, we've built two packages for Node.js to do this, ndef and mifare-classic. Using these packages, you can write node web apps like the one you wrote in Chapter 7. If you're using a BeagleBone, you can also use these packages in combination with BoneScript, the BeagleBone's Arduino-like JavaScript framework for controlling the physical I/O of the BeagleBone.

You can find the full sources for these two packages on GitHub, where Don has repositories for NDEF messages (*https://github.com/don/ndef-js*) and Mifare classic tags (*https://github.com/don/mifare-classic-js*). They're both available through the node package manager npm as well, which is how you'll load them for the following examples.

The NDEF package enables you to read and write NDEF messages in Node. The main functions in this package are encodeMessage(), for encoding an NDEF message into a byte stream to write to a tag, and decodeMessage(), which converts an incoming byte stream into an array of NDEF records. It contains most of the functions you're familiar with from the NDEF object in the PhoneGap-NFC plug-in as well, as you'll see in the examples that follow.

The mifare-classic package gives you a JavaScript interface to libfreefare. As such, it will only work with Mifare Classic tags, since it relies on libfreefare to do the reading. It has three functions as of this writing, read() and write() for reading and writing tags, and format(), which formats a tag as an NDEF tag.

There are a few basic examples included with both packages, in the *examples/* directory. The steps to install and run these examples should be the same on the BeagleBone, Raspberry Pi, and other Linux-based boards, as long as you've installed libnfc and libfreefare successfully. You'll use npm to install them after you make your project files.

Reading, writing, and formatting an NDEF-formatted tag is fairly simple using these two packages. To start with, make a new directory for your app and create a *package.json* file inside it:

```
$ cd ~
$ mkdir NodeNdefBasics
$ cd NodeNdefBasics
$ nano package.json
```

When nano's open and ready for editing, add this to your file:

```
{
    "name": "NodeNdefBasics",
    "author": "Your Name",
    "version": "0.0.1",
    "description": "Read, write, or format a tag",
    "main": "read.js",
    "keywords": [
        "NDEF",
        "NFC"
    ],
    "dependencies" : {
        "mifare-classic": "0.0.1",
        "ndef"    :  ">=0.0.4"
    },
        "engines": {
        "node": ">=0.8"
    }
}
```

Press Ctrl-X and then press Y to save this file. Then open a new file, *read.js*:

```
var ndef = require('ndef'),          // require ndef package
    mifare = require('mifare-classic');  // require mifare-classic package

mifare.read(function(error, buffer) {  // read tag
    if (error) {                       // if there's an error result
        console.log("Read failed ");   // let user know about the error
        console.log(error);
    } else {                           // you got an NDEF message
        // decode the message into a JSON object:
        var message = ndef.decodeMessage(buffer.toJSON());
        // print the message's records:
        console.log("Found NDEF message with " + message.length +
            // add "record" if there's only one, "records" if there's more:
            (message.length === 1 ? " record" : " records" ));
        // print the message:
        console.log(ndef.stringify(message));
```

```
    }
});
```

As you can see, the `mifare.read()` function from the mifare-classic package has a success callback as its parameter. When it's read a tag successfully, you can use the `ndef.decodeMessage()` function to convert the buffer to an array of NDEF records.

To install the ndef and mifare-classic packages, make sure you're connected to the Internet and type:

```
$ npm install
```

Once the packages have installed successfully, place your reader about a centimeter from a tag that you've already written NDEF messages to, then type:

```
$ node read.js
```

After a second or so, you should get a reply like this:

```
Found Mifare Classic 1k with UID bb60ee65.
NFC Forum application contains a "NDEF Message TLV".
Found NDEF message with 2 records
URI Record
http://nfc-tools.org

Text Record
Hello from nodejs
```

Formatting using the mifare-classic package is very similar to formatting with libfreefare, as you might expect. The package is just a light wrapper around that library. Create a new file, *format.js*:

```
var mifare = require('mifare-classic');    // require mifare-classic

mifare.format(function(error) {            // format tag
    if (error) {                           // if there's an error,
        console.log("Format failed ");     // report the error
        console.log(error);
    } else {                               // if the format works out OK
        console.log("Tag formatted OK");   // report that
    }
});
```

Once you've installed with npm, place your reader near a tag you want to format, and run. You should get the following:

```
Found Mifare Classic 1k with UID 52d55be4.
Formatting 16 sectors [...4...8...12...16] done.
Tag formatted OK
```

It will take a few seconds to format, and if you move the reader before the formatting's done, you'll get an error, so hold still. Once it's done, you've got a tag that's ready for writing, so create a new file, *write.js*:

```
var ndef = require('ndef'),                        // require ndef package
    mifare = require('mifare-classic'),            // require this package
    message,                                        // an NDEF message
    bytes;                                          // the bytes stream to write

message = [
    ndef.uriRecord("http://nfc-tools.org"),        // make a URI record
    ndef.textRecord("Hello from nodejs"),          // make a text record
    ndef.emptyRecord()                             // make an empty record
];

bytes = ndef.encodeMessage(message);               // encode record as a byte stream

mifare.write(bytes, function(error) {              // write function
    if (error) {                                   // if there's an error,
        console.log("Write failed ");              // report the error
        console.log(error);
    } else {
        console.log("Tag written successfully");// report that tag was written
    }
});
```

The full source code for these last three examples can be found on GitHub (*http://bit.ly/node-basics*).

The mifare.write() function takes a byte stream and a callback function as parameters, like read(). If it succeeds, the callback doesn't return anything. If there is an error, the callback returns that. When you install and run this with a tag in range, you should get the following if the write is successful:

```
NDEF file is 45 bytes long.
Found Mifare Classic 1k with UID 52d55be4.
Tag written successfully
```

If the tag isn't written successfully, you'll get something like this:

```
NDEF file is 45 bytes long.
Found Mifare Classic 1k with UID 52d55be4.
Write failed
mifare-classic-write-ndef: No known authentication key for sector 0x0e

mifare-classic-write-ndef: No known authentication key for sector 0x0a

mad_write: Mifare Authentication Failed
```

As with reading and formatting, the key to success is holding the tag near the reader and keeping it still while the write is in progress. If you read this with the reader example, you'll get this output:

```
Found Mifare Classic 1k with UID 52d55be4.
NFC Forum application contains a "NDEF Message TLV".
Found NDEF message with 3 records
URI Record
```

```
http://nfc-tools.org

Text Record
Hello from nodejs

Empty Record
```

Now that you understand the main functions of these two node packages, it's time for a few examples of what you can do with them.

Web Interface for Tag Writer

Node.js works easily as a web server, as you saw in Chapter 7, so it makes sense to create a web interface for a tag writer with the packages you've just learned (this is a variation on "A Browser Interface for the Arduino NDEF Writer Device" on page 165). In fact, you can use the same *index.html* page from that project.

Start off by making the directory and the *package.json* file as usual:

```
$ cd ~
$ mkdir NodeNdefWriterWeb
$ cd NodeNdefWriterWeb
$ nano package.json
```

The main difference between this package file and the one for the writer script is the addition of express.js as a dependency:

```
{
  "name": "NodeNdefWriterWeb",
  "author": "username",
  "version": "0.0.2",
  "description": "Write a tag from a browser",
  "main": "index.js",
  "keywords": [
    "NDEF",
    "NFC"
  ],
  "dependencies" : {
    "express": ">=3.0",
    "mifare-classic": "0.0.1",
    "ndef"    :  ">=0.4"
  },
  "engines": {
    "node": ">=0.8"
  }
}
```

The *index.js* file is very similar to the *index.js* from "A Browser Interface for the Arduino NDEF Writer Device" on page 165, but with a few changes, noted at the end of this script:

```
/*
   NodeNdefWriterWeb.js

*/
var ndef = require('ndef'),              // require ndef package ❶
    mifare = require('mifare-classic'),  // require this package
    express = require('express'),            // make an instance of express
    app = express(),                         // start Express framework
    server = require('http').createServer(app), // start an HTTP server
    record = {},                             // NDEF record to send
    deviceMessage = "";                      // messages from writer device

app.use(express.bodyParser());           // use bodyParser middleware for express
server.listen(8080);                     // listen for incoming requests on server
console.log("Listening for new clients on port 8080");

// respond to web GET requests with the index.html page:
app.get('/*', function (request, response) {
  response.sendfile(__dirname + '/index.html');
});

// take anything that begins with /submit:
app.post('/submit', function (request, response) {
  var days = request.body.days,          // get the number of days from the body
      today = new Date(request.body.checkin),   // get the time from the body
      // calculate the checkout timeStamp:
      departure = new Date(today.valueOf() + (days * 86400000)),
      nfcResponse,                         // the response from the NFC reader
      message,                             // the NFC message to write
      bytes;                               // byte stream to write it with

  record.name = request.body.name;       // get the name from the body
  record.room = request.body.room;       // get the room number from the body
  // convert to unix time in seconds:
  record.checkin = Math.round(today.valueOf()/1000);
  record.checkout = Math.round(departure.valueOf()/1000);

  message = [
      ndef.textRecord(JSON.stringify(record)), // make a text record ❷
  ];
  bytes = ndef.encodeMessage(message);   // encode record as a byte stream

  mifare.write(bytes, function(error) {  // write function ❸
      if (error) {                          // if there's an error,
          nfcResponse = "Write failed"; // report it
          nfcResponse += error;
      } else {
          nfcResponse = "Tag written successfully" + JSON.stringify(record);
      }
      console.log(nfcResponse);// report that the tag was written
      // write the HTML head back to the browser:
```

```
        response.writeHead(200, {'Content-Type': 'text/html'});
        // send the data:
        response.write("Wrote the following to the card:<br>");
        response.write(nfcResponse + "<p>");
        // send the link back to the index and close the link:
        response.end("<a href=\"/\">Return to form</a>");
    });            // end of mifare.write()
});                // end of app.post()
```

❶   You're adding mifare-classic and ndef instead of serialport.

❷   You're creating a text record using the helper from the ndef package and encoding it as a byte stream.

❸   You're calling `mifare.write()` to write the message to the tag, and waiting for the response.

The full source code can be found on GitHub (*http://bit.ly/node-writer-web*).

The user interaction for this is identical to the browser interface project we mentioned before. You enter the data in the form, press the submit button while holding the guest's card over the reader, and the NFC reader writes to the tag. You should get the NDEF record as a JSON string in the browser if the write succeeds, and a failure message if it doesn't.

Tags Controlling Physical Output

One of the more interesting things you can do with an embedded Linux board like the BeagleBone or the Raspberry Pi is to use its *general purpose I/O* (GPIO) pins to sense and control the physical world. These are the physical input and output pins of the board. The hotel door lock in Chapter 7 is one possible application of this. Rather than reading the guest's door key card on the Arduino and opening the lock, you could read it on a BeagleBone or Raspberry Pi.

The following example shows the bare minimum to connect the mifare-classic and ndef-js packages with the GPIO of your board. It turns on LEDs connected to the board's GPIO to indicate how many records are in the NDEF message read from a tag.

On the BeagleBone, you'll use the BoneScript package, which gives you control of the GPIO pins using an API that's similar in style to the Arduino API. On the Raspberry Pi, you'll use the `onoff` npm package.

BeagleBone Version

On the BeagleBone, the general purpose IO pins (GPIO) can be controlled using Bone-Script, a node package developed by Jason Kridner, the software architect of the BeagleBoard products. BoneScript has many commands that are similar to the Arduino commands for GPIO control, like `pinMode()`, `digitalRead()`, `digitalWrite()`, and so forth. It's built into the BeagleBone distribution of Ångström. In fact, if you open up your web browser and go to "http://beaglebone.local:3000" while your board is on the same local network as your computer, you'll get the built-in Cloud9 IDE for the BeagleBone. From it, you can run, stop, and debug any BoneScript projects you write.

The Cloud9 IDE stores all your projects by default in */var/lib/cloud9/*. You won't need to worry about a *package.json* file when you write in the Cloud9 IDE. That's both convenient and inconvenient, as it means you can't easily include modules that aren't native to the IDE. You can, however, use BoneScript in your own packages, so for this project you'll skip the Cloud9 IDE and work the same way you have been all along. Because BoneScript is installed in the distribution, you won't need to put it in your *package.json*. Node will automatically use the local version.

This example is a variation on the tag reader you saw earlier. To get started, set up the directory as usual:

```
$ cd ~
$ mkdir NodeTagToLed
$ cd NodeTagToLed
$ nano package.json
```

Here's the *package.json* file:

```
{
  "name": "NodeTagToLed",
  "author": "username",
  "version": "0.0.1",
  "description": "Read a tag, light LEDs",
  "main": "index.js",
  "keywords": [
    "NDEF",
    "NFC",
    "Bonescript"
  ],
   "dependencies" : {
    "mifare-classic": "0.0.1",
    "ndef"    :   ">=0.0.4"
    // note: Bonescript is built into the BB distribution.
    // if you include it in your package.json, it will cause errors
  },
  "engines": {
    "node": ">=0.8"
  }
}
```

As you can see, not a lot changed from the read tag example. Even the keyword mention of BoneScript is optional. The *index.js* file starts just like the one from that project too, but you're going to add four new pieces of code:

```
var ndef = require('ndef'),              // require ndef package
    mifare = require('mifare-classic'),  // require this package
    io = require('bonescript');          // bonescript is built into the BB ❶

io.pinMode('USR0', 'out');               // set LED I/O pins as outputs ❷
io.pinMode('USR1', 'out');
io.pinMode('USR2', 'out');
io.pinMode('USR3', 'out');

setInterval(readTags, 2000);             // read every 2 seconds ❸

function readTags() {
    mifare.read(function(error, buffer) {  // read tag
        if (error) {                       // if there's an error result
            console.log("Read failed ");   // let user know about the error
            console.log(error);
        } else {                           // you got an NDEF message
            // decode the message into a JSON object:
            var message = ndef.decodeMessage(buffer.toJSON());
            // print the message's records:
            console.log("Found NDEF message with " + message.length +
                // "record" if there's only one, "records" if there's more:
                (message.length === 1 ? " record" : " records" ));
            // print the message:
            console.log(ndef.stringify(message));

            // loop over the LEDs and turn on one for each record:  ❹
            for (var pinNum=0; pinNum<4; pinNum++) {
                var pin = 'USR' + pinNum;      // set pin name, USR0 - USR3
                if (pinNum < message.length) { // USR0=1 record, USR1=2 records...
                    io.digitalWrite(pin, 1);   // turn on pin
                } else {
                    io.digitalWrite(pin, 0);   // turn off pin
                }
            }
        }
    });
}
```

❶ This is where you include BoneScript in your file.

❷ The labels USR0 through USR3 refer to the four built-in LEDs on the BeagleBone Black. For more on the naming of the GPIO pins, open a browser and go to "http://beaglebone.local/Support/BoneScript/". The reference material is on the board itself.

❸ In order to keep the script running infinitely, you're setting an interval to read for tags every two seconds. Then you're wrapping `mifare.read()` in a function called `readTags()` that gets called by the interval.

❹ This is where you loop over the four LEDs and turn on one for each record in the NDEF message you just read. First you concatenate the pin name (USR0 through USR3), and then you turn on or off the pin depending on the record count.

The full source code can be found on GitHub (*http://bit.ly/node-tag-led*).

When you have this project installed on your board using npm, run it as usual. It should run infintely, so you can read multiple tags. When you read a tag, it will count the number of records and use that to turn on the appropriate number of LEDs. Any of the tags you've already written will do the job.

Raspberry Pi Version

For this version, you'll need:

- 4 LEDs
- 4 220Ω resistors
- 1 small solderless breadboard
- 4 female-to-male jumpers
- 4 header pins

Although BoneScript is not ported to the Pi as of this writing, there are a few alternative node libraries for controlling the GPIO. None of them are as fully featured as BoneScript, but they do allow you to turn on and off the GPIO pins. Here's a variation on the BeagleBone example, but for the Pi, using the onoff npm package.

Set up the directory as you did for the BeagleBone Black. The *package.json* is the same except for one addition in the dependencies:

```
"dependencies" : {
 "mifare-classic": "0.0.1",
 "ndef"    :   ">=0.0.4"
 "onoff" : ">=0.1.6"
},
```

The onoff package works by writing to virtual files in the system directories that control the GPIO pins. For more details on it, see NPM's onoff page (*https://npmjs.org/package/onoff*). Since BoneScript does basically the same thing on the BeagleBone, the two libraries are similar, and the code for this example is similar.

The GPIO pins of the Pi are labeled as shown in Figure 9-1.

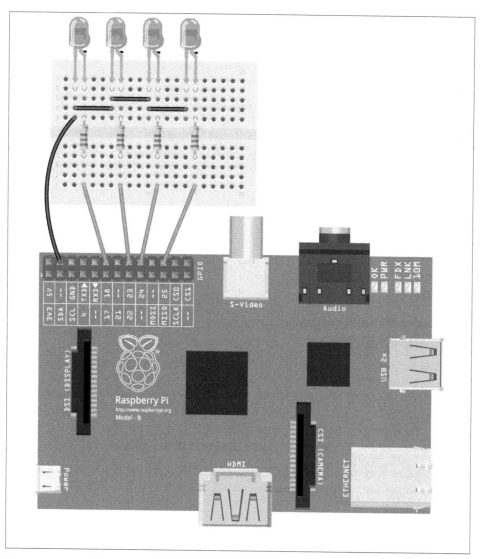

Figure 9-1. Raspberry Pi with LEDs attached to GPIO pins 18, 23, 24, and 15; the resis-
tors are 220Ω

In order to make onoff work on the Pi, you'll need to enable the pins as an administrator.
To do this, here's a short script that will do it:

```
var Gpio = require('onoff').Gpio,
    led = [];
    led[0] = new Gpio(18, 'out'),    // set LED I/O pins as outputs
    led[1] = new Gpio(23, 'out'),
```

```
    led[2] = new Gpio(24, 'out'),
    led[4] = new Gpio(25, 'out');
```

Save this as *suexport.js*, then install the whole project using npm install. Then run the script like so:

```
$ sudo node suexport.js
```

You won't see any output, but the script will enable the following script to run as a regular user.

Here's the *index.js* for the Raspberry Pi version, with changes from the BoneScript version noted:

```
var ndef = require('ndef'),              // require ndef package
    mifare = require('mifare-classic'),  // require this package
    Gpio = require('onoff').Gpio,        // require onoff package
    led = [];                            // array of LEDs ❶

led[0] = new Gpio(18, 'out'),            // set LED I/O pins as outputs ❷
led[1] = new Gpio(23, 'out'),
led[2] = new Gpio(24, 'out'),
led[3] = new Gpio(25, 'out'),

setInterval(readTags, 2000);             // read every 2 seconds

function readTags() {
  mifare.read(function(error, buffer) {  // read tag
    if (error) {                         // if there's an error result
      console.log("Read failed ");       // let user know about the error
      console.log(error);
    } else {                             // you got an NDEF message
      // decode the message into a JSON object:
      var message = ndef.decodeMessage(buffer.toJSON());
      // print the message's records:
      console.log("Found NDEF message with " + message.length +
        // "record" if there's only one, "records" if there's more:
        (message.length === 1 ? " record" : " records" ));
      // print the message:
      console.log(ndef.stringify(message));
      // loop over the LEDs and turn on one for each record:
      for (var pinNum=0; pinNum<4; pinNum++) {
        console.log(pinNum);
        if (pinNum < message.length) {   // LED0=1 record, LED1=2 records...
          led[pinNum].writeSync(1);      // turn on pin ❸
        } else {
          led[pinNum].writeSync(0);      // turn off pin
        }
      }
    }
  });
}
```

❶ Require *onoff* instead of *bonescript*.

❷ Use an array for the four LED pins. Make a GPIO object for each. Pin numbers come from the Pi GPIO header.

❸ Use `Gpio.writeSync()` instead of `digitalWrite()`.

When you install and run this script, it will run identically to the BeagleBone version: one LED will light for every record you read in an NDEF message on a tag.

Onoff package on the BeagleBone

It is possible to run this project on the BeagleBone as well as the Pi, with some modifications and caveats. You can't control the built-in LEDs, but you can control the regular GPIO pins with onoff. You can find the GPIO pin numbers for the BeagleBone on their website (*http://bit.ly/pin-headers*). Any of the GPIO pins can be used to output to LEDs.

As of this writing, there's an issue with semver, the version checking tool used by npm's build tool node-gyp. In order to use npm to install any scripts using onoff, you'll need to edit the configuration file related to semver as follows:

```
$ nano /usr/lib/node_modules/npm/node_modules/node-gyp/lib/configure.js
```

Look for the following lines (likely lines 104–108):

```
if (semver.gte(version, '2.5.0') && semver.lt(version, '3.0.0')) {
    getNodeDir()
} else {
    failPythonVersion(version)
}
```

Replace all four lines with this line and save the file:

```
getNodeDir();
```

Once you make this change, onoff will compile and install on the BeagleBone. You may still find it more convenient to use BoneScript, however.

Although this example is relatively simple, it hints at the possibilities afforded by these embedded boards for physical interaction from NFC. For example, the hotel door lock in Chapter 7 could easily be duplicated for the Raspberry Pi or BeagleBone. The lighting control from Chapter 6, and even potentially the music playback, could be done from either of these boards, with some more work. For more on control of the GPIO for either of these boards, see Matt Richardson's books mentioned previously, or Adafruit's excellent tutorials on both boards.

NFC on embedded Linux is still rather nascent in its development, as you can see from these examples. Libnfc offers great potential as a basis for further development, however,

---

and we hope to see further work on it and its spinoff projects. In particular, more development on broadening the range of compatible tag types, and on the peer-to-peer exchange libraries like libllcp will advance the technology considerably on this platform. The potential for NFC-driven physical applications using embedded boards is broad, and the platforms shown here provide a robust, inexpensive, and straightforward way to develop such applications.

Conclusion

You've seen NFC in action on three different platforms: Android, using PhoneGap; Arduino, using the NDEF library; and embedded Linux using libnfc. You've gotten to know the structure and affordances of NDEF, learned about the various tags that are compatible with NFC, and used peer-to-peer exchanges with NDEF. As you can see, the technology offers some interesting improvements on RFID, most notably a data format that's independent of the tag technology and the ability for device-to-device communication without tags as well.

There is room for improvement in the various NFC APIs currently available. If you're a low-level developer, we encourage you to get involved by helping to expand the range of tag types available to higher-level libraries, and to develop NDEF-level APIs for platforms where support for NDEF does not yet exist. If you're more of a high-level interface designer, we encourage you to use NFC in a wide variety of applications as inspiration for others on the technology's possibilities.

NFC Specification Codes

There are a number of NFC Specification codes that you might use frequently. They're all available in the NFC Specification (*http://bit.ly/nfc-tech-specs*) on the NFC Forum site, but some of them are reproduced here for handy reference.

The NFC Forum Specification list provides handy summary definitions of all the NFC specifications. When you find yourself struggling to remember what acronyms such as LLCP, SNEP, TNF, and RTD mean, go to this page for the quick reference.

Table A-1. Type name formats

Type Name Format	Value
Empty	0x00
Well-Known type [NFC RTD]	0x01
MIME media-type [RFC 2046]	0x02
Absolute URI [RFC 3986]	0x03
External type [NFC RTD]	0x04
Unknown	0x05
Unchanged	0x06
Reserved	0x07

Table A-2. Common record type definitions

Record Type	RTD code
Text	T
URI	U
Smart Poster	Sp
Alternative Carrier	ac
Handover Carrier	Hc

Record Type	RTD code
Handover Request	Hr
Handover Select	Hs

Table A-3. URI identifier codes

Decimal	Hex	Protocol
0	0x00	None. The URI is added exactly as written.
1	0x01	http://www.
2	0x02	https://www.
3	0x03	http://
4	0x04	https://
5	0x05	tel:
6	0x06	mailto:
7	0x07	ftp://anonymous:anonymous@
8	0x08	ftp://ftp.
9	0x09	ftps:/
10	0x0A	sftp://
11	0x0B	smb://
12	0x0C	nfs://
13	0x0D	ftp://
14	0x0E	dav://
15	0x0F	news:
16	0x10	telnet://
17	0x11	imap:
18	0x12	rtsp://
19	0x13	urn:
20	0x14	pop:
21	0x15	sip:
22	0x16	sips:
23	0x17	tftp:
24	0x18	btspp://
25	0x19	btl2cap://
26	0x1A	btgoep://
27	0x1B	tcpobex://
28	0x1C	irdaobex://
29	0x1D	file://

Decimal	Hex	Protocol
30	0x1E	urn:epc:id:
31	0x1F	urn:epc:tag:
32	0x20	urn:epc:pat:
33	0x21	urn:epc:raw:
34	0x22	urn:epc:
35	0x23	urn:nfc:
36...255	0x24.,0xFF	Reserved for future use. (URI will be saved exactly as written).

Index

We'd like to hear your suggestions for improving our indexes. Send email to index@oreilly.com.

W

well-known TNF values, 51
WiFi vs. NFC, 12

workflow, editing, 200
write mode, 97

About the Authors

Tom Igoe teaches courses in physical computing and networking at the Interactive Telecommunications Program in the Tisch School of the Arts at New York University. In his teaching and research, he explores ways to allow digital technologies to sense and respond to a wider range of human physical expression. He is the author of *Making Things Talk* and *Getting Started with RFID*, and he co-authored *Physical Computing: Sensing and Controlling the Physical World with Computers* with Dan O'Sullivan. He is a contributor to MAKE magazine and a co-founder of the Arduino open source microcontroller project. He hopes to visit Svalbard and Antarctica someday.

Don Coleman is a lifelong engineer who has come full circle from mechanical to software and now to hardware, bridging the gap between all disciplines. He is a seasoned PhoneGap developer who has embraced it since its inception, and has spoken across the country about the benefits and advantages of using PhoneGap. As the Director of Consulting for Chariot Solutions, a software consulting company near Philadelphia, PA, he works with teams and clients to reinvent their existing technology and lay the groundwork for the future.

Brian Jepson is a book editor with MAKE, a hacker, and a co-organizer of Providence Geeks and the Rhode Island Mini Maker Faire. He's also a geek-at-large for AS220, a nonprofit arts center in Providence, RI. AS220 gives Rhode Island artists uncensored and unjuried forums for their work and also provides galleries, performance space, fabrication facilities, and live/work spaces.

Colophon

The animal on the cover of *Beginning NFC* is a Central American squirrel monkey (*Saimiri oerstedii*). This small monkey has a distinctive black and white face mask, making it very identifiable in its native Panamanian and Costa Rican habitats. Squirrel monkeys are social animals that live in groups of 20 to 75 individuals; they have one of the most egalitarian social structures seen in the monkey kingdom. Females do not form dominance hierarchies, and males only become aggressive during breeding season.

It has been found that the males of a Central American squirrel monkey group are usually related, so they display marked affection toward one another. This behavior, coupled with the fact that neither sex takes dominance within the group, is unique to the Central American species of squirrel monkey. In contrast, bands of South American squirrel monkeys always have a strict social hierarchy, with one sex winning supremacy over the other and much fighting and competition between males.

Central American squirrel monkeys are omnivorous, and their diet includes insects, spiders, fruit, leaves, bark, flowers, and nectar. They also have a very unusual method for capturing tent-making bats; a monkey will locate a roosting bat by finding the tented leaves that provide it shelter, and then drop down onto the bat from above, hoping to startle it into emerging. Given the vegetarian aspect of its diet, the Central American squirrel monkey is a very important seed disperser and pollinator of certain flowers, including the passion flower. There are even several species of bird that have learned to follow the squirrel monkey around in hopes of catching extra insects and small vertebrates that the monkey flushes out of trees and undergrowth.

The current population of Central American squirrel monkeys is estimated at 36 monkeys per square mile in Costa Rica and 130 monkeys per square mile in Panama. It is believed that their current status as "vulnerable" is a direct result of deforestation, hunting, and capture for the pet trade. Habitat loss especially has fragmented the monkeys' favored living areas and made it difficult for them to establish large breeding groups. Although the population is doing slightly better than it was forty years ago, there are still conservation and reforestation efforts underway to try to expand the current population within Panama, especially in the country's national parks and wilderness reserves.

The cover image is from Riverside's *Natural History*. The cover fonts are URW Typewriter and Guardian Sans. The text font is Adobe Minion Pro; the heading font is Adobe Myriad Condensed; and the code font is Dalton Maag's Ubuntu Mono.

Get even more for your money.

Join the O'Reilly Community, and register the O'Reilly books you own. It's free, and you'll get:

- $4.99 ebook upgrade offer
- 40% upgrade offer on O'Reilly print books
- Membership discounts on books and events
- Free lifetime updates to ebooks and videos
- Multiple ebook formats, DRM FREE
- Participation in the O'Reilly community
- Newsletters
- Account management
- 100% Satisfaction Guarantee

Signing up is easy:

1. **Go to: oreilly.com/go/register**
2. **Create an O'Reilly login.**
3. **Provide your address.**
4. **Register your books.**

Note: English-language books only

To order books online:
oreilly.com/store

For questions about products or an order:
orders@oreilly.com

To sign up to get topic-specific email announcements and/or news about upcoming books, conferences, special offers, and new technologies:
elists@oreilly.com

For technical questions about book content:
booktech@oreilly.com

To submit new book proposals to our editors:
proposals@oreilly.com

O'Reilly books are available in multiple DRM-free ebook formats. For more information:
oreilly.com/ebooks

O'REILLY®

Spreading the knowledge of innovators   oreilly.com

Have it your way.

Milton Keynes UK
Ingram Content Group UK Ltd.
UKHW010652130824
446857UK00008B/108

9 781449 372064